8/14/19

PLEASE RETURN
I Am foRTuNATE To
have moRE NAvy friends who
will ENjoy.
I Thank you

SEA STORIES:

Tales of epic adventures recounted by sailors returning home from a long voyage; usually told over a bottle of rum with good friends and good intentions.

SEA STORIES

MY LIFE IN
SPECIAL OPERATIONS

★ ★ ★ ★

ADMIRAL
WILLIAM H. McRAVEN

(U.S. Navy Retired)

GRAND CENTRAL
PUBLISHING

NEW YORK   BOSTON

Grand Central Publishing
Hachette Book Group
1290 Avenue of the Americas, New York, NY 10104
grandcentralpublishing.com
twitter.com/grandcentralpub

First Edition: May 2019

Grand Central Publishing is a division of Hachette Book Group, Inc. The Grand Central Publishing name and logo is a trademark of Hachette Book Group, Inc.

The publisher is not responsible for websites (or their content) that are not owned by the publisher.

The Hachette Speakers Bureau provides a wide range of authors for speaking events. To find out more, go to www.hachettespeakersbureau.com or call (866) 376-6591.

LCCN: 2019931174
ISBNs: 978-1-5387-2974-8 (hardcover), 978-1-5387-2972-4 (ebook), 978-1-5387-1553-6 (large print hardcover), 978-1-5387-1643-4 (signed hardcover), 978-1-5387-1642-7 (B&N special hardcover)

Printed in the United States of America

LSC-C

10 9 8 7 6 5 4 3 2 1

And then I heard the voice of the Lord saying, "Whom shall I send and who will go for us?" And I said, "Here am I. Send me!"

—Isaiah 6:8

I dedicate this book to the men and women of the Special Operations community who said, "Send Me," and who have sacrificed so very much in the defense of this nation. It was the greatest honor of my life to have served with you.

Life is either a daring adventure, or nothing.
—Helen Keller

CONTENTS

AUTHOR'S NOTE

The events in this book are as I remember them. Any inaccuracies in the stories are a result of the passage of time or my advancing age. While I have taken some literary license with the dialogue, I believe the conversations depicted accurately capture the spirit of the moment. Additionally, I have changed some of the names out of concern over privacy, at the request of the individual, or because I was unable to contact the person in question.

CHAPTER ONE

THE GREATEST GENERATION

FONTAINEBLEAU, FRANCE

1960

I pushed the swinging door open just a crack and peeked out into the large, smoke-filled room. Jean Claude, the tall young French bartender, was shuttling from table to table taking drink orders from the American officers who filled the club on a Friday night.

Moving through the door, I crawled on my hands and knees to a place just behind the bar. From there I was hidden from view but could still see the entire room.

The American Officers' Club, located in the heart of Fontainebleau, France, was a three-story structure built in the French Provincial style with ornate molding, winding staircases, a small caged elevator, and large oil paintings of Napoleon, Louis XVI, and countless battle scenes.

As a child of five, to me the club was a special place. There were banisters to slide down, closets to hide in, and hallways to run through. I roamed freely, imaginary sword in hand, fighting pirates and Prussians, Nazis and Russians.

Using the hidden passages inside the building, I could move from the kitchen to the bar completely undetected. The dumbwaiter, which connected the kitchen to the second and third floors, served as a means to slip past the waitstaff, my two sisters (who were charged with keeping me out of trouble—rarely successfully, I might add), my parents, and the scores of other officers who knew I prowled the halls unattended.

While it was an American club, officers from every allied nation

1

were welcome. Impressive in their uniforms, straight in their bearing, they had a swagger and a confidence that was unmistakable to the victors of World War II.

It had been almost fifteen years since the end of the war, but France was still rebuilding and the Europeans looked to the North Atlantic Treaty Organization (NATO) to protect it from the Soviets. The military arm of NATO was the Supreme Headquarters Allied Powers Europe (SHAPE)—to which my father was assigned and the reason we were living in France.

As I moved to the other side of the bar, Jean Claude spied me and gave me that look, a look I had seen a hundred times before. *I see you*, it said. But there was always a twinkle in Jean Claude's eye. Like all men grown older, he appreciated the mischief in a young boy's heart, and I sensed there was a longing to be that lad again. In my mind, Jean Claude was my protector, the keeper of my secrets, the Watson to my Holmes.

Across the room, my father was sitting at an oval table with three other men. They all wore the uniform of an Air Force officer: a collared light blue shirt, a dark tie, slightly loosened at the neck, and a deep blue coat with silver wings on the chest.

With Dad were "Easy Ed" Taylor, "Wild Bill" Wildman, and "Gentleman" Rod Gunther, all colonels, all fighter pilots.

Ed Taylor, his hands in the air, one in pursuit of the other, was fending off an attack from a German Messerschmitt. A cigarette hung loosely from his lips and he only paused from the story to take a sip from the scotch snifter at his elbow. Ed was one of the pioneers of jet aircraft, at one point the fastest man in the world in aerial flight. He was Hemingwayish, with a flair for the dramatic, a love of good whiskey, and a need to fill every minute of life with something exciting. A fighter pilot in World War II and Korea, he would go on to serve in Vietnam and end his career as a three-war veteran. He drank hard, smoked unfiltered Camel cigarettes, loved to be in combat, and seemed to enjoy every person he ever met.

On his wall at home were personalized pictures with Presidents FDR, Truman, and Eisenhower, Generals Douglas MacArthur and George Patton, ballplayers Mickey Mantle and Roger Maris, kings and princes, tyrants and despots, and every average Joe he ever served with. Every picture came with a story.

Ed was married to Cordelia, or Cordie, as everyone called her. A southern girl from Texas who served as the Wives' Club president and was always in charge of the children's plays and adult social functions, Cordie liked to party as much as Ed, and their marriage, which lasted for over fifty years, was a constant struggle between his love of combat and a domestic need for normality. Combat always won out.

Bill Wildman also served in the European theater during the war, but like the rest of the men, he was now flying a desk at SHAPE. Bill was married to everyone's favorite wife, Ann. Ann was the best-looking woman in France: petite, shapely, smart, and always the life of the party.

Rod Gunther was a southern gentleman, prematurely gray, with a slow friendly drawl and a knack for making everyone around him feel special. His wife, Sadie, and their three girls were like part of our family. I had a crush on their youngest daughter, Judy, thinking she liked me too until I mistakenly put a firecracker in her hat that was meant for my sister Nan. Somehow, after that the romance went out of our relationship.

As Ed Taylor finished his story, with one hand diving sharply into the tabletop, all the men roared with laughter, though I knew they'd heard the story before. My father took a drag on his cigarette, rubbed it out in the ashtray, and waited for the next tale.

Among the men at the table, my father was the most reserved, although that wasn't saying much. Dad loved to tell stories as much as the rest of them. He was blessed with "movie star" good looks, as the women would frequently tell my mom (although I never could tell how she took the compliment).

He had jet black hair, made darker with the touch of Brylcreem he added every morning, along with a prominent nose, a slight cleft in his chin, and steel blue eyes that twinkled when he smiled—and he smiled often.

At five foot eleven, Dad stood tall, but not overbearing. In his younger days he was a remarkable athlete, receiving honors in football, baseball, basketball, and track at Murray State Teachers College in Kentucky. He worked his way through college by gambling on Mississippi riverboats, teaching tennis to "old ladies," and racing against Kentucky thoroughbreds—man against beast. Exceptionally fast for his day, he ran the hundred-yard dash in 9.8 seconds. At that speed he could beat most horses in a short sprint (sixty yards), and he often gambled a few bucks against local trainers to make his point.

After college, he played two years of professional football with the Cleveland Rams, and in one promotional shot, highlighting their new Murray State running back, the Rams had a picture of Dad bolting from the starting line with a horse and rider in hot pursuit. He later confided in me that he lost that race, "but only by a nose."

Football was "lucrative" employment. Dad made $120 a game and with Wheaties radio commercials cleared almost $130 a week. But as the possibility of war in Europe loomed larger, he left football and drove to California to sign up for the Army Air Corps.

When I asked him years later why he joined the military, he said that as a boy he watched soldiers march through the streets of his home town of Marston, Missouri, and board a train bound for the trenches of France. His father, an Army surgeon, was one of those men. He knew then that he wanted to be a soldier.

After graduating from aviation officers' school at Brooke Field in San Antonio, Texas, he received orders to the 309th Fighter Squadron, 8th Air Force. The 309th was part of the first American contingent to be posted in the United Kingdom. At the time, the

Americans were still working to build a fighter aircraft that could compete in aerial combat against the German Messerschmitt. So when Dad arrived in England he and the other pilots of the 309th were given British Spitfires.

The "Spits," equipped with the powerful Rolls-Royce engines, new guns, and sleek aerodynamics, were good enough to go toe to toe with the Germans. Dad flew the Spitfire throughout the war, going on to fight in the campaigns in North Africa, Sicily, Salerno, and eventually at the Normandy invasion.

He registered two confirmed kills during the war, but would himself be shot down over France in 1943. The saga of his escape and evasion from France back to England was told many times during our posting in France, not by Dad, who rarely talked about his wartime service, but by the French resistance fighter who helped him back to freedom and now lived near us on the outskirts of Paris.

Jean Claude suddenly appeared behind the bar. He reached for a glass, poured it halfway to the top with Coca-Cola, and then added a heavy dose of cherry juice. A Roy Rogers, he announced, handing me the drink. He knew not to call it a Shirley Temple. I sat cross-legged behind the bar as he fixed other drinks and then moved out to serve the patrons. Soon my mother and the other wives arrived.

As with all wives of that era, you didn't come to the club unless you were "dressed to the nines." Their hair was large and starched to perfection, with not a strand out of place. Each cocktail dress showed just enough neckline and just enough leg to be sophisticated but not showy. With a cigarette in one hand and a drink in the other, they took their place by their men. But while they were "the wives," there were no demure shrinking violets in this group. These were women who married men of adventure—fighter pilots. They knew what they were getting into when they said, "I do," and in spite of all the hard times that were to come (and there would be a lot of them), every marriage survived until death parted them.

As the ladies sat down, Jean Claude headed to the table for more drink requests. As he bent over to take an order I saw him nod his head in my direction.

Traitor.

My mother turned around, smiled, and waved me over to the table.

I put down the Roy Rogers, ran to the table, and hopped on my mother's lap. She hugged me tightly and kissed me on the cheek. With Mom there was always the subtle scent of perfume and cold cream. I can still smell it to this day.

Rod Gunther rubbed my crew cut ("one like the astronauts had...") and in his soft voice said, "Billy, my boy, what have you been up to tonight?"

It was an invitation to tell a story, to be part of the adult conversation, to try to match my adventures with bomber missions over France, dogfights over North Africa, traveling with Chiang Kai-shek or dancing with Vice President Nixon (my mother's favorite). Stories filled the rest of the evening, with my mother occasionally covering my ears when the men said something "too adult."

After last call, when the drinks were finished and the packs of cigarettes lay crumpled on the table, the men stood up abruptly, as if completing a mission brief, shook hands, and laughed about something in an earlier story. The wives hugged and kissed each other on the cheek, promising to meet again on Monday for some social function.

Friday nights at the Officers' Club were a ritual during our three years in France. The stories of air-to-air combat, life on the front lines, and daring escapes all fueled my longing for adventure. The stories never focused on pain and sorrow. Even when they recounted lives lost, there was generally a glass raised, a toast made to a good man who fought hard and died gloriously.

In late 1963, Dad had a mild stroke (something to do with cigarettes and Jim Beam whiskey, the doctor would say). He recovered, but our family was reassigned to Lackland Air Force Base in San Antonio, to be near Wilford Hall Air Force hospital. Ed, Cordie, and the four Taylor boys were right up the road in Austin, and we kept in touch with the Gunthers and the Wildmans for many years to come.

In Texas, my parents made new friends, and with them came new and better stories. There was Colonel David "Tex" Hill, one of the original Flying Tigers who served with General Claire Chennault in China. Tex was military royalty in San Antonio. Tall, gentle, with an easy way about him, he was a legendary pilot in both Air Force and Navy history, with over twenty-eight confirmed kills. Along with his wife, Maize, he became part of our large family of friends and the vibrant social scene that revolved around the military in the 1960s.

There were also Jim and Aileen Gunn. Promoted to full colonel when he was twenty-five years old, and then shot down a week later in a combat mission over Romania, Jim managed to escape from a prisoner-of-war camp in Bucharest in the belly of a Messerschmitt—flown by a member of the Romanian royal family.

Jim almost died from exposure as the unpressurized fighter made its way over the Alps to Italy, but upon landing, he thawed out, contacted the American military, and gave them the precise location of the POW camp. Had he been a day later, German aircraft would have bombed the camp, hoping to destroy the evidence of POW abuse. Seventy years later Jim Gunn was awarded the Silver Star for his heroism.

Along with Tex Hill and Jim Gunn, there was Major Joe McCarty, who worked for U.S. intelligence during the war, Colonel Bill Strother, a decorated bomber pilot, and Bill Lindley, the only general in the group. All were part of the families that raised me. Their wives, Betty, Ann, and Martha, respectively, were like surrogate mothers, and often, as in the case of Ann Strother, told me bawdy jokes and adult stories at an age well before my mother would have approved.

The years at Lackland Air Force Base were filled with dove hunting in the fall, deer hunting through the winter, bridge for the women, poker for the men, golf on the odd weekends, and frequent trips to the Gulf Coast for fishing and more storytelling. I'm not really sure when the men got any work done, but as a kid, I thought it all seemed part of the rhythms of life—and I loved it.

Like all the men and women of their generation, they were children of World War I, lived through the Depression, and the men all fought in World War II and Korea. They were survivors. They didn't complain. They didn't blame others for their misfortune. They worked hard and expected the same from their children. They treasured their friendships. They fought for their marriages. They wore their patriotism on their sleeve, and while they weren't naïve about America's faults, they knew that no other country in the world valued their service and sacrifice as much as the United States did. They flew their flags proudly and without apology.

But I'm convinced that what made this generation so great was their ability to take the hardships that confronted them and turn them into laughter-filled, self-deprecating, unforgettable, sometimes unbelievable stories of life. My father used to tell me, "Bill, it's all how you remember it." The stories in this book are how I remember my life. I think I could sit at that table in Fontainebleau now . . . and tell a story or two.

CHAPTER TWO

OPERATION VOLCANO

SAN ANTONIO, TEXAS

1966

I pushed the spring-loaded knife back into the bottom of the black attaché case. It clicked firmly into place. Rotating the dials to the coded numbers, I turned the two buttons horizontally and the lid to the case popped open, exposing my Luger pistol and a twenty-round magazine. A spotting scope was lashed to the inside along with my passport and several thousand dollars in unmarked bills.

Confident that everything I needed was there, I closed the case, checked the safe house one final time, and then stepped outside into the fading sunlight.

Traffic on the street was light. I looked over my shoulder to ensure no one was following me. A lot was riding on this mission and there was only one thing that could stand in my way.

"Bill, time for dinner!"

Mom . . .

"In a minute," I yelled back.

"Five minutes, no more. Your food is getting cold."

Pulling the spotting scope from the James Bond Attaché Case, I looked for my sidekick, Dan Lazono. Dan was supposed to be concealed in the bushes across the street, ready to provide backup if the mission went awry, but apparently his mom had called him back inside as well.

Mothers.

★   ★   ★

The sun began to set over the small military housing complex on the outskirts of Lackland Air Force Base. Home to about a hundred officers and their families, Medina Annex sprawled across the rolling hills that overlooked the Officer Training School.

Every morning at sunrise the sound of reveille blared through the loudspeakers, echoing throughout the housing area, and every night at sunset the sweet, haunting sound of "Taps" told me it was time to stop playing and go home.

Throughout the year, hundreds of young Air Force cadets arrived at the school, heads shaved, backs straight, purposeful in their gaze, Vietnam in their future.

The mid-1960s was the height of the Cold War and ushered in the era of movie and TV spies: those men from U.N.C.L.E., Napoleon Solo and Illya Kuryakin; Derek Flint of *In Like Flint*; Matt Helm; and of course, everyone's favorite, James Bond. Being in Texas, you couldn't escape Cowboys and Indians, but being a spy was so much "neater."

In addition to training new cadets, Medina Annex also housed a large ammunition storage facility—dozens of hardened, aboveground structures hidden in the backwoods far from prying eyes. These "Gravel Gerties" looked like small volcanoes, a hundred feet in diameter and rising twenty-five feet from the ground. Named after a character in the *Dick Tracy* cartoon, the bunkers stored every high explosive in the U.S. Air Force inventory, including nuclear weapons—if you believed Dan Lazono.

Security around the ammunition site was extensive. Air Police with their K-9 dogs patrolled the area on a regular basis, checking in with the command post when anything irregular was spotted. Around the perimeter of the facility were three concentric eight-foot-high chain-link fences, each topped with barbed wire. The layered defenses would be quite a challenge, even for 007.

*   *   *

"Have you been climbing in the trees again?" Mom asked.

"No ma'am," I said sheepishly.

Lifting my shirt, she inspected the large bandage that covered my stomach. "The doctor said no strenuous activity for one month. Not until the wound heals. If you keep running around like this you will have a scar for the rest of your life."

I do.

Three months earlier, while scouting out the Gravel Gerties for a possible spy mission, I climbed high into a nearby tree to get a good look at the security. Below me, Billy McClelland and Jon Hopper stood watch. *Somehow, they always stood watch.*

As I slowly stepped out onto an old branch, it gave way, sending me plummeting twenty feet to the ground, but not before I ripped my stomach open on a broken limb that jutted out halfway down the tree. It was two miles through the woods back to my house and Billy took off running to get my mother. Jon, the youngest of the three of us, kept pressure on my gut while we walked as far back as we could to shorten the distance home.

Mom arrived in the car just as Jon and I broke out of the tree line. A frantic look on her face, she piled me into the back of the old station wagon and raced to Wilford Hall Air Force hospital.

Wilford Hall and I were old friends. It seemed like every week I was in the emergency room for something: a broken arm from falling off a large fence, a slit wrist from running through a sliding glass window ("You better stop running in the house or you're going to crash through that window!" How did Dad know that?), a busted knee from Pop Warner football, a broken ankle from basketball, a broken nose from, well…we were well acquainted. But this accident seemed to top the rest.

The branch ripped a ten-inch gash in my stomach, but fortunately, it didn't puncture any internal organs. The doctors stitched me up and put a large bandage over my stomach. All of this would have been fine, except a month later while riding the Air Force shuttle bus home from the new James Bond film, I fell out of the bus (it's a long story) onto the street and ripped open the sutures.

Back to Wilford Hall.

"Give me that rock," Billy said, pointing to a shot-put-sized stone in the nearby creek. He brushed a small lock of blond hair out of his eyes and with a determined look tossed the heavy stone into a bucket suspended from a tall oak. The bucket slowly began to sink, bringing with it the rope that lowered the "drawbridge" onto our island fort.

"Nice toss," Jon yelled. Jon yelled enthusiastically about everything. To him, everything we older boys did was exciting.

I grabbed the rope and pulled down on the counterweight. The wooden plank settled easily between the mainland and the island—which was only separated by four feet, with a water depth of two feet. Any one-legged man could have forded our moat, but after building an elaborate tree fort, we had to find a way to protect it.

We were ingenious. The tree fort was a miracle of wooden engineering. Every usable piece of plywood and two-by-four we could find went into its construction. Four walls, two windows, a solid floor, and a door that said KEEP OUT!!!

We ran out of nails before the fort was complete, so the pieces of two-by-fours forming the ladder on the side of the tree were just the sort of thing my mother would not have liked. Billy climbed up the wobbly rungs and announced his arrival in the fort.

"I'm in. Come on up!"

I quickly scaled the tree and joined Billy. Jon stood at the bottom peering through his glasses, trying to gather his courage to make the climb.

"Come on, come on. We don't have all day," I said.

Jon grabbed the first step and began to climb. His knees were shaking and he squinted through the glaze of his fogged-up lens. Jon was a follower, and our club of three needed at least one good follower. Always working to overcome his fear of the woods, the rules we broke, and the trouble we might get into, Jon still followed us, and as young boys trying to be men, having a friend like Jon made us stronger.

As Jon reached the final rung, Billy grabbed one side of his belt and I the other and with a noticeable grunt we hauled him into the fort.

We had come to the fort to make final preparations for our upcoming mission—a mission to infiltrate the ammunition storage facility.

It seemed like a good idea—*at the time.*

We were certain that there was something nefarious going on at the Gravel Gerties, something that was a threat to U.S. national security. It was up to us to save the world.

I pulled out the makeshift map and began the briefing.

"We'll call this—Operation Volcano," I announced.

Billy and Jon smiled broadly. It was a cool name. "M" and Moneypenny would have approved.

"Billy, we'll need to move the planks into place tomorrow. Can you get your dad to bring them to the fort?"

"Sure," Billy said. "I told him we needed some extra wood to reinforce the treehouse. He said he could bring it by on Saturday, but we'll have to move it from the fort to the outer fence."

"Are you sure the planks are long enough?" I asked.

"I think so," Billy said, not filling me with confidence.

"They have to be long enough to stretch from the top of one fence to the top of the other," I said. "It's the only way we can get past the electric fence in the middle."

"Electric fence?" Jon said.

"Of course it's electric," I said. "They always have an electric fence."

Billy nodded. Of course they did.

"Jon, what about your dad's binoculars?"

Jon squirmed uncomfortably.

"Never mind," I said. "I'll get my father's deer hunting binoculars. He won't miss them for a day."

Jon sighed and glanced downward.

"It's all right," Billy said. "You have a real important part of the mission. You are going to be our security."

Jon liked that.

"You have to keep alert, alert at all times," Billy said. "If the APs catch us we'll be in real trouble."

Jon wiped the sweat from his forehead and adjusted his glasses. "Do you think we'll get caught?"

Billy and I looked at each other. Frankly, the thought had never occurred to us. I mean, how much trouble can you get into breaking into a high-security compound?

"Nah, we won't get caught," I said with conviction.

"Who's bringing the hot dogs?" Billy asked.

"I have two whole packages," I answered.

The hot dogs were essential. Once we scaled the outer fence and used the planks to bridge across the two other fences, we would need something to protect us from the K-9s. Jon thought we needed steaks. Every movie hero used steaks, he argued, not hot dogs. Big steaks, T-bones, I think. Jon's point was a good one. No self-respecting spy used Oscar Mayer hot dogs—ever. But my mother just didn't understand why we needed steaks at the "clubhouse," and I couldn't tell her about the mission, so the hot dogs would have to do.

And it was a fort, not a clubhouse.

"It's agreed, then," I said. "We will meet tomorrow afternoon at my house and begin the mission." Everyone nodded. "This is going to be great! Just like the movies."

"Who's going to be James Bond?" Jon asked.

It was something else we had never thought about. But it had to be decided. Billy was actually way cooler than I was. All the girls at elementary school liked him, he had a pet raccoon, *and* his dad drove a Corvette Stingray.

"We can both be James Bond," Billy offered.

"You can't both be 007," Jon countered.

I thought about it for a second. "I'll be Napoleon Solo, and Jon, you can be my sidekick, Illya Kuryakin."

Everyone was happy. The plan was complete. We were ready for Operation Volcano.

"Don't move," I whispered.

The eyes of the big diamondback rattlesnake were firmly fixed on Jon. The snake, curled tightly in a striking pose, was five feet from Jon's face, its rattle high in the air warning our three-man patrol to stay clear.

"Back away," I said.

Jon followed my instructions.

Slowly I reached down and picked up a piece of limestone shale that formed the bedrock of the washed-out gully we were in.

"Don't do that!" Billy said in a raised voice. "Don't do that!" he repeated.

Ignoring his warning, I tossed the flat shale rock in the direction of the snake. The rock landed just in front of the rattler's head, and the snake launched forward, scattering us in three directions.

"Ahhh!" Jon yelled as the snake slithered past him into another clump of rocks.

I started laughing uncontrollably.

"It's not funny," Jon said.

"I know, I know," I apologized. But it *was* funny.

Snakes were part of life in Texas, and all of us had grown up with some story of rattlers or moccasins creeping into our backyard, hiding underneath a woodpile, or crossing our paths while we were hunting deer. And this washed-out gulley was full of rattlers. In the heat of the day they would come out to warm themselves on the rocks. Unfortunately, the only way to get to the ammunition depot undetected was down this dry creek bed.

The walls of the creek bed were about six to eight feet high, with rocks and old tree roots jutting out of the soil, providing good footing to climb out quickly. Ten feet wide in some parts, the creek bed narrowed to a few feet as it approached our exit point. In the spring the waters that filled the gully would rush through, creating a funnel effect.

The three of us were well armed for the mission. Jon had Old Betsy, a Davy Crockett rifle that he carried slung over his back, and he wore a coonskin cap, which was far too big for his head and was always falling off.

Stuffed into my holster was my Roy Rogers pearl-handled cap gun, and Billy was armed with the best weapon of all: a Red Ryder BB gun.

After the snake scare, I took the lead and Billy and I put Jon in the middle. As we moved farther into the woods the noises of the nearby neighborhood began to fade away. There was an eeriness to our surroundings even though we had walked this path a dozen times before.

"I hear a truck!" Jon yelled.

"Be quiet," Billy said. "Listen."

It was a truck all right, and not far away. I pulled out my six-shooter, motioned to Billy and Jon to stay put, and climbed up the side of the creek.

The truck was moving slowly in our direction, but I couldn't see anything through the thick mesquite trees.

"What do you see?" Jon whispered nervously.

"Nothing," I said. "Give me the binoculars." I had entrusted Jon with my dad's binoculars and he had dutifully packed them away in his knapsack.

Billy grabbed the binoculars from Jon and scurried up the side of the hill to deliver them to me. "Look, over there," he said.

There was a break in the tree line and the truck had come to a stop about fifty yards away.

"Oh shit," Billy said, inching closer to the fallen log I was hiding behind.

We all liked to say "shit." It was the only cuss word we knew and we said it often.

I looked through the binoculars. In small letters on the side of the blue pickup truck were the words *Air Force Police*. Inside the cabin I could see a gun rack with an M-1 rifle and a shotgun hanging on the hooks. The Air Policeman driving the vehicle opened the door and stepped out.

"What's going on?" Jon asked.

Billy backed off from behind the log and waved at him to be quiet.

On the other side of the vehicle, the Air Policeman stood motionless for a few moments. I adjusted the zoom on the binoculars. Smiling, I handed the binoculars to Billy.

"He's just taking a pee," Billy said, snickering.

We watched as the airman finished his business and began to get back into the cab.

Suddenly from behind us there was the loud snap of a branch breaking, and I could hear Jon tumbling down the hill. The sound echoed through the woods, and beside the truck the airman paused to listen. Billy and I froze.

My heart was pounding, and even though we were not inside the perimeter fence, I knew this was a restricted area. After a few seconds the airman hopped into the truck and drove off. Billy and I hustled back down the slippery hill to see if Jon was all right.

"My cap. Where's my cap?" Jon said, wiping the mud off his face.

Hanging on the broken branch like some bushy-tailed squirrel was Jon's coonskin cap. We retrieved it and continued our patrol. Thirty minutes later we arrived at the planks of wood that Billy and I had moved earlier in the day. *Jonny Quest* was on TV at ten o'clock or Jon would have helped us move the planks, but we knew that he never missed Saturday morning cartoons, and certainly not *Jonny Quest*.

"Are you sure we should do this?" Jon asked.

Billy and I looked at each other, hoping one of us would acknowledge it was a bad idea. But we didn't.

"Just grab the first plank," I said.

We had scouted out this location over the past few months. The woods were thick on both sides of the fence line and I knew that there was a Gravel Gertie about seventy-five yards away. I had seen it three months earlier, right before the branch gave way, sending me to the hospital.

Grabbing the first plank, we laid it at a forty-five-degree angle against the fence. Billy pushed against the wood to see if it was secure.

"Okay, who's going first?" he asked.

Both Billy and Jon looked at me. After all it was my idea, my plan, my mission, and even though I wasn't the designated James Bond, it was my responsibility.

"I'll go," I said, stepping onto the bottom of the plank.

The Chuck Taylor high-tops I was wearing seemed to grip the wood well. Slowly, I climbed my way up the board until I reached the top, balancing myself with one foot on the barbed wire and one foot on the plank. I could now see the top of the Gravel Gertie rising above the trees.

"Quick, quick. Hand me the next plank!"

Billy and Jon picked up the next board and started to hand it to me.

"It's too short," I yelled. "Give me the next one."

Every board was too short. The distance between the fences was way too long, but we had come too far to stop now. The world still needed saving.

My feet were beginning to wobble and it was hard to stay balanced eight feet in the air with nothing to hold on to.

Suddenly the Chuck Taylors lost their traction. My left foot slipped out from under me and I teetered on one leg, waving my arms frantically trying to get my footing.

"Jump! Jump!" Jon screamed.

"Oh shit, oh shit, oh shit!" I yelled, tumbling off my perch and falling spread-eagle into a patch of high grass. I hit the ground with a thud and lay there momentarily to catch my breath.

"Uh-oh," Billy said softly.

I was now inside the fence line with no way out.

"You okay?" Jon asked.

"I'm fine," I said, peering through the chain-link fence. "Throw me another board. I'll use it to climb out of here."

Jon and Billy heaved another long plank over the barbed wire and I quickly propped it against the fence. I wiped the mud off my Chuck Taylors and began to climb up the plank. "Hey, this works," I said triumphantly as I reached the top of the fence.

As I turned to look back, I could see the Gravel Gertie. To me it was like the evil mastermind's lair in some great adventure story. Our hero had been thwarted in his first attempt, but I knew Napoleon Solo never gave up on a mission. *Neither would I.*

"Hand me another board," I said.

"What!" Billy asked.

"Quick, quick, quick! Hand me a plank. I'll just make another bridge."

Jon and Billy grabbed two more long boards and slid them over the top of the barbed wire. I placed the third board against the middle fence, and after a few tries managed to get the fourth board over the middle fence and into the grass on the other side.

It was hot, Texas hot, and the sweat began to roll down my forehead. I cleaned off the Chuck Taylors, extended my arms for balance, and tightroped my way to the top of the "electric" fence. *Clearly, I had not thought this through.* Unlike at the first fence, I couldn't use the barbed wire to balance myself for fear that a million volts would fry me. I assumed a million volts because it was a government fence and a million was a big number. Teetering at the top of the board, my only option for getting to the other side was to jump over the three strands of wire, hit the dirt, and do a cool, secret agent somersault. *Yes, clearly, I had not thought this through.*

Jon and Billy were peering through the fence like they were watching a baseball game from outside the park.

"Be careful!" Jon yelled, his high-pitched voice cracking with fear.

As I inched closer to the top of the board, I could feel the plank give a bit. It was starting to slip from the ground up.

"Hurry, hurry!" Billy screamed.

Bending my knees, I took two steps and pushed off the board, launching myself over the top of the fence. I knew from the start that my leap wasn't high enough. The heel of my Chuck Taylors caught the top of the wire just enough to alter my flight. Hands and feet flailing erratically, I tumbled out of control into the grass below. Landing on all fours, I rolled sideways down a slight knoll. I hopped up quickly and dusted myself off. Jon was clapping gleefully, but Billy was pointing to the board on the other side of the fence. It now lay buried in the grass, having fallen from the fence as I jumped. My escape route was compromised.

I picked up the plank on my side of the middle fence and leaned it back against the barbed wire. The mission was getting considerably harder.

"Come on, guys!" I whisper-yelled. "Climb over."

Jon looked at Billy and said in a panic, "I'm just the lookout. You told me you just wanted me to stay here."

"Yeah, yeah. You can stay and keep watch," Billy responded. Jon immediately picked up the binoculars, grabbed Old Betsy, and moved about twenty yards down the fence line. There was nothing to see from that position but more trees.

"Are you coming?" I asked Billy, but I could see that look in his eyes. The rickety planks and the fear of the electric fence were not his idea of an adventure. This was real danger, not the made-up stuff we usually played.

"Maybe I should stay here and keep watch with Jon," Billy said, somewhat weakly. Then he paused for a second, wiped back his mop of blond hair, and smiled. "You can be James Bond," he offered.

"I get to be James Bond?"

"Yeah, yeah. You can be James Bond," Billy said.

"Cool. Okay, you can be Napoleon Solo," I said.

It seemed like a good trade to me. After all, this really was a mission for 007, not the Man from U.N.C.L.E.

There was no way to get to the Gravel Gertie now, but at least I could get to the top of the third fence and see if any nefarious activity was taking place at the top-secret installation.

Grabbing the plank from the middle fence, I dragged it to the final barrier and laid it at an angle against the barbed wire. Wiping off my Chuck Taylors one more time, I got a running start and bounded up the plank. As my weight hit the board, the plank slid slightly to the right and tossed me off halfway up. I readjusted the plank, securing it against a metal strut, and backed off even farther to get up more speed. I looked over my shoulder and could see Billy's face pinned against the chain-link fence, a real look of concern in his eyes.

"Be careful!" he yelled.

I just nodded and started my sprint.

As I hit the plank I sprang forward and in a few steps found myself balancing on top of the board. Like Sir Edmund Hillary on Everest, I looked around and surveyed the land before me. The Gravel Gertie was almost completely visible now and it was everything we thought it would be: a sinister-looking fortified bunker, with concertina wire and warning signs posted at every corner. But looking around, there was no one in sight. No guards, no dogs, no henchmen with steel blades in their hats, no nothing.

I looked back at Billy and waved. He still didn't seem happy.

"That was easy," I muttered to myself.

Suddenly, a siren began to sound, the noise so loud I had to cup my ears. A red light at the entrance to the Gravel Gertie was spinning at high RPMs, and in the distance, while I couldn't make out the words, I could hear a loudspeaker blaring a call to arms.

"Hurry, hurry!" Billy started yelling.

"They're coming!" Jon shouted.

And they were coming. I could hear the rumble of a truck not far away and soon the most frightening sound I had ever heard—*a dog, a massive Hound of the Baskervilles, barking, angry dog.*

"Shit, shit, shit!"

I slid down the plank, grabbed the piece of wood, and charged toward the middle fence. Laying the slat against the fence, I backed off and tried to run up the board. I slid back. Once, twice, three times.

Now both Billy and Jon were at the first fence, their hands clinching the chain link, yelling for me to hurry up.

The sound of the K-9 was getting closer. I couldn't tell if he was on the inside or the outside of the fence, or if he was on a leash or running wildly toward his prey, but I knew what I had to do. Reaching into my small knapsack, I tore open the package of Oscar Mayer hot dogs and began tossing them in every direction. *If only I had steaks*, I thought.

Backing off one final time, I got down into a starting position, hands on the ground, butt in the air, and then, with a loud yell, launched my body into a sprint. I hit the plank, arms pumping, legs churning, and quickly dashed to the top. Without hesitation, I raised my knees high and leaped over the barbed wire, landing on all fours in the soft grass.

"This is the Air Police," a voice from a bullhorn announced. "You are in a restricted area. Use of lethal force is authorized."

"Hurry, hurry!" Billy yelled again.

Running to the final plank, I hit it at full speed, but only managed to get halfway. Grabbing the sides of the board, I clawed my way up the remaining few feet, balancing precariously at the top. Looking toward the Gravel Gertie, I could see something moving through the woods, a man and his dog driven by the scent of fear and Oscar Mayer.

As I started to ease my body over the final strand of barbed wire, my Roy Rogers pearl-handled six-shooter fell from my holster onto the ground below. I looked at Billy and then down toward the pistol.

"Come on! We gotta go!" Billy screamed.

Billy held the last plank and I slid down from the top of the fence, tumbling the last four feet to the ground. Jon was about to wet his pants. He was jumping up and down and pointing wildly in the direction of the approaching K-9.

"Run, run!" I yelled.

Flailing with arms and legs, we took off at a gallop, dashing through the woods back to the dry creek bed. The siren was still blaring and I could hear more instructions coming over the loudspeaker.

The sound of the truck grew louder as we got to the gully and moved back toward the housing area. "This is the Air Police. Stop or you will be fired upon." I remember thinking the airman's voice was very matter-of-fact. I guess if you're the guy doing the shooting and not the guy getting shot at, then you can be calm. *We were not calm.*

"They are going to start shooting at us," Jon cried.

"No they're not," I said, trying to act confident.

"I think they are," Billy said, not helping my case.

"We're outside the fence. They can't shoot us now," I responded.

Suddenly the sound of a shotgun echoed through the woods, the pellets raining down on the other side of the creek.

"Maybe we should stop. Give ourselves up," Jon suggested.

"It's only another mile to the housing area," I said. "Keep moving. We're not giving up."

We were past the opening where the truck was visible, but we could hear the engine and it was beginning to move away, back toward the Gravel Gertie. No one said anything. We just kept moving.

Two hours after the mission began, we broke through the tree line and made our way back to my house. We cowered in the garage for several hours, waiting for the police to come and take us away, but no one ever showed. I peeked out the side door several times, but the neighborhood was quiet. The siren and loudspeakers had stopped before we left the woods, and now it seemed like just another Saturday afternoon.

Jon was sniffling quietly, worried that his parents would find out and take away Saturday morning cartoons. Billy and I had other worries. Both our dads were old school and we would get more than a stern lecture.

As "Taps" sounded that evening, Billy and Jon headed home. I left the garage and walked into the kitchen. Mom was cooking fried chicken and Dad was in the living room reading the newspaper. Mom gave me a big hug and asked where I had been all day.

"At the clubhouse," I answered.

"That's nice," she said.

I washed up, had dinner, and then the whole family settled in to watch NBC Saturday Night at the Movies.

On Sunday, Billy, Jon, and I gathered at my house and recounted the mission a dozen times. We were worthy secret agents. "M" would no doubt be giving us another mission sometime soon. Not too soon, though, Jon worried.

By Monday, everything seemed to be back to normal—until Dad came home.

"Bill, I need to talk to you," he said, summoning me into the living room. "There was an attempted break-in at the ammunition storage facility this weekend. Do you know anything about it?" he asked.

Before I could answer, he started talking again. "Do you know how serious breaking into a restricted area can be? The APs have orders to shoot to kill."

I swallowed hard.

Then I saw something in his eyes that I had never seen before—fear. Fear for me. Fear that I could have been shot. Fear that he might have lost his son.

"The police think it might have been some kids from the neighborhood. Is there anything you want to tell me?"

"No sir," I replied.

"Do you know anything about this?"

And then, for the first and last time in my life, I lied to my father.

"No sir," I said.

He looked sad. And I knew why.

He just nodded, said okay, and let me go.

That evening I finished my bath, kissed my parents good night, and went to my bedroom. As I pulled back the sheets and started to get under the covers, there, resting on my nightstand, was my Roy Rogers pearl-handled six-shooter.

CHAPTER THREE

IT'S A WONDERFUL LIFE

SAN ANTONIO, TEXAS
1973

The oval running track beneath my feet felt hard and unforgiving. There were three hundred yards left to go. It was time for my kick. Time for my kick. *Where is my kick?*

"Now!" I screamed, pumping my arms to gain some momentum.

The runner beside me edged into the second lane, forcing me to swing wide.

Twenty men left. I would take them down one at a time. Nineteen. Eighteen. Seventeen.

I could hear the crowd at the stadium screaming. On the grass infield, my coach, looking down at his stopwatch, was yelling at the top of his voice, "Faster! Faster!"

Sixteen. Fifteen. Fourteen. Thirteen. Twelve. Eleven. Ten. Nine. Eight. Seven. Six.

Two hundred yards left. I had to make my move if I was going to break the school record in the mile.

Five. Four. Three.

I was running out of fuel. I started my kick too soon. Behind me a runner began to catch up.

No one catches me on my kick! My lungs were burning and my legs were dead. *No one catches me!*

He caught me. He passed me.

The last hundred yards seemed like forever. I crossed the finish line and stumbled onto the infield, collapsing in pain. Drenched from sweat in the Texas heat, I rolled onto my knees and threw up the steak dinner I had eaten just three hours earlier.

"Well, you were close," the coach said, trying to console me.

"Time? What was the time?" I asked between gasps for air.

"It could have been better," the coach answered, handing me the stopwatch.

Wiping the sweat from my eyes, I looked down at the watch. "4:37.20."

"Four minutes, thirty-seven seconds, and two-tenths." It was almost a full five seconds off the record of 4:32.70. A dismal time.

My friends and teammates, Mike Morris and Mike Dippo, came dashing across the infield. "What was the time?" Morris asked excitedly.

The coach handed him the watch.

"Oh," he said, disappointed for me. "Man, it looked like such a good race."

"Hey, don't sweat it, Bill," Dippo said. "You've got one more race. You'll get it. You'll get the record."

Five seconds, I thought. In the mile, five seconds was an eternity. I had been closer to the record before: within two seconds. Lately, however, my times had been increasing rather than decreasing. I was losing my confidence and my opportunity to put my name in the school record book.

For years I had dreamed of being an Olympic-caliber runner. I read every book on the great high school and college star Jim Ryun. I watched old film of Roger Bannister, the first man to break the four-minute mile. Kip Keino and the wave of African runners thrilled me and motivated me to work harder. With every step I took on the back roads of San Antonio, I imagined I was on the final stretch of the 1500-meter gold medal race. Keino had begun his surge. Ryun was on his heels and I was about to make my move. I would let them take the lead, tire themselves out, and then I would begin my kick. *The world-famous McRaven kick.* No one could out-sprint me in the final three hundred meters. No one.

Today's race had taken its toll on me. The clock had beaten me. Maybe I was just a mediocre runner. Maybe I would never make the Olympics. Maybe none of this was worth it. I grabbed my gym bag and headed home.

"Bill, phone call!" Dad yelled from the other end of the house.

"Who is it?" I yelled back.

"I think it's one of your coaches!"

Strange, I thought. I had just come home from Thursday track practice. Coaches didn't say anything.

I picked up the phone. "Hello?"

"Bill?" came a vaguely familiar voice.

"Yes sir."

"Bill, this is Coach Turnbow," he said in a slow, soft Texas drawl. "How are you doing tonight?"

For a moment I was stunned. Coach Jerry Turnbow had been the assistant head football coach at my high school. He had departed Theodore Roosevelt two years earlier to take a head coaching job at a school across town. To those of us on the track team, the high school football coaches were like minor gods. They molded the young men in pads who would lead the school to victory. Football was the only real sport in Texas. Track was just a diversion. And football coaches, well…football coaches never associated with those of us who ran in circles. Besides, I didn't think Coach Turnbow even knew who I was.

I stumbled for a minute. "I'm fine, Coach," I answered.

"Well, Bill, I hear you have one race left to break the school record. Is that right?"

Okay, now I was really amazed. How did he know that? Why did he even care? I was a miler on a track team, a track team that hardly anyone in the school knew we had and…the coach wasn't even at the school anymore.

"Yes sir. I have one race left."

"Bill, look now, son. You can do this. You can break that school record. All you have to do is run hard. Run hard and you can break that record. I know you can do it!"

"Yes sir," I said, trying to sound confident. "I'll give it my best."

"You do that, Bill." He paused. "Well, good luck, son."

"Thank you, sir."

I hung up the phone and just sat on the edge of the bed. Coach Jerry Turnbow had just called me to wish me luck. Coach Turnbow!

Run hard, he said. *Just run hard. I know you can do it!*

Twenty. Nineteen. Eighteen. Seventeen. Sixteen. Fifteen. Fourteen.

"Run! Run!" Dippo yelled, sprinting through the infield, Morris on his heels.

I was swinging wide on the last curve. Two hundred yards to go. My lungs were screaming. My arms were pumping. My legs were churning. My kick was there.

"Faster! Faster! Faster!" the coach shouted, waving his arms in a circular motion.

Ahead was the finish line—a thin yellow tape marking the end of the race.

Thirteen. Twelve. Eleven.

My eyes were glassing over from sweat. The pain had left me. The body was in runner's shock. A wonderful feeling of numbness and euphoria, but it wouldn't last. Any second now, the lactic acid building up in my body was going to cause my muscles to seize up, and the only thing that would get me across the finish line was pure willpower.

Run hard, Bill. Just run hard. I know you can do it!

One of my favorite movies of all time is Frank Capra's Christmas classic, *It's a Wonderful Life*, starring screen legends Jimmy Stewart and Donna Reed. The movie is set in the mythical town of Bedford Falls in the 1930s and '40s. Stewart plays George Bailey, a young man who has taken over his deceased father's Savings and Loan. Reed plays his wife, Mary. Other characters in the movie are George's younger brother, Harry, whom George saved from drowning when Harry was just nine, and George's forgetful Uncle Billy. The villain in the film is the mean old Mr. Potter, a soulless banker who only lives for the money he can make off people.

George longs for the day when he can leave the small town of Bedford Falls and see the world. He wants to do big things with his life, really big things. But as the movie progresses, George never makes it out of Bedford Falls. Instead he stays in the town, going about his daily life and trying to keep the old Savings and Loan from being taken over by Mr. Potter. But eventually, bad luck befalls George Bailey and he decides that it is better to end his life and leave the insurance money to his family.

George goes to a nearby bridge, ready to jump off, when God sends an angel to help. The angel is an awkward fellow named Clarence. He tries to convince George not to end his life. George won't listen and tells Clarence that his life has been worthless and it would have been better had he never been born.

Clarence the angel decides to show George what life would have been like—*had George never been born.* They head back into town, and, much to George's surprise, the town is no longer the quaint Bedford Falls but a run-down, seedy place called Pottersville. Mary, his wife, never married and is an old maid librarian. Other things in the town have changed, and not for the better. As the scene continues to unfold, Clarence takes George to the town cemetery. There, barely visible through the overgrown grass, is the tombstone of his younger brother Harry. The tombstone shows that Harry died when he was nine.

George, not understanding what Clarence has done, screams that this isn't right. He yells, "That's a lie! Harry Bailey went to war. He got the Congressional Medal of Honor!" He stopped a kamikaze from sinking a ship. "He saved the lives of every man on that transport."

Then comes the seminal moment in the movie. Clarence says, "But George, you don't understand. Because you were never born, Harry died that day on the ice. Harry wasn't there to save all those men, because you weren't there to save Harry."

And that's when it hits you. The actions of one man, George Bailey, changed the lives not just of those he touched, but also of so many others. All the men on that ship, and their children and their children's children, were alive because of George Bailey. The town of Bedford Falls had thrived because of the kindness of George Bailey, and the people he befriended lived full and happy lives—because of George Bailey.

One hundred yards. Ten. Nine. Eight. Seven. Six.

"Push it! Push it!" I screamed out loud.

Everything I had, I gave.

The crowd was on its feet—the yelling inaudible but loud, driving me harder.

I leaned forward, pumping my arms and willing my legs to move faster and faster and faster.

Five. Four. Three.

Fifty yards. Just a few seconds. I had to hold on. Just a few more seconds.

Two. Two. Two.

Stumbling, reaching, sprawling, I fell across the finish line and tumbled onto the hard cinder track, rolling onto the infield to avoid being trampled. I couldn't breathe. The sound of my heart pounding in my ears blocked out all noise. Mike Morris was standing in front of me. I couldn't make out what he was saying, but I could see the look on his face. He handed me the stopwatch.

4:31.40.

A new school record.

Later that evening my mother would hug me. My father would tell me how proud he was, and the following week I would get a few congratulations. The record was shattered the next year by a better runner. But it didn't matter. That race would forever change my life. Knowing I could set a goal, work hard, suffer through pain and adversity, and achieve something worthwhile made me realize that I could accomplish anything I put my mind to. It made me realize that I could be a Navy SEAL. Over forty years later, I know that my life and the lives of the thousands of men and women I commanded were changed by a phone call. One act of kindness.

If we are lucky, somewhere in our lives there is a George Bailey—a person who helped us along the way. A man or woman, who, probably without even knowing it, changed everything about our own future, and in doing so, changed the lives of so many others.

Jerry Turnbow was my George Bailey, and I will be forever grateful that he took the time to call.

Thanks, Coach!

CHAPTER FOUR

THE ONLY EASY DAY WAS YESTERDAY

CORONADO, CALIFORNIA
1977

W aaater!"

"Dig! Dig harder!"

The twelve-foot wall of water was beginning to crest, and all seven men in the Inflatable Boat Small (IBS) knew they had to paddle for their lives or the wave would crush the tiny boat and send us all crashing back onto the shore. As the coxswain, my job was to hold the IBS into the oncoming wave and hope we could keep the bow centered. If the rubber boat turned sideways, we would surely dump and the few moments of dryness we had experienced over the past hour would vanish and once again we would be soaked to the bones from the cold Pacific Ocean.

The wave was upon us and my fellow SEAL trainees from Class 95 were paddling as hard as they could as I yelled the stroke cadence.

"We're losing it!" shouted one of the men.

I could feel the strain on my paddle as the wave bore down upon the tiny raft. The only thing keeping us from capsizing was my oar, which was planted firmly in the water, steadying the IBS.

We were just about over the crest of the wave. We were going to make it, I thought. Over the wave and into calm water. We just had to hold on for one more second.

Craaack! The sound was unmistakable. Wood splintering in two, like a slugger's bat snapping as a hundred-mile-an-hour fastball caught the middle of the pine.

Suddenly the rudderless boat spun sideways. Men and oars tumbled out of the IBS, caught in a vortex of water and foam, plunging beneath the wave and rolling violently on the sandy bottom off Coronado, California.

One by one the trainees popped to the surface and struggled to make their way to the beach. Each man had a chemlite taped to his life jacket, and I took a quick head count to make sure all my men were present and accounted for.

Dejected and wet, we gathered together in the surf zone and retrieved the bobbing IBS, which had been pushed down the beach and was floating aimlessly toward Tijuana, Mexico.

"All right. You guys know the drill," I said. They all nodded.

Grabbing the IBS, we mustered back on the beach in front of the SEAL training instructors. In true military fashion, we aligned the IBS with the bow facing the ocean and all seven men stood at rigid attention next to their spot on the boat. Every man had recovered his paddle...but me. I was at the stern, my green fatigues sagging from the weight of the water, my jungle boots oozing sand from the tiny eyelets, and my orange kapok life preserver pushing my head backward at an awkward angle.

Looming over me was Senior Chief Dick Ray, a highly decorated SEAL from Vietnam. Tall, with broad shoulders, jet black hair, and a pencil-thin mustache, Ray was the epitome of a Navy SEAL. Everyone respected him and everyone feared him.

"Ensign McRaven. How would you evaluate your performance?" Ray said without a hint of anger.

Before I could answer, Doc Jenkins, a large, heavyset African American corpsman, jumped in. "Pathetic. That's what it was. Just fucking pathetic!" Jenkins screamed, closing to within inches of my face. "I can't believe your boat crew couldn't get past that tiny little wave." He grabbed the man next to me by his kapok life jacket and shook him hard. "You guys are weak and none of you belong in the Teams. You make me sick to look at you."

"Mr. Mac," Ray asked calmly. "Do you have all your men and equipment?"

"No, Senior Chief," I responded.

"No! No!" Jenkins yelled. "Not only can't you get past a piss-ant wave, you can't even keep track of your men and equipment." He stomped around waving his hands fanatically. "Has someone drowned, Mr. Mac? Are you missing one of your crew?"

"No, Instructor Jenkins."

"Then what the fuck are you missing?"

"My oar, Instructor Jenkins."

"Your oar! Your oar!" he yelled in my ear. "You can't paddle a fucking IBS without an oar!" Shaking his head, Jenkins looked at Ray and asked, "Well, Senior Chief, I don't know what we should do about this."

Somehow I knew where this discussion was going. Senior Chief Ray walked over to me and in a whisper asked, "What do you think we should do, Mr. Mac? I can't go back to Commander Couteur and tell him we lost government property. We have to be good stewards of the taxpayers' dollars. Don't you think, Mr. Mac? Don't you think we need to be good stewards of the taxpayers' dollars?"

"Yes, Senior Chief."

I could see Jenkins out of the corner of my eye. He was trying not to laugh. He and Ray were the perfect good cop, bad cop.

"I tell you what we need to do, Mr. Mac. We need to find that paddle. Don't you think?"

"Yes, Senior Chief."

"Good, good. So, you and your boat crew get back in the IBS, get back in the water, and see if you can find that missing paddle."

Jenkins turned around and yelled at the top of his voice, "Hit it!"

Without hesitation, we grabbed the hand straps on the IBS and charged back into the surf zone, knowing that we would never find the broken paddle, but in an hour or so the instructors would get tired of our efforts and return us to the barracks. It was 2100 hours. The end of another long day of runs, swims, obstacle course, more runs, more swims, and constant harassment. Tomorrow would bring more of the same, and though only three weeks into SEAL training, I had learned already that "the only easy day was yesterday."

After graduating from the University of Texas I spent two months in Austin on recruiting duty before the Navy transferred me to Coronado to begin SEAL training. Basic Underwater Demolition/SEAL (BUD/S) Training was reportedly the toughest physical training in the entire military, but in August 1977, it was difficult to find out anything about SEALs or SEAL training. Even the military orders I received were cryptic—a school course number with no title. At the time, BUD/S training was just another class at the Naval Amphibious School in Coronado. While the legacy of Navy frogmen extended back to World War II, the evolution from the frogmen to the Vietnam-era SEALs was not well known to the public.

I was assigned to Class 95. The class started with 155 trainees: 146 enlisted men and 9 officers. By the end of the second week of training we were down to 100 enlisted men and 4 officers. The officers in the class included Lieutenant (Junior Grade) Dan'l Steward, who was the senior officer and therefore the class leader. There were also two other ensigns besides myself, Marc Thomas and Fred Artho. Dan'l was a Naval Academy graduate, Marc from VMI, and Fred from the University of Utah. Dan'l was a superb officer with tremendous leadership skills and physically very strong. Marc and I would end up as "swim buddies" and spend most of BUD/S lashed together during our dives and long swims. Marc was one hell of a runner, but swimming wasn't his strong suit. Together we were a great match.

Fred Artho was indestructible. With an incredible tolerance for pain, he was far and away the best runner. Together the four of us bonded quickly.

After nine weeks of training, the class was down to fifty-five total "tadpoles" and the infamous Hell Week had yet to begin. Six days of no sleep and constant physical and mental harassment, it was the second-to-last week of "First Phase." During the Second Phase of training the students learned to dive with various scuba rigs, and Third Phase was all about land warfare. Most trainees thought that if you could make it through Hell Week you were almost certain to finish BUD/S, but statistically that wasn't true. A lot of men failed the tough academics of dive phase or were uncomfortable at night underwater. Still others lacked the leadership and quick decision making necessary for the immediate action drills so prevalent in land warfare. Statistically, only 25 percent of the enlisted men made it through training and in 1977 less than 50 percent of the officers. In all, BUD/S training lasted six months, after which time you were assigned to a SEAL or Underwater Demolition Team (UDT). Then you had another six months of advanced training before you received the coveted SEAL Trident.

It was the Friday before the start of Hell Week when Dan'l Steward called us all together in the large BUD/S classroom. A Naval Academy gymnast and rower, Steward was five foot nine, with classic washboard abs, a thin waist, powerful legs, and broad shoulders. He was also a "rollback" from Class 94. The Wednesday before Class 94's Hell Week, his bicep was ripped from his arm when the rubber sling used to recover swimmers aboard a fast-moving boat caught him too high and pulled the muscle clear of the bone. After a few months of recovery, he was placed in Class 95.

Standing on the small stage, Steward came to parade rest. After four years at the Academy, it was a natural stance for him.

"Gentlemen, on Sunday night we will begin Hell Week. It is the most challenging, grueling, gut-wrenching test that most of you will ever encounter in your lives."

You could feel the anticipation in the room.

"If you finish it, you will likely go on to be Navy SEALs, the most elite warriors in modern time. You will be part of a brotherhood of men like no other the world has ever known."

He stepped down from the stage and walked into the huddled group of men. "But—the only way you can complete Hell Week is if we stay together as a team." He scanned the crowd to make sure everyone was listening. "At some point during the week all of us will falter. At some point, each of us will think about quitting. We will be enticed by the instructors to leave the ice-cold water and go someplace warm and cozy where we can relax and forgo the pain of Hell Week. They will tell you that all you have to do to get a good meal and warm bed is to ring the bell. Ring the bell three times and you're out. You won't even have to face your fellow tadpoles again."

Looking around the room, I could already see fear in the eyes of some of the men. Not fear of pain or exhaustion or even death. They feared failure.

"We must stick together!" Steward shouted. "Don't think about quitting. Don't think about how hard it's going to be in an hour or a day or a week." He paused and entered the center of the huddle. Calmly, with a look of complete confidence, he said, "Just take it one evolution at a time."

One evolution at a time. One evolution at a time. These words would stick with me for the rest of my career. They summed up a philosophy for dealing with difficult times. Most BUD/S trainees dropped out because their event horizon was too far in the distance. They struggled not with the problem of the moment, but with what they perceived would be an endless series of problems, which they believed they couldn't overcome. When you tackled just one problem, one event, or, in the vernacular of BUD/S training, one evolution at a time, then the difficult became manageable. Like many things in life, success in BUD/S didn't always go to the strongest, the fastest, or the smartest. It went to the man who faltered, who failed, who stumbled, but who persevered, who got up and kept moving. Always moving forward, one evolution at a time.

"Never quit. Never quit. Never quit!" The class picked up the refrain and came together in the center of the room. Steward yelled out, "Class 95!" Fifty-five men answered in unison, "Hooyah Class 95!"

But in one week many of those men would no longer be in Class 95.

Machine-gun fire erupted outside the small barracks room in which Steward, Thomas, Artho, and I were berthed. It was Sunday evening—the start of Hell Week.

"Muster on the grinder!" came the commanding voice of Senior Chief Ray.

As we darted out of our room, an instructor poised at the end of the hallway tossed a grenade simulator in our direction. It exploded with the force of a hundred large firecrackers, rattling the windows and almost knocking me off my feet. Standing by the stairway, another instructor tossed a smoke grenade, while a third instructor moved through the hall firing the M-60 machine gun into each room, blank brass casings falling everywhere. It was chaos. Exactly how it was intended to be.

Running behind Steward, I dashed down the two flights of stairs and into the chilly night air. Anticipating the start of Hell Week, all the men had slept in their green utility uniforms. Steward began to muster the men in five lines of ten to twelve trainees each, but the instructors would have none of it. The concrete area upon which we did daily physical training was named the grinder, and it had a reputation for grinding men down to their breaking point. The grinder was filled with BUD/S instructors, some with automatic weapons, others tossing grenade simulators, still others with hoses to soak the trainees.

"Drop down, Ensign McRaven!" yelled a familiar voice behind me.

It was Senior Chief "Bum" Grenier—a tobacco-chewing, hard-ass southern boy who said "fuck" every other word. More than any other instructor, Grenier loved to screw with the trainees. He was constantly dropping us for push-ups, spitting tobacco in our hats, and asking the trainees questions, the answers to which would get us in more trouble.

Questions like, "Mr. Mac, do you think my girlfriend is pretty?"

"Yes, Senior Chief."

"Well, then you're a liar. She is the ugliest-looking woman in California. Hit the surf!"

Of course, if you countered with, "No, Senior Chief, I think she's ugly," then you hit the surf anyway for questioning the senior chief's choice of women.

Dropping to the concrete grinder, I assumed the push-up position and began my mandatory twenty-five push-ups.

"Mr. Mac, do you think you are going to get through Hell Week?"

"Yes, Senior Chief!" I yelled over the sound of machine-gun fire.

"Your class is weak, Mr. Mac. You'll be lucky if half of them make it through tomorrow."

As he completed his sentence, I could hear the sound of the brass bell ringing three times. Someone had already quit and we weren't five minutes into Hell Week.

"See. Fucking quitters," he said, his tobacco breath hot on my face. "I'm going to make you quit, Mr. Mac. All week long you are going to see me and tremble with fear. Because all week long I am going to bring you pain."

Out of the corner of my eyes I could see the hose. He shoved it into my mouth before I could move and the full force of the water pressure blasted down my throat. I immediately turned away, but he followed my face back and forth as I shook from side to side.

"You're going to quit, Mr. Mac. You might as well do it now and save yourself the pain. Just quit now!" *Another three rings on the bell. Two men gone. Another three rings. Three men.*

"They are dropping like fucking flies. Might as well join them, Mr. Mac. Just quit!"

The water was beginning to choke me. Struggling to get a breath, I jerked the hose out of Grenier's hand. "I'm not going to fucking quit!"

Grenier reeled back, a look of surprise and anger on his face. You never challenged an instructor and got away with it. Pain was coming.

"Get on your feet, Mr. McRaven," he demanded.

I promptly came to attention and the senior chief closed to within an inch of my nose, the tobacco-stained teeth and pock-marked face filling my entire view. Suddenly, I noticed a twinkle in his eye.

"Get back with your class, Mr. Mac, and don't you dare quit on me."

I smiled. "I won't quit on you, Senior."

"Hooyah, Mr. Mac," he said softly.

The rest of the class was doing more push-ups when I joined them, but before I could get into position, I heard, "Hit the surf!" It was a familiar refrain in BUD/S training. Anytime anyone did anything that didn't meet the instructor's standards, which were very vague and quite arbitrary, the trainee, fully clothed, ran at full speed and dove into the Pacific Ocean, ensuring every part of his body was submerged. This drill was routinely followed by the "sugar cookie," during which the trainee, thoroughly soaked, rolled around on the beach so that his uniform and his body were caked with sand—wet and sandy, a particularly uncomfortable feeling as the sand had a way of chafing you throughout the rest of the day.

"Hooyah," we yelled as a sign of our class unity. Then, en masse, we ran to the beach, linked arms, and walked into the pounding surf. The instructors' job was to break us. To find out who was weak and sort them from the strong.

"Lie down," came the next command. Together we lay in the surf, head facing the ocean, feet toward the beach. The waves rolled over the top of us, cold water blasting across our bodies.

"Now," Doc Jenkins began, "you will stay in this water until someone quits. Who wants to be the first?"

Arms linked, we held each other tight and whispered from side to side, "No one quit. Never quit."

We held firm for thirty minutes, until someone in the ranks broke. I couldn't see who it was from my prone position, but seconds later I heard the sound of the bell. *Three rings. Down another man.*

As promised, the instructors brought us back to the beach. After some obligatory yelling, we were ordered to change into dry uniforms and muster on the grinder in three minutes, which we all knew wasn't enough time to switch uniforms.

Nevertheless, we sprinted back to the barracks. I had time to put on a dry T-shirt, grab a hidden Snickers bar, and dash back downstairs. Two and half minutes later, we were still late.

"Mr. Steward, do you have any control of this class?"

"Yes, Instructor," came the reply.

"Then why aren't they fully mustered on the grinder as I asked?"

"Sir, we still have thirty seconds."

Never question an instructor.

"Then you know what you can do with those thirty seconds, Mr. Steward?"

Steward didn't reply.

"Hit the surf!"

Once again, we all ran to the surf, plunged in, and returned to the grinder. The bell rang again.

Within minutes after returning we were in formation jogging to the other side of the Naval Amphibious Base. NAB Coronado was the home of BUD/S training. The BUD/S compound was on the beach side, but the main base was on the bay side. After shivering for the past hour, we were all happy to be jogging across the highway onto the main base.

Arriving at the piers that moored our Special Boat Squadron small craft, the class was now down to fifty men. The shock of the first hour had caused five men to ring the bell. They quit because they couldn't conceive making it through another six days of being cold, wet, and miserable.

No sooner had we halted the formation than the order came to "hit the bay." Once again, fully clothed and soaked to the bone, we plunged into the cold water of Coronado Bay.

"Mr. Steward, Class 95 will stay in the bay until two men quit. Do you understand me?"

"Yes, Instructor," Steward said stoically.

Swimming over to a group of five trainees, I circled the men and said to each one, "No one quits. They can't keep us in here forever."

"Are you sure?" came a reply.

"There's one!" Senior Chief Grenier, standing on the pier, laughed.

Sure enough, climbing the ladder out of the bay was one of my original boat crew members. I had always questioned this sailor's motivation, but had hoped for the best. He lifted himself onto the pier, approached the instructor, and asked to quit. To us trainees, the instructors were all sadists who wanted nothing more than for you to quit and never be seen again. In reality, they were all good men who wanted each trainee to succeed. I watched as the instructor pulled the sailor aside and asked him, man to man, "Are you sure you want to quit? You've come a long way. You can still do this." I couldn't hear the response, but the body language gave away his answer. With head down and shoulders slumped, the trainee nodded, then came to attention and promptly jogged to a nearby bus—the quitters' bus. I would never see him again.

Moments later, another, then another, then another. In all,

three more trainees quit and we weren't even into the third hour. Six hours later, the night would turn into day and three more men would ring the bell. Over the next two days we were kept constantly cold, wet, and fatigued. Just about the time you dried off and began to get "comfortable," some instructor would yell, "Hit the surf," and we would charge into the waves like crazed lunatics. By Wednesday evening, most of us were operating on automatic. We went where we were told, without question, without emotion, and just pushed through the pain. But with Wednesday also came the mudflats, the most tiring event of the week and the one that broke most of the men.

The mudflats were part of the Tijuana slews, a swamplike drainage area that ran from South San Diego into Tijuana. The mud was deep and thick, with a stench that permeated the entire area.

Late in the afternoon we paddled our IBSs from Coronado down to the mudflats. By the time we arrived the sun was getting low on the horizon.

"Mr. Steward, your class looks entirely too clean. Are you clean, Mr. Steward?"

"No, Instructor Faketty. We are dirty, filthy tadpoles." Petty Officer First Class Mike Faketty was our class proctor for First Phase. While he had to perform his duties as an instructor, it was also his job to get as many guys through First Phase as possible. Faketty was one of the few instructors who was not a Vietnam veteran, but as we would find over the course of the next few months, he was still one of the best SEALs at BUD/S. But for now his job was simple. Weed out the weak.

"No, Mr. Steward. I have conferred with my fellow instructors, and they agree, you are all way too clean." He paused and had that sadistic grin that instructors got before they hammered you. Then very quietly he said, "Hit it."

We all waded into the mud, which sucked you in up to your

waist and made movement extremely difficult. The mud had been a way of life for the Vietnam-era SEALs. The Mekong Delta was filled with mud. The Viet Cong hid in the slews of the Mekong River thinking they were safe. But the SEALs earned their reputation by going where no else would go or could go—into the VC camps. Into the mangrove and mud bogs where the enemy felt they had sanctuary. Mud was a great equalizer of men. Big or small, weak or strong, if you fought the mud, it fought back, and it was tireless.

Over the next few hours, as the sun went down and the night got cold, we stayed in the mud. There were mud relay races. Mud diving. Mud wrestling. Mud swimming. Anything to keep us in the mud. By 1900 hours, the sun was going down and every inch of our bodies was covered with mud. Then the fun began.

At the edge of the mudflats the instructors had built a small campfire—a lure, an enticement, the flames calling us to quit.

"Man, it's warm here by the fire. How's your coffee, Doc?"

"Coffee's great, Fak. How's your chow?"

"Oh, I got the beans and franks. Great chow."

Huddled at the edge of the mud pool, we sat shivering uncontrollably, hanging on every word the instructors said, but under our breath we whispered encouragement to each other.

Faketty approached the edge of the mud. "Gentlemen, I have to tell you it's really nice and warm by this fire."

I could see some of the other trainees eyeing the flames as they jumped upward with each draft from the ocean breeze.

Faketty continued, "You can come join me. All I need is for five men to quit. Just five men and you can all come sit by the fire and have some coffee."

The trainees had linked arms both for warmth and for support. Faketty paced the edge of the mud. "Just five guys. I just need five quitters."

I could feel the student beside me begin to loosen his grip. He was ready to bolt for the dry ground. "Don't quit, man," I whispered. "Hang tough, this will be over soon." His arm broke free of mine and he started to push forward through the mud.

Suddenly, from the far end of the line of trainees came a familiar tune. One man began singing loudly. It was not a song for tender ears.

"Hey!" Faketty yelled. "Keep quiet! I didn't say you could sing."

Steward joined in, then another man and another. Before long the entire class was singing. The instructors threatened us with more time in the mud. But the singing persisted and the man next to me returned to his place.

From the light of the fire, I could see the instructors smiling contentedly. They knew the class was coming together, in spite of the pain. But the evening was just beginning and the night would get worse with each passing hour.

By 2100 hours we were out of the mud and sitting on the cold ground as the instructors continued the harassment.

"Mr. Steward, Mr. Mac, Mr. Thomas, and Mr. Artho. Front and center." I unfolded my legs, struggled to my feet, and joined the other three officers next to the fire.

"Warm, isn't it?" Faketty said.

None of us spoke.

"So, here are the rules for tonight's follies. When I say, 'Hit it,' the entire class has five minutes to get as far away from here as possible. Then when you hear the sound of the air horn you will turn around and try to make your way back to the base camp. If you successfully elude the instructors, who will be out hunting for you, then you can sit by the fire and have some chow. If you get caught, however, you will spend the rest of the evening in the mud. Am I clear, gentlemen?"

"Yes, Instructor Faketty," we yelled in unison.

"Good. Just remember—it pays to be a winner."

After Steward gave a quick brief to the class, Faketty yelled out the start command and like drunken mice we all took off in different directions. The night sky was clear and cold. The stars were bright but there was no moon. It was dark, but my eyes had already adjusted to the ambient light.

Instead of running far, I decided that tactically it would be better to stay close to the camp, making the distance I had to elude the instructors much shorter. After about a hundred yards I stopped and found good concealment behind a mound of sand and scrub brush.

The starlight illuminated shadows of trainees dashing in every direction—freezing, coated with mud, slow-witted from exhaustion, their reasoning was elementary at best. Suddenly a figure came from my blind side and dove over the mound, settling down beside me. It was my fellow trainee, Seaman Marshall Lubin. Lubin was quite a character. The oldest man in the class at age thirty-two, he was a '60s-style hippie who had traveled the world "escorting" women to exotic locations. After his last relationship went south, he decided to join the Navy and become a diver. During one of our classroom sessions on sentry stalking, Lubin approached me afterward with a stunning revelation—to him. "Mr. Mac, they're teaching us to kill people," he said with a look of horror. "Yes, Lubin," I responded calmly, noting that SEALs in Vietnam often had to take out Viet Cong sentries in order to get to their objective. "What did you think this course was all about?" I asked.

"I thought we were learning to be scuba divers. Nobody told me we were going to kill people." He was a lover, not a fighter. But, like most who came to BUD/S, witting or not of the product it produced, Lubin wanted to test his inner strength. To his credit, he stayed the course, would graduate a SEAL, and later leave the Navy to be a civilian chiropractor.

"Damn, I'm cold, Mr. Mac. I can't last out here too long. We have got to get back to the fire."

"Patience, Marshall. If we hurry we'll get caught and spend the rest of the night in the mud."

Suddenly another figure came out of the shadows. "Hey, you guys want some hot chocolate?"

"What?"

"Hot chocolate. You guys want some hot chocolate?"

It had to be a trick, I thought. Or maybe the hallucinations had already started, those thoroughly exhausted moments when your mind visualized what you really hoped to see. It was a well-known phenomenon during Hell Week. I could smell the warm chocolate and hear the milk pouring into a canteen cup.

"Here, here. Drink it. I've got to go." Without hesitation, Lubin and I drank what was given to us and the shadowy figure departed. I watched as the apparition moved from mound to mound like Gunga Din, pouring cups of hot chocolate into freezing trainees. The sweet taste on my swollen tongue told me the experience was real, but still very strange.

Lubin and I began to move closer to the fire. Bounding from one small mound to the next, we closed the distance until we were within sight of the fire and could hear the instructors. But this was the danger zone. Close enough to see the prize—close enough to be caught.

Lubin was shaking so hard it was making me colder. "Lubin, stop shaking, man. You're making noise," I whispered.

"I can't stop, sir. I've got to get to the fire."

"Not now," I warned. "There are too many instructors moving around." But before I could stop him, Lubin was on the move.

I could see his lanky figure slithering across the sand trying to make it to the next mound, but I could also see an instructor, eyeing his prey. Hunkering down next to a small bush, Lubin was within twenty-five yards of the fire.

"Well, well, what do we have here?" yelled Petty Officer Faketty. "Seaman Recruit Lubin."

Lubin stood up and faced the music. As I watched, the instructors surrounded him. I thought it was my time to make a dash for the fire.

"Lubin, where is your swim buddy? Surely you are not out here alone without a swim buddy. That would be a violation of BUD/S regulations."

Swim buddy. I was screwed and I knew it. In BUD/S you always, always swam, ran, dived, ate, and, in the field, slept with a swim buddy. But the rules of this nighttime folly had not mentioned swim buddies.

"Here's the deal, Lubin. Either you give up your swim buddy or every trainee will spend the evening in the mud."

I knew that there was no way Lubin was going to give me up, but the instructors were going to make it very painful for him. I stepped forward and identified myself.

"Mr. Mac," Faketty said with a chuckle. "Looks like you and Seaman Lubin have a date with the mudflats."

I sighed.

"Hit it," Faketty yelled.

Lubin and I nodded and we plunged into the waist-deep mud, where we would stay for the next hour, watching as our fellow trainees sat by the fire and ate C-rations.

When we were finally set free of the mudflats it was about 0100. We had been assigned "tents," which were actually lean-tos whose open side faced the ocean breeze, making them no better than sleeping outside.

Now, barely able to move with a core temperature well below normal, I fell into the tent and was immediately grabbed by my tentmate, Petty Officer Earl Hayes. A former junior college running back, Hayes, a large, muscular African American from Alabama, was one of the best enlisted men in the class. He had natural leadership abilities and was a two-time rollback, making this Hell Week his third. To my knowledge, no man had ever completed three Hell Weeks.

Draping his large body over mine, Hayes tried to stop my shaking. It was uncontrollable, though. For the next several hours Hayes lay on top of me, transferring what little body heat he had to me.

By 0600, the sun was up and I had survived another day. Hump day was over. Only three more days to go.

Over the course of the next two days, we continued with the unending series of physical events. As every day passed we lost a few more men, but with the strong leadership of Dan'l Steward and the senior enlisted men in the class, we were actually doing quite well.

Friday evening brought the infamous Treasure Hunt, a string of clues that led each seven-man boat crew on a long hike and paddle around Coronado Island. Ordinarily, this wouldn't have been a difficult evolution, but by Friday evening most of the trainees could barely walk from swollen feet, chafed groins, and just pure exhaustion. Additionally, many of the men had begun to hallucinate from the fatigue: sharks on the beach, sea monsters rising from the waves, bikini-clad women waving to us from imaginary boats. It made for interesting conversations.

My boat crew, comprised of the "big men," those trainees over six feet tall, had already found three of the six clues. We were paddling our way across San Diego Bay in our IBS searching for the next clue when one of the men on the bow called out.

"Mr. Mac, look out for that fence. About one o'clock."

We were in the middle of San Diego Bay, I thought. *There was no fence.* Then another trainee called out. "It's about a hundred yards out."

Steering the boat, I squinted into the darkness and peered outward at the one o'clock direction. We were in the middle of San Diego Bay—there *was* no fence.

A third man in my boat crew then said softly, "Come left about ten degrees."

I looked again. We were in the middle of San Diego Bay. *There was no fence.* As we paddled onward, I continued to get updates on the fence from every member of my crew, except the guy sitting right in front of me who was watching a Padres game in his mind. They had gone into extra innings.

It had been five days since I last closed my eyes, but I felt my wits were still strong—but I just couldn't see the damn fence.

"Fifty yards ahead, sir."

"Come a little more to the left."

What the hell, I thought. I shifted my paddle and steered the IBS to the left. Moments later, in complete unison, the entire crew looked to the starboard side of the IBS and watched as we passed the "fence." We were in the middle of San Diego Bay. *There was no fence!*

Thirty minutes later we reached the rocky shoreline of the Naval Amphibious Base. We found the next clue, which led us back to the BUD/S compound. With the rubber boat on our heads, we jogged the two miles back to BUD/S, where we picked up the last and final clue. The men could barely walk and our objective was two miles away, up the beach to the North Island Naval Air Station fence. We had been dry for the past several hours and nothing felt better than being dry, but carrying the IBS to the fence two miles away seemed a daunting task.

"We paddle down to the fence," I said.

The boat crew let out a collective groan. "Sir, we can't get back in the water. What if we dump? We'll be wet the rest of the night."

"Do you guys really think you can walk the two miles to the fence and then two miles back?" I asked.

"It's better than being wet. Yeah," came the refrain.

"Let's go, guys," I said without further discussion. "To the beach."

It was 2300 and the tide was out and the surf low. It was a good decision, I thought. We entered the water and everyone immediately jumped into the IBS, not wanting to get any wetter than they had to.

We negotiated the first wave without a problem. Only two more waves to go and we would be out in calm water. After that we could take our time paddling down to the North Island fence.

The second wave seemed a little bigger, but only the bow men got splashed and we paddled onward, confident in our seamanship.

As I saw the third wave building, the poem "Casey at the Bat" flashed through my head: *"There was no joy in Mudville—mighty Casey has struck out."*

"Waaater!" came the familiar yell.

"Stroke! Stroke!" I screamed.

It was too late. Tossing the tiny IBS in the air, the wave sent us hurtling into the surf, paddles and men flying everywhere, fully clothed, deeply fatigued, swollen and raw from chafing. The hundred-yard swim back into the beach felt like an English Channel crossing. Crawling out of the water, I looked around and saw the men starting to emerge from the surf.

Body language is an interesting study. Even at midnight, soaked from head to toe, covered in sand with their utility uniforms sagging around their ankles, I could see the frustration in each man's posture. They were cold and wet...again—and it was my fault. On top of the sand berm, which separated the BUD/S compound from the beach, I could hear the booming voice of Doc Jenkins broadcasting over the bullhorn.

"What the fuck were you thinking, Mr. Mac?" He laughed maniacally just for theatrical emphasis. "Now you're all wet again. It would have been a lot easier to walk—and much, much dryer. I bet your boat crew loves you for that decision." He laughed again.

It was certainly not the first mistake I had made in BUD/S, but somehow it seemed to be the most egregious because it affected other guys—and we were cold and wet. We hated being cold and wet.

Within a minute all the men were on the beach with their paddles and mustered beside our IBS. I expected a small mutiny on my hands, or at least a full ration of shit. But with Doc Jenkins' laughter echoing off the compound walls, my boat crew—my fellow trainees, my teammates—grabbed the rubber straps and with an act of defiance picked up the IBS and charged back into the surf. It was all I could do to keep up. Each man leaped into the boat exactly on time and began stroking hard with a determination we didn't have during the first attempt.

"You'll never make it, Mr. Mac!" Jenkins yelled from the berm. But we did.

Within a minute we had cleared the set of three waves without incident and found ourselves paddling easily toward the North Island fence. Whether from exhaustion or out of spite, we began laughing as loud as we could. Loud enough for Doc Jenkins to hear that we had not been beaten. Forty-five minutes later we crossed back through the surf and arrived dry and spirited at the fence. There, waiting for us, were Jenkins and Senior Chief Grenier. They had driven to the fence.

We placed the IBS with the bow facing outward, came to attention at our spots, yelled a hearty "Hooyah," and stood by for instructions.

"Don't be so fucking cocky," Jenkins said. "The night is young and you still have another day of Hell Week. In fact, we may just extend it an extra day."

There were always rumors that the instructors had the authority to make Hell Week seven days long. Start on Sunday, finish on Sunday. No one could ever remember a time when that happened, but the threat scared all of us and we quickly quieted down.

Grenier came around to the bow of the boat and faced my crew and me. "Mr. Mac, the Treasure Hunt is over. Proceed back to the compound, and you had better hurry. The other crews are already moving in that direction and the last boat crew to arrive will regret their tardiness. Move it!"

This time we decided to walk back to the compound carrying the IBS on our head. While defiance was all well and good, none of us wanted to be wet again.

On the way back, I could see one of the other boat crews several hundred yards ahead of us. Just off to the left of the beach was the famous Hotel del Coronado. This grand old Victorian landmark had been around for almost a hundred years and guests had included presidents, kings, movie stars, and sports figures. Jutting off from the beach was a concrete pathway that took visitors right up to the entrance of the hotel. As my boat crew plodded painfully back to the BUD/S compound, I looked up and noticed that the boat in front of me was gone. Shifting my head, I tried to look through the glaring lights of the hotel and the Coronado Shores condominiums, which lay just beyond the Del. Where had that boat gone? Was there a shortcut I didn't know about? At this point, even a few hundred yards made a huge difference.

We continued on down the beach until we came abreast of the hotel. It was a little after midnight on a Friday and there were still a lot of tourists milling about. I heard the commotion before I could see anything. There in the glare of the Hotel del Coronado lights, the missing boat was being escorted out. In a state of complete oblivion, the boat crew had walked up the concrete path into the hotel lobby, coming to rest in the middle of a large crowd of partiers. The Del's manager, who was a Coronado resident and well acquainted with Hell Week, very gently eased the men back onto the path and down to the beach, much to the amusement of the hotel guests.

By 0100 all the boat crews were back at the compound. It was Saturday morning and, barring any extension of Hell Week, we had just one day to go.

By Saturday, your feet were so swollen you couldn't get your boots off without cutting them clear. Your hands were so enlarged that you couldn't close them to grasp things. Your thighs were chafed raw from the constant exposure to sand and water. But, interestingly enough, most of us had caught our second wind— no sleep for five days, constantly cold and wet, nonstop harassment, physically exhausted. Still, we were young and incredibly motivated, and at this point the only thing that would stop us was death—and the instructors wouldn't allow that.

"Muster on the grinder in five minutes," Steward yelled, his voice hoarse from a week of giving orders.

With IBSs firmly planted on our heads, we jogged to chow, ate, and then spent the rest of the morning doing relay races at the base athletic field. By noon, most boat crews were unable to walk at all. While no one was going to quit, we also couldn't complete the events. Finally, out of anger because of our apparent "lack of effort," Instructor Faketty marched us from the athletic field to the bay and ordered everyone into the water. One by one the boat crews set down their IBSs and waded into the harbor.

We were just about at our breaking point and the instructors knew it. We were bone tired: the kind of fatigue where every breath takes effort. We had no energy reserves left. The cold water sapped every last ounce of strength. Huddled together in the bay, the remaining men were just barely holding on.

"You guys are pathetic," Jenkins yelled. "I can't bear to look at you. Everyone turn around so I don't have to look at your face."

As directed, we slowly turned from the beach and faced outward, treading water and looking toward the south end of San Diego Bay.

"We still don't have our quota of quitters yet," Jenkins announced. "So the class will stay in the water until five more men quit."

The threat of quitting brought us closer in the water, like a herd protecting itself from an outside threat. "Don't quit. Everyone stay together." Whispers of encouragement spread across the class.

"I figure in thirty minutes at least five of you will quit. Let's start the clock now."

Thirty minutes. We couldn't make thirty minutes and we all knew it. Maybe now was the time we died. Would they let us die? Because no one was going to quit. Not now, not this class. Not after six days of hell.

"What are you whispering about?" Faketty shouted. "Stop the fucking whispering and give me five quitters."

We got closer.

"Turn around, you maggots!"

Slowly the class did a pivot in the water, and there, standing beside Instructor Faketty, dressed in starched green utilities and standing at parade rest, were all the instructors who had put us through Hell Week.

Faketty smiled. "Congratulations, Class 95. Hell Week is over."

None of us moved, none of us cheered. The past six days had been one test after another. Was this another test? To lift us up and then break us down again?

"Mr. Steward. Get the class out of the water. Hell Week is secure. Well done."

It was over. As a class we had survived. As men we had pushed ourselves to our limits and found the inner strength to carry on. The remaining men could barely exit the water. Tired well beyond exhaustion, we helped each other to the beach and once again lifted our IBSs atop our heads and made our way back to the barracks.

For the next thirty-seven years I would compare every tough situation I was in to the rigors of Hell Week. Throughout the rest of my career I was never as cold, or wet, or exhausted as I was in Hell Week, and therefore I knew whatever life threw at me, I could make it.

But BUD/S was far from over. In the next five months the class would lose another fifteen good men. Phase Two, the diving portion of training, weeded out most of them. Those who hadn't been raised around the water struggled with the long nighttime dives and the claustrophobia that came with diving under ships in the harbor.

The land warfare phase took out the final few, men who had trouble maintaining their situational awareness in the middle of live fire exercises. By the end of February 1978 we were down to thirty-three men and only two days from graduation. There was one final training evolution—helicopter cast and recovery.

The evolution was simple. Two squads of eight men each would load a twin-bladed CH-46 helicopter and fly from the athletic field to a position over the bay. Once in position, the helo would lower its ramp, and one by one the men in the first squad would leap from the helo into the water. This would be followed by the second squad. Soon thereafter, the helo would come around, dangle a rope ladder from a hole in the center of the aircraft, and the swimmers would climb up the ladder back into the helicopter. Simple.

In fact it was so simple and fun to watch that the families of the graduating frogmen were invited to view the event from the beach.

"Bill, your squad ready?" Steward asked.

"Good to go, sir!"

The haze gray Navy helicopter set down on the football field and lowered its ramp. Steward and his squad loaded up first and I motioned to my squad to follow. The roar of the engines made communication difficult, but the crew chief standing on the edge of the ramp directed us to our places on the nylon bench.

The helo held about sixteen troops, eight on each side. We sat on nylon benches that folded up when not in use. As with most Navy helos, the overhead piping dripped hydraulic fluid, and a thin film of slick brown liquid covered the metal floorboard, making walking tricky.

The Navy cast master, the enlisted man in charge of the evolution, gave us the buckle-up sign, and soon after we lifted off. Looking out the small porthole, I could see the families sitting on bleachers anxiously awaiting the first cast of swimmers.

It was a beautiful San Diego day, clear blue skies. The winds were softly blowing out of the south. The bay was flat and the water no longer seemed like our enemy. Our spirits were sky high, knowing that we were only forty-eight hours from becoming full-fledged Navy frogmen.

The helo banked to the north and the cast master gave us the two-minute warning. Steward's squad unbuckled, stood up, and began to move toward the ramp. Dressed in swim trunks, a wet suit top, a mask and fins hooked on their web belts, they looked like real frogmen. The helo dropped down to about six feet off the water and slowed to ten knots. Hooked into a gunner's belt securing him to the helo, the cast master leaned over the edge of the ramp and waited for the aircraft to slow. Raising his hand, the cast master looked toward Steward and yelled, "Go, go, go!"

Leaping from the ramp, Steward held a tight body position and entered the water smoothly. The rest of his squad followed, splashing into the bay and then swimming apart to ensure they were properly separated for the helo pickup. Minutes later, my squad received the order to unbuckle and stand up.

I moved to the edge of the ramp and the cast master gently put his hand on my chest, stopping me from going any farther. I looked out the back end and could see the spray kicking up as the helo dropped to several feet off the water. My heart was pounding, not from any fear of jumping out the back, but from the excitement of knowing that I was really going to be a frogman.

This was the last event. No more harassment. No more forced entry into the cold water. More important, I felt like I had earned the respect of the Vietnam-era SEAL and UDT instructors. I was about to become part of the Teams. Just this one final event.

"Stand by!" came the order from the cast master.

He looked down, checked the height of the helo, and then turned to me, gave a clear, definitive hand signal, and yelled, "Go, go, go!"

Tucking my head into my chest, crossing my arms and gripping my thighs tightly, I leapt from the ramp and plunged about ten feet into the water. A second later I popped to the surface and saw the helo moving away, still dropping the rest of my squad.

I got a quick head count and a thumbs-up from each swimmer

to make sure everyone was okay. We were straight and lined up evenly behind Steward's squad.

The helo had already swung around and the cast master had lowered the rope ladder out the "hell hole."

As the slow-moving helo approached each man, they grabbed the ladder and muscled their way up the rungs back into the helicopter. Within minutes all of Steward's men had been collected. I was the first swimmer in the second squad, and as the helo approached I could see the helmeted faces of the pilots flying the aircraft.

The ladder was down, but the twin blades of the helo blasted the water with such force that it shrouded the aircraft in a cloak of spray and mist. Pulling my mask over my face, I braced for the blast as the helo approached. The ladder was well over ten feet long and dragged over the top of me. Reaching for one of the wooden rungs, I pulled myself up the short distance and into the helo. Scrambling through the hell hole, I made my way into my assigned seat on the bench.

Something was wrong! Water was lapping at my feet. Suddenly, a wave of water rushed down the aisle and now we were waist deep and the helo was sinking. Looking toward the cockpit, I could see the crew furiously trying to get control of the aircraft. Power in the number one engine was lost and the helo had settled into the bay and was going down fast. As trainees, we were briefed that if the helicopter went in the water to sit tight and wait for the blades to stop moving. Then we could exit the side door in an orderly fashion. Right...

Out the side door I could see the blades just several feet off the water, spinning at full speed. It looked like a blender, and any attempt to exit out the side could get us all cut to pieces. We waited for a signal from the cast master. The ramp and the tail section were underwater and there was no way out the back. Struggling to keep the helo afloat, the pilots were trying to nudge it toward land

and beach it to save the aircraft—but there was too much weight in the tail end. Either we got out or all of us would perish.

Eyes wide and looking for options, the cast master knew there was only one choice. Pointing to the side door, he screamed, "Out, out, out!" I looked at the men surrounding me and nodded. We had to go! It was either out or down.

Steward waved his hand. "Follow me!"

The blades were only three feet off the water, turning at a blinding speed, trying to get all the torque they could to lift the drowning aircraft out of the water. Without hesitation I dove out the side door, driving my body as deep underwater as I could. The neoprene wet suit top was incredibly buoyant and fought my efforts to get deeper.

Dig, dig! I yelled in my brain. Kicking as hard as I could, I stroked underwater, knowing that if I came up too soon the blades would decapitate me. Above me I could see the shadows of the blades, *whop, whop, whop,* as they tried to grab air.

Deeper, deeper, deeper! You have to get deeper. I was losing my breath fighting the wet suit. Finally, I could see the shadow of the rotors behind me and I surfaced a good twenty meters beyond the tip of the blades. Everywhere beside me my men were popping up, and once again, I looked around for a thumbs-up and counted heads. We had all made it out safely.

"Mr. Mac! Mr. Mac!" Lubin, who was about ten yards ahead of me, was frantically waving his hands, urging me to look over my shoulder. Like some maniacal out-of-control machine, the helo was moving in our direction, the blades beating just above the water, and the pilots couldn't control it.

"Holy shit!" I turned and began stroking as fast I could. Churning the water around me, I clawed as hard as I could to gain some distance between the helo and me. Within a few moments the helo turned back away from the clump of swimmers and we were out of danger. Minutes later a small safety boat picked us up out of the bay and returned us to the shore.

The parents who were attending the final exercise rushed toward the safety boat, hugging their sons as they disembarked and wondering what their boys had gotten into. The rest of us were laughing. We had responded well under pressure and we were giddy with pride. An hour later the pilot, with a fully flooded fuselage, managed to maneuver the helicopter to the beach and the crew got out unharmed.

"One hell of a way to end your training," Faketty said to me.

"Well," I replied. "Let's just hope it's not an indication of things to come."

We all boarded the bus, headed back to the barracks, and two days later thirty-three men from Class 95 graduated from Basic Underwater Demolition/SEAL Training. I could never have imagined that thirty-six years after graduation I would still be a frogman, having served longer than any other SEAL on active duty. And that our final evolution at BUD/S was in fact an indication of many things to come.

CHAPTER FIVE

THE HAND OF GOD?

Subic Bay Naval Station, Philippines

1981

The point man took a knee. Behind him the squad of SEALs immediately stopped, each man taking up a security position along the narrow jungle path. It was hot. It was humid. The mosquitoes swarmed. The sounds of night life in the tropics chirped and cawed and buzzed, and the giant palms with their outstretched fronds seemed to inhale and exhale with every gust of evening breeze.

Peering through an AN/PVS-2 Starlight Scope, the point man scanned the opening in front of him. One hundred yards away, three men, guns carried at low port, paced before a small thatched two-room hut.

Time was getting short. The SEAL squad was hours behind their intended schedule. Two days earlier, they had been inserted into the jungle by helicopter and linked up with a Negrito scout. The Negritoes, pygmy-like natives who lived in the rain forest, were the world's greatest trackers. Indigenous to this part of the Philippines, they knew every break in the mountain, every clean watering hole, and, most important, every path through the triple canopy jungle.

Five days earlier, Colonel Bernard B. Brause, commander of the Marine barracks at Subic Bay Naval Station, had been kidnapped on his way home from work. The Moro National Liberation Front (MNLF), an Islamic terrorist group, had claimed credit. They issued statements threatening to kill Brause unless five of their compatriots were released by the end of the week. SEALs from SEAL Team

One, stationed at Naval Special Warfare Unit One (NSWU-1) in Subic, had been given the mission to rescue the colonel. Intelligence indicated that the terrorists were going to move Brause at daybreak. *One hour away.*

Sliding back into the jungle, the point man and the SEAL platoon commander huddled under a small green poncho. Pulling out a red-lens flashlight and a map, the point man began to brief the platoon commander. The basic mission was unchanged. The guards were as expected. The SEAL snipers would engage the guards. If the intelligence was right, the hostage would be inside, guarded by another two men. But once the snipers fired the first rounds, all hell would break loose. The remaining SEALs would rush the building, clear the rooms, and rescue the hostage. *Simple...*

Crawling on their bellies, their M-14s laid across their arms, two SEALs, their faces streaked with green-and-black camouflage, emerged from the tree line. Behind them the other men crouched down low, ready to move at the first shot.

Breathing deeply, the first sniper peered through the grainy green scope, trying to put his crosshairs on the guard farthest from the hut. The night was so dark that what little ambient light existed was useless. Sweat dripped from his forehead, stinging his eyes and obscuring the front lens of the scope.

Suddenly, shots rang out. The guard at the far end of the shack had spotted the SEALs and began to yell, firing erratically in the direction of the jungle.

"Fire, fire, fire!" came the call from the SEAL platoon commander.

From the tree line, the SEALs opened up on full automatic, rushing the small shack, leapfrogging forward in pairs to maintain the volume of fire.

"Move, move!" screamed one of the SEALs.

Diving underneath the shack, one guard began shooting wildly at the oncoming SEALs. "Kill the hostage! Kill the hostage!" he yelled in broken English.

From inside the shack, a burst of automatic fire rang out. Running full speed, the point man crashed through the door.

On the other side, two men, guns raised, immediately opened fire on the SEAL, the flash from their AK-47s sending blinding light throughout the small hooch.

"You're fucking dead!" said one of the "terrorists."

The point man lowered his rifle and shook his head. "Shit."

From the other end of the jungle opening, I watched as the training exercise unfolded. The mission was a disaster. The SEALs were late in arriving to the target. They had been compromised in the tree line, and once the shooting started, they failed to move quickly enough to rescue the "hostage."

It had been a long couple of weeks and this hostage rescue training mission was the culmination of Special Warfare Exercise 1981, or SPECWAREX 81. As the Naval Special Warfare Unit One assistant training officer, my job had been to help plan this particular scenario, arrange the opposition force, coordinate the logistics, and escort our VIP "hostage," Colonel Barney Brause.

Brause was the senior Marine officer at Subic Bay Naval Station. The station had been used as an American naval base for almost a hundred years and had a long and sometimes salacious history of taking care of Marines and sailors. The city of Olongapo was just outside the main gate. With over a thousand bars and four thousand Filipino "hostesses," Olongapo was made for weary sailors and Marines coming off long deployments.

As the commander of the Marine barracks, Brause was in charge of both the Marine combat contingent in Subic and the Office of the Provost Marshal, which served as the local law enforcement agency. Brause himself was a combat-tested Marine. A former member of the famed 1st Reconnaissance Battalion, he had served as an advisor to the Vietnamese reconnaissance units. He was a tough, rugged, no-nonsense Marine.

On base, the SEALs and the Marines had not always gotten

along. Fights out in Olongapo were a daily occurrence. Invariably one of my SEALs ended up in the overnight brig, having served notice that we were "tougher than the Marines." I recruited Brause to play our hostage in hopes of building some rapport with the senior Marine, while at the same time showcasing just how capable the Navy SEALs were at hostage rescue. *Clearly, this was not going as planned.*

Brause lifted himself off the plywood floor of the makeshift hut. "Well, that was fun!" he said casually.

"I'm sorry, sir," I responded. "The SEALs were compromised as they approached the target and the bad guys opened up on them."

Brause straightened up, tucked in his shirt, and smiled at me. "Well, at least the OPFOR played it straight. I've been on these exercises before where the assault force never loses. It's way too canned. This was good. Hopefully your guys will learn something from their mistakes."

I was somewhat taken aback. I had expected Brause to crow about how badly we screwed up. As a young officer, watching the colonel deal with an awkward situation was a learning moment for me.

"Hey, Mac, don't worry," he said, slapping my arm. "I've been on dozens of training and real-world missions that didn't work out half as well. Your guys will be fine."

"Okay," he said with authority. "What's next? Where do we go from here?"

"Well, sir. The plan calls for us to link up with the allies and then do a vehicle extraction to Cubi airfield. We have two MC-130 Combat Talon aircraft due to land in about twenty minutes. The SEALs are all getting on the first aircraft, but you and I are on the second bird with our foreign partners."

SPECWAREX was a joint, combined exercise that, in addition to the Navy SEALs, included Special Forces from the Army Green Berets, the Australian Special Air Service and New Zealand Special

Air Service, and Filipino SEALs. The SEALs involved in the hostage rescue mission were tasked with handing off Colonel Brause to our allies.

I looked at my watch. It was 0400. The planes were due to land at 0430 and then conduct three hours of low-level flying through the mountains and over the water. We were way behind schedule, and I suspected that after the training was over, the colonel still had a long day ahead of him.

I looked at my watch again. "Sir," I said, trying to be respectful of his time. "Why don't we call it a night? We aren't scheduled to do anything other than ride in the back of the bird, and I know it's been a long day for you."

One.

Brause looked at me somewhat disappointed. "Mac, look. I intend to play this all the way through. If the SOF guys are going to ride around for hours, so will I."

Exactly what I expected.

"Roger, sir. Let's get moving, then."

I nodded to the point man and we continued the scenario.

Outside, the SEALs formed a security perimeter and Brause was moved into the center of the circle. The corpsman did a cursory check to ensure the "hostage" didn't need immediate medical care. Satisfied that Brause was well enough to walk, the platoon began moving back into the jungle. After a short patrol through the thick underbrush, we came to a small opening and linked up with the New Zealand SAS and our other allied partners. Waiting in the opening was our ride out of the jungle: several World War II–style jeeps and a couple of large four-by-four trucks that could hold all the troops.

"Hey, mate!" came the whispered voice of the Kiwi warrant officer. "I hear the rescue was a fucking goat rope."

The SEAL platoon commander dropped his head a bit and acknowledged the obvious.

"What the fuck do you want us to do from here?"

I drew close and said in a low voice, "Follow through with the plan. The birds are due to arrive in thirty minutes. The SEALs will board the first aircraft and you guys are on chalk two."

"Right-oh," he said, turning to his sergeant. "Rally the boys and let's get moving."

The SEALs passed off the colonel to the Kiwi warrant officer and then the entire force boarded the vehicles for the short ride out of the jungle. I hopped in the truck with the colonel and squeezed in between him and a Filipino SEAL.

Inside the truck the heat was oppressive, made worse by the fact that we lowered the canvas flap to hide our presence. Sweat poured down my face and I could barely see through the thick cloud of mosquitoes that had followed us into the bed of the truck. Beside me, Brause, wearing his Marine camouflage utilities, seemed unperturbed by either the heat or the bugs.

The convoy commander stopped momentarily to check his bearings. Looking at my map through a red-lens flashlight, I realized we were within a few hundred yards of the airfield. I took a quick sip from my canteen and offered the colonel a drink.

It was almost 0415. The two C-130s were due to arrive exactly at 0430.

Minutes later, we broke through the jungle and onto a hard-packed road at the far end of the runway. Everyone jumped out of their vehicles and immediately took up security positions. The Filipino SEAL, who had been sitting beside us, grabbed the colonel and moved him to the center of the semicircle, ensuring that our VIP was well protected. I followed closely behind.

We were on the top of a small hill that provided a clear view of the entire Cubi Naval Air Station. Cubi was colocated with Subic Naval Base and served as the main airfield for the Pacific Fleet in the South China Sea. The runway sat on a long peninsula that jutted out into Subic Bay. Across the bay was Green Beach, a large swath of sand and jungle that served as the main training area for deployed Marines. Beyond the beach rose the mountains that protected the bay from the monsoon storms that ravaged the Pacific during the summer, and far in the distance lay the bustling town of Subic Bay with its twinkling lights and hundreds of fishing boats.

The night was quiet now. There was no movement and the insects seemed to have retreated back into the jungle. I could hear the faint voice of an Aussie radioman talking on his PRC-25 with the crew of the MC-130. Murmurs. More murmurs.

"Pssst. Pssst."

Someone was motioning to me in the dark. I moved to the outer circle.

"What?" I whispered to the New Zealand officer.

"The Hercs are running late," he said.

"Shit." I looked at my watch. "How late?"

"They say another five minutes."

"Okay. Nothing we can do but wait."

I returned to the center of the formation. "Colonel. The birds are running a few minutes behind schedule. They should be on the ground in about five."

He nodded without saying a word.

Five became ten and ten became fifteen. I turned to the colonel again.

"Sir. Are you sure you don't want to forgo the last part of this exercise?"

There wasn't an immediate response. I could tell he was now starting to think about my offer.

"No," he said somewhat reluctantly. "Let's see it through."

Two.

Fifteen minutes later the muffled rumbling of a four-engine C-130 could be heard in the distance.

"Inbound." The word spread throughout the force.

Getting to our feet, the colonel, the Filipino SEAL, and I fell in behind the Kiwi formation. The moon had fallen behind the crest of the mountains and it was pitch black. If not for the dim lights of Subic Bay, the commandos would have been almost invisible.

The sound of the engines grew louder, but the MC-130s were still undetectable against the night sky. Thirty minutes earlier, the two aircraft from the 1st Special Operations Squadron at nearby Clark Air Base had departed for the short hop to Cubi. Flying at 180 knots, just above the rice paddies north of Subic, they would bank west, come in between the mountains, and then, using their advanced avionics, conduct a blacked-out landing in less than three thousand feet onto Cubi airfield. There was something unnatural about a large cargo plane with a giant wingspan maneuvering so deftly in the sky.

"Here they come!" said the Kiwi, his voice rising with a sense of anticipation.

The two aircrafts' outlines were almost imperceptible. I craned my head trying to locate the birds with my ears. The screech of the wheels and the roar of the engines announced their arrival, and we began to move off the small hill toward the runway. The SEALs were already out of the jungle moving toward "chalk one"—the first aircraft.

It was about two hundred yards to the ramp of the second aircraft, and now everyone was running at a double-time pace. As the birds turned on the tarmac to line up for their quick takeoff, two crewmen exited off the ramp and, using red-lens flashlights, signaled the approaching forces.

I looked over at the colonel and could see that the past several days were starting to take their toll on him. He hadn't slept in days. He was dehydrated from his time in the jungle and probably hadn't eaten a decent meal in the past forty-eight hours. The next three hours were not going to help matters. We would take off from Cubi and immediately rocket upward to avoid "enemy" gunfire. Then the two MC-130s would head west toward the mountains behind

Green Beach. Once there, we would begin hours of low-level flying up and down, up and down, up and down, and up and down, thousands of feet of changing elevation. After the first few minutes of up-and-down flying, the back of the plane would be filled with the putrid smell of vomit, which would cause more vomiting, but the up and down would not stop. To me, flying in the back of a Combat Talon doing low-level terrain following was one of the most exhilarating experiences in special operations. However, not everyone shared my enthusiasm.

Heat from the engines blasted across my face and the noise of the props made any real communication impossible. As we started to board the airplane I grabbed the colonel one final time. It was 0500.

Pointing to my watch, I yelled over the noise, "0500!"

The Green Berets and allied commandos were boarding behind us.

The colonel grabbed my wrist and looked at the time. I knew that Brause would board the plane unless I gave him a reason not to. The whole point of asking him to be our "hostage" was to build rapport between the SEALs and the Marine leadership. Somehow I didn't think low-level flying for an additional three hours was going to help my cause.

Shaking my head, I waved a knife hand across my throat. "Let's call it a day, sir," I mouthed.

Three.

Without saying a word he nodded reluctantly.

Grabbing the loadmaster, I pointed to the colonel and me and indicated that we were not boarding the plane. The loadmaster acknowledged and quickly went back to preparing the aircraft for departure.

Brause and I returned to a waiting jeep. I shook his hand, thanked him for helping out with the exercise, and watched as a young petty officer escorted him back to Subic. Exhausted, I jumped in another jeep and drove home. It had been a long couple of days.

Half an hour later, aboard the MC-130, call sign Stray 59, the pilot checked his instruments. Like the rest of us, the preceding days for him and his crew had been long and tiring. Adjusting his night vision goggles, he could see the water just a few feet below him. The water was closer than expected . . . *too close to recover.* The tip of the left wing caught the top of a small wave and in an instant the plane tumbled forward, exploding in a fuel-injected ball of flame as it violently ripped apart from the impact of aircraft and sea. Of the twenty-four men aboard—eight crew members and sixteen passengers from the United States, Australia, New Zealand, and the Philippines—all but one, Air Force first lieutenant Jeffrey A. Blohm, died in the crash.

Life in the SEAL Teams always seems to revolve around fate or destiny or the hand of God. Why do some men live and others die? Why were some men saved that day? Did God have a different plan for us? What about the crew and passengers of Stray 59? Surely their families would have wanted them longer in their lives. They were all brave and honorable men, all worthy of a full and prosperous life.

I think about them often.

Twenty years later, as I rose to the rank of admiral and combat in Iraq and Afghanistan became a daily activity, I thought a lot about Stray 59. The role of the MC-130s, and their sister aircraft, the AC-130s, became more and more important to our special operations missions. With every plan I reviewed and every plan I approved, I asked myself silently whether the risk to the crew and the aircraft was worth the reward. I can only hope that the sacrifice of the men aboard Stray 59 saved lives—lives of men and women who have no idea that their destiny rested with a plane that took off from Cubi airfield in 1981 and never returned.

May God rest their souls.

CHAPTER SIX

A GORILLA WALKS INTO A BAR

SAN ANTONIO, TEXAS
January 1986

The last breath. It's sudden. It's short. It has a deep pitch to it, full of exasperation and a touch of regret. I always thought last breaths came with words, but they don't. They just come and life is over.

As I sat across from my dying mother, she exhaled one final time and passed away. My father gently stroked her hair and kissed her forehead, tears flowing down his cheeks. They had been man and wife for forty years, and both always assumed, with Dad's heart condition, that he would be the first to go. They were wrong.

Lying on our living room couch, she was twenty pounds lighter and the cancer had robbed the color from her skin. But she would have been happy to know that not a starched hair was out of place. We buried her the following Monday under a beautiful tree in the Fort Sam Houston National Cemetery. It rained all day.

Dad didn't understand why I had to rush back to work, and nothing I could offer him made sense. We were planning a highly classified mission to disable three oil-pumping facilities off the coast of Libya. Intelligence showed that Libyan leader Mohammar Gadhafi was responsible for supporting terrorist action including the bombing of a Berlin discotheque. The SEAL option was part of a larger operation to destroy the Gadhafi regime.

At the airport Dad leaned in and shook my hand firmly. My family was never much for hugging, except my mom, who loved to put her arms around me and kiss me on both cheeks. But men, particularly military men, didn't hug.

"I'll be all right," he said. "I don't know what you're up to, but be safe."

"I may not be able to write for a while, Dad. Or call. But don't worry. I'll be fine."

I saw a lump rise in his throat. He couldn't lose anyone else right now—certainly not his only son. Still, Dad knew that I was a man, and men had responsibilities—and that made him proud.

He wrapped his arms around me, kissed me on the cheek, turned around, and walked away. I never forgot that feeling, and as a father I hug my children every chance I can. I am a hugger now.

The flight took me from San Antonio to Dallas to San Juan, Puerto Rico. Seat 32A next to the bathroom. Somehow the military travel planners always put me in 32A. Did they think I had a small bladder or liked getting off last? After thirty-seven years I never did figure it out.

USS *Cavalla* (SSN 684), a *Sturgeon*-class nuclear submarine, had transited from Hawaii through the Panama Canal and was now moored at Roosevelt Roads Naval Station in Puerto Rico. The *Cavalla*'s passage through the canal raised the interest of a Soviet intelligence vessel that parked itself off the coast of San Juan listening for reflections of American intent.

A week earlier, on a midnight flight out of Norfolk, Virginia, a large covered shipment arrived by C-5 transport plane at Roosevelt Roads and was immediately moved to a nearby hangar, away from prying eyes. During the ensuing days, this Dry Deck Shelter (DDS) was mounted on the hull of the *Cavalla* and would be the underwater garage from which we would launch our minisubmarines called SEAL Delivery Vehicles (SDVs).

The SDV was a wet submersible. It was jet black in color, shaped like a long cigar with a cockpit in front and a passenger compartment in the rear. Water flowed freely through the SDV, requiring each SEAL to wear a scuba rig and a thick wet suit. Technically, the "boat" could carry up to eight men—albeit small men—but for this mission there would be only three: a pilot and navigator in the front, and a mission commander, who sat in the back and directed the operation.

Commander Bob Mabry had just relinquished command of SEAL Delivery Vehicle Team Two (SDVT-2) to Commander Tom Steffens, but owing to Bob's experience in SDVs, the Pentagon left Bob in charge of the overall mission, while Tom had command of the SDVs alone. For several months now, we had been planning and rehearsing the operation. Still, only a handful of SEALs and submariners knew the actual target. When directed by the President, the *Cavalla* would leave Puerto Rico undetected, transit the Atlantic, pass through the Strait of Gibraltar, and come to a position off the coast of Libya. Once there, we would conduct a submerged launch of the SDV. The SDV would travel underwater to the first of three Libyan oil-pumping stations.

Diving down deep, the SEALs would place explosives on a critical component of the pumping station. Once the explosives detonated, the facility would be inoperable for six months to a year. In an effort to ensure that no oil leaked into the Mediterranean, the engineers were very specific about where we had to place the explosives.

That all sounded good when you were looking at blueprints at Naval Intelligence, but at night, at depth, breathing through a scuba regulator in enemy waters, it didn't seem so simple. Consequently, for our training, Bob Mabry convinced the Navy to build three mock-up training devices, which we lowered into the waters off the coast of Vieques Island, Puerto Rico. For the past two months, three SDV crews had been diving constantly in preparation for the mission. I was the mission commander on the third crew.

Tonight, however, we were rehearsing a different part of the operation: combat search and rescue (CSAR). Mabry and Steffens agreed that if the SDV had mechanical problems inside Libyan territorial waters and couldn't return to the *Cavalla*, we would have to send a helo in to quickly extract the SEALs. Technically, this was a challenging scenario. It required the SDV to carry a large sonar buoy that had a transmitter affixed to the top. Once activated, the transmitter sent a signal to a P-3 reconnaissance aircraft orbiting well outside Libyan airspace. The P-3 radar could get a general location on the beacon, but in order to triangulate the exact position of the transmitter we needed a slow-moving SH-3 Sea King helicopter with a passive receiver. Once triangulated, the Sea King would fly to our position, lower a "horse collar," and hoist us into the helo. *Simple.*

"Starting flood up procedures."

"Roger, starting flood up procedures."

Turning the large valve in the Dry Deck Shelter, the ship's diver opened the pipe and seawater began to flood the forty-foot chamber. The air in the shelter was humid, smelling of saltwater and neoprene from our wet suits. Movement was almost impossible as the SDV filled up the shelter with only a two-foot pathway on either side of the boat. It took forty-five minutes to fully flood the DDS, so I reviewed my mission checklist to ensure everything was in order.

The Dry Deck Shelter was a spin-off from the giant Regulus missile chambers that were part of the Vietnam-era submarine USS *Grayback*. For two decades the *Grayback* had launched earlier versions of the SDVs, but now we had the technology to have a mobile Dry Deck Shelter, which could be transported worldwide and mounted on specially configured submarines. The *Cavalla* was the test bed for this capability. No one ever anticipated putting the DDS into a real-world operation this quickly.

"Sir, all systems are good to go. I have the first course at 270 degrees for ten thousand yards."

"Roger, Ron. I confirm 270 at ten thousand," I replied.

Ron Blackburn was the SDV navigator. A first class petty

officer, he was a superb SEAL and very comfortable on these long dives. Ron's only problem was that he was tall and slim, and having 3 percent body fat was never a good thing when you were spending twelve hours underwater. No wet suit in the world could make up for a nice layer of body fat. Every time we returned from a long dive, Ron was bordering on hypothermia, but he never complained.

Once the shelter was flooded, the submarine crew from inside the *Cavalla* began to pressurize the chamber, equalizing it to the outside depth. With the pressure equal, the large shelter doors began to slowly open and the ship's divers scurried about unhooking the SDV from the cradle in which it sat. Bioluminescent sea life filled the shelter and streams of glowing green protoplasm flowed off the edges of the submarine.

A ship's diver swam up beside me and gave me the okay sign. They were ready to launch us from the *Cavalla*.

"Okay," I mumbled through the full-face mask. "Dave, stand by to push out."

"Roger, sir, standing by to push out," came the reply.

Smart, hardworking, never a problem he couldn't solve, Dave Roberts was the SDV pilot. A second class petty officer, he had been in SDVs his whole SEAL career and was just damn good at what he did.

The ship's divers grabbed the side of the now neutrally buoyant SDV, pushed it out of the shelter, and maneuvered it onto the deck of the *Cavalla*. The submarine's conning tower, which was forward of the DDS, created a shield from the four-knot current pushing over the bow of the submarine. This made for calm waters on the deck.

Pushing back the sliding hatch, I looked outside the SDV, checked to ensure the ship's divers were ready, and gave the order to launch the SDV.

"Stand by to launch," I announced.

"Roger, sir, standing by to launch," Dave replied.

Each command given was always repeated to ensure the order received was understood exactly. Our face masks were equipped with a communications system, but understanding muffled words spoken inside a rubber mask took some effort.

Dave powered up the electric motor and with a slight push from the divers we eased off the side of the *Cavalla* and were underway.

Like some giant gray whale returning to the depths, the *Cavalla* faded from view as Dave steered a course perpendicular to the submarine's heading. We rose to fifteen feet, which was our normal submerged transit depth.

"Must be a little choppy topside," Dave said, to no one in particular.

I could feel the swells pulling at the boat, sucking it upward and then casting it down again. Having been a pilot for years, I knew that Dave was fighting to keep the SDV level. The variations in pressure no longer bothered any of us. Our eardrums were so pliable that we could go from zero to thirty feet and back again without even having to clear them. Still, it was a matter of pilot pride to keep the boat as level as possible.

"I'm going to bring her down a few feet."

"Roger," I replied.

We had ninety minutes to go before we surfaced and began our escape and evasion exercise. Just enough time for a little nap. I repositioned my legs between the two sonar buoys, four haversacks of demolition, and two extra diving rigs, curled up, and started to snooze. Cramped, cold, wet, and breathing into a Darth Vader mask, somehow to me everything felt completely natural. It was the nature of being a frogman, particularly an SDVer.

Most SEALs hated the idea of being in SDVs: confined in a small space, no room to move, underwater for hours on end, long hot showers at the end of the dive being the only respite from the bone-chilling cold. But for me, the SDV recalled the glory days of the Italian frogmen of World War II or the British X-craft sailors who sailed their minisubs into the deep fjords of Norway chasing German battleships. I dreamed that someday the call would come for me to defeat the Soviets in a daring SDV attack on the Russian shipping in Vladivostok—someday.

"Mr. Mac. Five minutes to our stop point," Ron announced.

"Roger, Ron. Five minutes," I replied.

Pulling my feet into my chest, I grabbed the larger of the two sonar buoys and maneuvered it into position for easy deployment. The flow of the water inside the rear compartment began to subside as Dave slowed the boat. Tiny swirls of green phosphorescence pooled in the air pockets of my hovering exhaust bubbles and I could feel the SDV begin to rise.

"Surfaced," came the call.

Reaching behind me, I grabbed the handle on the compartment door and slid the hatch to the rear. Immediately a wave poured over the boat, knocking me back into the aft area.

"Whoa. It's a bit rough up here," I muttered to myself.

"Hey, I thought the weather guy said the seas were going to be calm tonight," Dave said, opening the front canopy and climbing onto the top of the boat.

"Maybe he meant two hundred feet down on the *Cavalla*," Ron said, laughing.

Grabbing the buoy, I pulled a small pin, which initiated the buoy's saltwater activation. Immediately I could hear a pinging sound.

"Okay, start the clock," I said.

Ron looked at his watch. "It's now 2115. They said thirty minutes, tops, and we should be out of here."

"I bet we're lucky if they find us in an hour," Dave said.

"It's a little eerie being out here without a safety boat," Ron said, pulling off his wet suit hood.

No one wanted to say it, but Ron was right. Every training dive until now, we had a safety boat. On board the boat was a diving supervisor, a corpsman, a safety diver, and radio communications in case something went wrong. Tonight, we were all alone. We were training to go on a real-world mission, Mabry had lectured. *You won't have a safety boat off Libya. You might as well get used to it now.*

"I can't see squat," Dave said.

The fog was beginning to roll in and the swells were getting bigger.

"How far to Vieques?" I asked.

"Looks like we're about ten miles off the coast," Ron said. "But my Doppler navigation isn't working in these water depths, so the more we drift the less confident I am in where we are."

"Well, it shouldn't be long now," I said, trying to sound confident. "Then we can turn the boat over to Lieutenant Snell and head back to Roosey Roads. I bet the master chief still has the bar open."

The plan called for a replacement crew to come out with the helo. They would jump in, assume control of the SDV, and return it to the *Cavalla*. We would get a free ride to the base and maybe, just maybe, a cold beer and a warm rack.

Thirty minutes came and went. Then an hour. Then two. Then three.

"I'm getting frickin' cold, Mr. Mac," Dave stated unemotionally.

"Yeah, me too, Dave," I agreed.

"Make that three of us," Ron stuttered, shaking uncontrollably.

Expecting to be in the water two hours tops, all of us were wearing "shorty" wet suits. Our usual one-inch-thick wet suits were fine for sedentary twelve-hour dives, but for short dives they caused overheating and you had to continuously douse yourself with cold water to avoid passing out. Even though the waters off Puerto Rico were in the eighties, anything below body temperature quickly drained your core temperature.

"It's been five hours since we launched. Maybe we should try to return to the *Cavalla*," Ron said.

"We don't have any idea where the *Cavalla* is right now, Ron. We've been drifting for three hours. I guarantee you, Mabry and Steffens have every airplane in the fleet looking for us. We just need to stay put and stick with the plan."

It wasn't a very good answer and I'm not sure I believed it myself. Ron was a good sailor, though. Through his shaking and stammering I heard him say, "Yes sir."

"Well, the good news is, it isn't raining," I said, as another small wave came rolling over the top of the SDV.

"Yeah, we wouldn't want to get wet." Dave smiled, clutching his arms tight to his chest.

"You sure that damn beacon is still pinging?" Ron asked.

"Yeah, it's still pinging," I replied. "Just no one's listening."

I lay back on the top of the SDV as we bobbed around lost in the middle of the Caribbean. As any leader would, I thought I needed to take charge and help us get through this long night. I made a mental list of our situation. Let's see, we had no communications. We only hoped the beacon was sending out a signal. We had no idea where we were and no way to get back to our host submarine. We were very cold and getting colder. The weather was continuing to deteriorate and the sun wasn't due up for another three hours. We weren't going to die—at least I didn't think we were—but we were going to be utterly miserable unless I came up with a good idea.

Let's see. I need a good idea. A good idea. A good idea.

Nope. No good ideas. Oh well.

"Have you heard the one about the gorilla that walks into a bar?"

"What?" Ron said.

I said, "Have you heard the one about the gorilla that walks into a bar?"

Ron shook his head. Dave uttered something unintelligible.

"So a gorilla walks into this bar," I started again. "Behind the counter, the frightened bartender sees the gorilla and runs to the manager in the back room. Panicking from the sight of this giant ape, the bartender shouts to the manager, 'A gorilla just walked into the bar!'

"The manager seems completely unfazed. 'Well,' he says calmly to the bartender. 'Go see what he wants.'

"The bartender returns to the counter, summons up his courage, and approaches the gorilla. 'Can I help you?' he asks."

Ron propped himself up on the bow of the SDV and through his weary, bloodshot eyes said, "Mr. Mac, this had better be good…"

"Let me continue."

Dave adjusted himself so he could hear through the waves slapping against the hull.

"So, the bartender says, 'Can I help you?'

"'Gin and tonic,' the gorilla replies.

"The bartender returns to the manager and says, 'The gorilla wants a gin and tonic. What should I do?'

"'Sure, sure,' the manager says. 'Get him a gin and tonic, but charge him nine dollars.'

"'Nine dollars!' the bartender roars. 'That's ridiculous! He'll tear me apart.'

"'No, no he won't,' the manager says. 'Gorillas aren't very smart. He won't know the difference.'

"So the bartender pours a gin and tonic, delivers it to the gorilla, and says reluctantly, 'That will be nine dollars.'

"The gorilla scowls and grunts, but eventually reaches into a small purse, pulls out a ten, and gives it to the bartender. The bartender opens the cash register, puts away the ten, and gives the gorilla a dollar change."

Dave was now on his elbows listening to every word and Ron was smiling through the cold.

"The bartender returns to the manager and says, 'You were right! That gorilla was really stupid.'

"A few minutes later, the gorilla pounds on the bar. The bartender approaches the counter and the gorilla says, 'Another gin and tonic.' The bartender pours another drink, hands it to the gorilla, says, 'That will be nine dollars.'

"The gorilla pulls out another ten. The bartender opens the cash register, puts away the ten, and gives the gorilla one dollar in change. Finally the bartender gets up his courage and says to the gorilla, 'You know, we don't get too many gorillas in here.'

" 'Well,' the gorilla says…"

"Hey," Dave yelled. "I hear a helo!"

I could hear it as well. "All right. Power down the boat. Dave, make sure we have the ballast tanks completely blown. Ron, you're first up."

We turned on a red flashing strobe light and saw the helo return the signal indicating he had seen us in the water. The weather was still touch and go and the helo struggled to maintain its hover. The downwash from the rotor blades was pummeling us, so I waved the helo away to a position about a hundred yards from the SDV.

Ron swam toward the horse collar, but every time he got close the winds pushed the helo off its mark, and Ron had to chase the sling for ten minutes before he finally caught the collar and was hoisted aboard.

The replacement crew jumped into the water and swam over to the SDV. Dave went next and then I followed. What should have taken ten minutes was now close to thirty. I knew the helo was running low on fuel, and just as I pulled myself into the side door the pilot banked the helo hard left and we headed back to Roosey Roads.

By the time we arrived back at our barracks it was around 0500. It had been a long night. We were still shaking from the cold and ready to get some rack.

"Well, let's hope we don't have to evade in Libyan waters," Ron said. "We'd all die of hypothermia before we could be saved."

Dave had already stripped off his wet suit and was heading to the showers. Ron was stowing his life jacket and I was jotting down some notes about the evening's events when a chief petty officer, in uniform, walked into the room.

"Are you Lieutenant McRaven?" he asked.

I nodded.

"Sir, the admiral would like to see you."

Ron and I exchanged looks.

"What admiral?" I asked.

"Sir, I was just told to come get you and deliver you to the admiral."

"Yeah, I understand that part, Chief, but I don't know any admiral."

"Sir, Commander Mabry told me to get you right away and take you to see the admiral. I have a car waiting outside."

"Okay," I said reluctantly. "Let me change and I'll be right with you."

"No sir. You need to come right now. Those are my orders."

I looked at the chief to gauge his seriousness. SEALs have been known to play elaborate jokes on each other, and right now I really, really wasn't in the mood for a prank. The chief wore the insignia of a master-at-arms. He was the Navy's version of a military policeman.

"Let me at least change out of my wet suit."

"Sir," the chief said, as if warning me for the final time.

Ron began to close ranks with me and I motioned him back a step.

"All right," I said. "Let's go. Ron, you and Dave get some rest. Hopefully this shouldn't take long. If I'm not back in a few hours give Commander Steffens a call and let him know what happened."

Ron acknowledged and the chief and I headed outside and got in the car. We drove for thirty minutes to the other side of the base and arrived at a deserted parking lot across from an old C-130 hangar.

Standing in the parking lot were two men. I recognized the large figure of Commander Bob Mabry, but the other man, who was significantly older and in civilian clothes, I didn't know.

The chief dropped me off next to Mabry and pulled away. It was still nighttime and there were no lights in the parking lot. Mabry walked up to me and made the introductions.

"Bill, this is Admiral Craig Dorman. He's running the show."

I came to a modified attention and shook hands with Dorman. He was in his early fifties, with fading blond hair, a wiry build, a strong grip, and piercing eyes, but with a friendly smile.

"You guys have done a great job here over the past three months, Bill. It's been very impressive to watch."

All I could do was say thank you. I still didn't exactly understand what was going on.

"I'd like you to come talk to a few folks about tonight's training operation. We need to make sure we can fix the problems with locating your position or we will never get approval from the Pentagon to launch this mission."

I looked around at the empty parking lot.

"This way," Mabry said, and we started heading to the hangar.

The admiral opened the door and Mabry followed quickly behind. As I entered the hangar bay I was stunned at what I saw. Two hundred people were arrayed in ten rows spread out across the length of the floor.

Mabry smiled.

"Sir, who the hell are all these people?" I whispered to him.

"They are all the people behind the curtain, Bill. They have been coordinating the aircraft, working the intelligence, tracking the submarine, jamming the Russian AGI, and passing daily situation reports to Washington."

The admiral walked me in front of the line of desks and made a short introduction. "Ladies and gentlemen, this is Lieutenant McRaven. He was the mission commander for tonight's CSAR exercise and I have asked him to provide a quick summary of the operation."

I started to speak, but before I could the admiral interrupted. "Oh, but before you give us your debrief, we're all dying to know one thing."

I looked into the crowd and everyone was leaning forward in their chairs as if expecting some revelation from me.

"What's that, sir?" I asked.

"The punch line," the admiral said. "What's the punch line?"

"What punch line?"

"The punch line to the gorilla joke."

My mouth dropped open and the crowd broke into laughter.

"Surely you knew that the sonar buoy had a microphone on it?" The admiral smiled, knowing damn well that I didn't.

"No sir," I responded, turning a bright shade of red thinking of everyone we had bitched about while waiting for the helo.

"Well you do now. Sooo…" The admiral didn't finish the sentence.

"So…" I continued. "The bartender said, 'You know, we don't get many gorillas in here.' And the gorilla says, 'Well, hell, for nine dollars a drink I'm not surprised.'"

The hangar erupted in laughter. Mabry and the admiral were almost bent over. The joke wasn't that funny and the delivery a little staged, but there was no denying the humor of the situation. Even though I was the butt of the joke, I couldn't help but laugh myself. Two hundred people had been listening to every word Ron, Dave, and I had said over the past six hours. Every complaint about the submarine crew, every snide remark about the late helicopter, every lurid story about some port call, everything that sailors talk about when they think no one is listening—*everything.*

I finished briefing the admiral and his folks and returned to the barracks. Mabry directed me not to tell Ron and Dave about the additional staff hiding in the hangar. I told them the chief had it all wrong and it was only Mabry who wanted to see me.

Two days later we received the word that the SEAL mission was canceled. The Pentagon decided to go with an airstrike option, and what was later to be Operation El Dorado Canyon was conducted on April 15, 1986. The air raid struck several targets, including the airfield in Tripoli, a military barracks in Bab al-Azizia, and a headquarters building in Bengazhi.

The *Cavalla* returned to Hawaii. The SEALs returned to Little Creek and we all got back to our daily lives. But two months later as I was driving in to work, scanning the local radio stations, I heard a disk jockey say, "And the bartender says, 'You know, we don't get too many gorillas in here.' And the gorilla said, 'Well, hell, for nine dollars a drink I'm not surprised.'"

Some jokes are just too good to be kept a secret.

CHAPTER SEVEN

THE GHOSTS OF TOFINO

CORONADO, CALIFORNIA
September 1989

I t says, 'George H. W. Bush, President of the United States.'"
"Bullshit, let me see that!" I said, grabbing the letter from the command master chief. "Well, I'll be damned. It does say George H. W. Bush."

Master Chief Bill Huckins pulled the White House letter back from me and began to read the memorandum. Huckins was the senior enlisted man at SEAL Team One. Tall, stocky, always red-faced, with a gregarious personality and a cutting wit, he had the respect of every man in the Team. I was the Executive Officer (XO), and with the commanding officer deployed to the Persian Gulf, that put me in charge of SEAL Team One, and Bill Huckins was my right-hand man.

"The President of the United States requests your assistance in locating a Navy P2V2 reconnaissance plane lost in British Columbia, Canada, in 1948. The plane departed Whidbey Island Naval Air Station on November 4, 1948, for a routine patrol and was never heard from again. A Navy search and rescue crew located pieces of the wreckage in 1962, but owing to the hazardous conditions, were unable to recover much. For the next twenty-seven years, the plane remained lost. Recently, a bush pilot flying in the region of Tofino, British Columbia, spotted a shiny metal object inside an extinct volcanic crater near Mt. Guenes. The base of the crater is filled with water and it is possible that the remains of the aircraft lie deep beneath this mountain lake. On board the plane were nine souls and it is our duty to locate them and return their remains to a proper resting place."

The master chief stopped reading. "The letter goes on to give the point of contact and directs us to respond to the President's request by this Friday," he said.

"Why would the President of the United States care about a plane that was lost over forty years ago?" Huckins asked.

"Bush is a former naval aviator," I answered. "My guess is one of the crew members' family must have approached the POTUS and asked for his help."

"Okay, XO, but why us? Why SEAL Team One?"

"Because who else can mount an expedition into the middle of nowhere Canada that requires climbing and diving?" I responded.

"Not just diving," Huckins said, unrolling a topographic map of the area. "High-altitude diving."

I surveyed the map as the master chief pointed out the terrain.

"Those mountains in that area go as high as eight thousand feet," he said. "And the crater lake the President is talking about sits at about three thousand feet. That means all our dive tables need to be revised."

The region was as isolated as any I had ever seen. The mountains around the suspected crash site were exceptionally steep, and there wasn't a level piece of ground within a hundred miles of the site.

"We'll need someone who knows his shit," I said.

Without hesitation the master chief said, "I'll give Barker a warning order."

Senior Chief Geoff Barker was the preeminent diver in all the SEAL Teams. Tall, heavyset, with dark hair and a big soft face, he could outswim and outrun most of the smaller, fitter guys in the team. He supervised our SEAL Team One dive locker and was one of the most professional enlisted men I had ever worked with. He *did* know his shit.

"Who else do we need?" I asked.

But before the master chief could answer, I knew who I wanted.

"Get me Pat Ellis," I said. "He's a lead climber and has the intel background to do the prep work."

The master chief nodded his approval.

Pat was everyone's image of a Navy SEAL, also tall, but with strong angular features and a sharp intellect. And with Pat, there was a level of maturity that wasn't common in most young petty officers.

"And let's add Greg Walker."

"Good choice," Huckins acknowledged.

Walker was a quiet fellow, with a dark complexion and large mustache. While not a SEAL, as a Navy First Class diver he was the most knowledgeable about the science of diving. He was the second in charge of the dive locker at SEAL Team One and had earned the respect of every frogman in the command.

"Finally, throw in Doc James, he's good all around," I said.

"Who do we put in charge?" the master chief inquired.

"The senior chief can lead it," I responded.

"Sir..." the master chief said, drawing out the word with a certain amount of derision. "You know there is no way Admiral Worthington is going to let the senior lead this effort. He's going to want an officer-in-charge."

"You don't need an officer to lead this operation," I argued. "Barker is more than capable of handling this mission."

The master chief didn't say a word. He just nodded politely as if to confirm that I was a lunatic.

"Screw you," I said, laughing. "Call Naval Special Warfare Group One and let them know that we have our team and we can be ready to go early next week. And stop giving me that look."

"What look?" the master chief asked, feigning surprise.

"Yeah, that look," I fired back. The master chief just smiled.

He had been right, of course. Admiral George Worthington,

the commander of Naval Special Warfare, not only insisted that an officer go along on the mission, but ordered me to be the head of our little expedition. I didn't complain too much. It was an opportunity to get out of the office and hike the outback of Canada. While none of us really expected to find an aircraft that had been missing for over forty years, it was another adventure, and who didn't want another adventure?

Doc James was on travel and unable to join us, so we added Petty Officer Chuck Carter to the team. The five of us—me, Senior Chief Geoff Barker, Petty Officers Ellis, Carter, and Walker—were boarding a C-130 bound for Naval Air Station Whidbey Island in Washington State. The plan called for us to land at Whidbey and transfer to a Canadian cargo plane for the final flight into Tofino, British Columbia. Once at Tofino we would rent a small helicopter and take turns lifting our gear and personnel into the suspected crash site.

The loadmaster motioned us onto the airplane. We were ready to take off.

"Look, XO," the master chief yelled above the noise of the spinning props. "I know this seems like a lot of fun to you, but you guys are heading into an area where no living being has set foot in decades."

"A little dramatic, aren't we?" I said.

"I'm only saying—be careful. You don't know what's out there, and if you get into trouble, help is a long, long ways away."

I could see it in his eyes—the master chief was genuinely worried. Worried like a mother sending her child off to their first day of school. I smiled, shook his hand, and said, "Gotta go. Hold down the fort until we get back."

The master chief nodded, gave a half salute, and turned away.

As the plane lifted off, Barker, Ellis, Carter, and Walker were already dozing. I pulled out a small laminated copy of the topographic map and looked at our destination one more time. It *was* a long way from anywhere, but we were five experienced sailors and

I was certain we could handle anything we might find. *Absolutely certain.*

"You're looking for what?" The bearded man laughed.

"That again, eh," his ruddy-faced partner roared.

I was beginning to regret stopping for dinner. The German-style restaurant with long picnic tables, wood-beamed ceilings, and several large grandfather clocks was the only place open for food and it was Oktoberfest in Tofino. The oompah music blared in the background and lederhosened men and large-breasted women danced the polka while my team and I downed some brats and sauerkraut. Barker, a teetotaler, sipped his Coca-Cola, while the rest of us guzzled a liter of hefeweizen.

"Do you Yanks know how many times pilots, trappers, fishermen, and tourists have said they saw some"—ruddy face paused to choose his words—"shiny object?"

At the words "shiny object," Geoff Barker took a deep, exasperated breath. They were the exact words the President had written in his letter to the command. We had rushed to pull together this small team, and Barker, in particular, had worked long hours to get the right climbing, diving, and camping gear ready for this operation. Now it seemed we were on a wild Canadian goose chase.

Trying to be positive, I defended our plan. "We have it on good authority that a large metallic item was spotted here," I said, pointing to the laminated map.

"A shiny object, you mean." Bearded man snickered, wiping the beer foam from his whiskers.

"Sonny, it's been over two decades since anyone spotted that wreckage," ruddy face said. "Even if a plane had crashed in those mountains, it would be buried under a hundred feet of snow and ice and you'd never be able to get to it."

"And the snow never melts in these parts," bearded man offered, tapping the map.

Bearded man was partly right. For almost the entire year the snow never melted in these mountains, except for two weeks in late September—and then only partially. If we had any chance of finding the plane, it would have to be in the next two weeks.

Suddenly, a large woman with massive cleavage grabbed my free hand and yanked me to the dance floor. "Let's polka!" she shouted, spinning me around.

"I don't dance," I objected, stumbling across the wooden floor.

"We polka," she said again in broken English.

Bearded man, ruddy face, and my four companions all began to clap loudly and yell encouragement. *What the hell*, I thought. The polka looked a lot like the Texas two-step.

Grabbing my large German fräulein by her plump hands, I began to move around the floor, bumping everyone in my path— much to the amusement of my fellow frogmen and the well-dressed band director, who kept yelling, "Everyone polka!"

As I looked over at the table, bearded man and ruddy face were laughing, but in the back of my mind, I knew their laughter had nothing to do with my dancing.

"Lower," I yelled. "You've got to get me lower!"

The pilot of the small Bell helicopter acknowledged my request and brought the helo down another six feet. Precariously balanced on a large boulder, Barker and Ellis reached for the scuba tanks as I handed them out the side door of the helo.

Walker passed me the remainder of the equipment, took one final look inside the helo, and announced that all the gear was out. I nodded to him to get out of the bird, and with one smooth motion he slid across the deck of the helo, out the side door, and onto the boulder below.

Tapping the pilot on the shoulder, I shouted, "Thanks for the lift."

Looking over the barren landscape, steep mountain peaks, and treacherous ice floes, he shouted back, "Be careful out here! If I don't hear from you in four days, I will be back."

I nodded thankfully, patted him on the back one final time, and slid out the side door into the waiting arms of big Geoff Barker.

We all watched as the helo banked slowly right and struggled to gain altitude. The blades were grasping at the thin air and the whine of the engines echoed loudly off the surrounding mountains.

Within minutes all was quiet. Dead quiet. With all of our gear heaped in a pile at our feet, the five of us stood precariously on the large rocks surveying our new surroundings. It was spectacular.

On three sides were peaks rising up to five thousand feet. Below us was an ice blue mountain lake that spilled off the open edge of the basin. How far the water dropped we couldn't tell, but it appeared to fall endlessly into another valley below. While a few pine trees dotted the landscape, there was no sign of other life— just rock. Big rocks.

As predicted, all the snow was gone, with the exception of a long, narrow ice floe that extended several thousand feet from the top of the mountain on the far side to a place about three hundred yards up from the lake.

"Well," Ellis announced. "We're here. Now what?"

It was only 1500 hours, but the light was fading fast as the sun slowly sank behind the tall mountain peaks.

"Let's set up camp for the night and we can begin our dives in the morning," I said.

"I found a spot over here," Barker said. "We can fit both tents on the same boulder and still have some room for a fire and a few camp stools."

"Well, we won't have to worry about bears or mountain lions," Ellis said, surveying the mountainside through the scope on the .300 WinMag. "Nothing lives up here."

"It's gonna be dark soon," Barker said. "Let's get moving."

Within an hour we had shifted all of our equipment to the only flat area inside the basin. Barker was right, though. The campsite worked nicely.

Barker and I shared one tent and Ellis, Carter, and Walker were in the other. By 1700 the sun was gone completely, but stars lit up the night sky. Comets dashed across the horizon just above the peaks, and the Big Dipper, normally the brightest stars in the sky, were consumed by the surrounding heavens. In all my years in the Teams, from the jungles of Panama to the mountains of Alaska to the middle of the South Pacific, I could not remember a night where the stars shined so very brightly.

Bundled in Gore-Tex jackets and wool pants, we sat around the fire trying to stay warm.

"Do you really think they're down in that lake, XO?" Walker asked.

"I don't know, Greg. Maybe we'll find out tomorrow," I said.

"Damn, that would be cool, wouldn't it," Ellis chimed in. "What if that plane is really still there, preserved in the icy waters, just waiting for us to find it?"

"As clear as that water is, it won't take too many dives to determine if it's there," Barker said, adding another pallet to the fire. We had bundled all our gear on small wooden pallets and had enough firewood to keep us comfortable for several nights.

"Can you imagine what it must have been like?" Carter said. "I mean, these guys are on a routine flight, nothing to worry about, and then *bang*, something goes wrong: a bad engine, icing, something, and within a matter of minutes they are struggling for their lives trying to keep this big ol' plane in the air."

"My guess is the pilot saw the lake and thought it might be an open pasture," I speculated.

"Yeah, must have really sucked when he got closer and realized it wasn't grass, but water," Barker said.

"Wait a minute, when did this accident occur?" Ellis asked.

"November 1948," I answered.

"Wouldn't the lake have been frozen in November?" Ellis continued.

We all looked at each other, surprised the question had never come up.

"Sure, sure it would've," Carter said excitedly.

"So..." Barker said, hoping someone would finish the sentence.

"So..." I said, jumping in, "if he actually made the lake, but couldn't stop, then the plane would have careened into the side of the mountain."

"At about 120 miles per hour," Ellis added.

"Yeah, but if that was the case, we would have seen remnants of the plane scattered all across the mountainside. And we saw nothing," Barker said.

"Ah, we're probably nowhere close to that crash," Walker mumbled. "I say we give it a day, and if we don't find anything we break out the radio and call the helo back."

At Walker's suggestion everyone went quiet. We were prepared to stay four days looking for the wreckage, but Walker was right. There was no plane anywhere in sight. If it wasn't under the water—it wasn't here.

"All right, guys, we have a big day ahead of us. Let's turn in," I said.

"Roger, sir," Barker answered. "I'm going to throw one more pallet on the fire, just in case Bigfoot is out there."

We all retired to our tents, jumped in our sleeping bags, and within minutes all I could hear was the sound of the crackling fire and the snoring of tired men.

As I rolled over in the bag, I couldn't help but wonder about the fate of those lost crewmen. I was hoping we would find some answers in the morning. But the morning was still a long ways off.

I was shaking uncontrollably. Pulling the fabric of the sleeping bag as close to my body as possible, I tried to get warm, but it just wasn't happening. We had underestimated how much the temperature would drop at night, and my bag clearly wasn't rated for this kind of weather.

As I rolled to my left, reaching for my spare jacket, I noticed something was missing.

Barker.

I opened my eyes and waited a minute until they adjusted. The shadow from the fire flickered against the tent and I could vaguely make out a silhouette by the flames.

Struggling out of my bag, I threw on my Gore-Tex jacket, unzipped the fly on the tent, and stepped outside into the bitterly cold night air.

Barker was sitting on a stool warming himself by the fire.

"You okay, Geoff?" I asked.

Without even looking in my direction he muttered, "I'm fine."

I looked around to see if there was a whiskey flask that Barker might have smuggled into our campsite. He was a tough, proud man, but the bottle had always haunted him. A year earlier, after several minor incidents, he had gone cold turkey. Since then he hadn't taken a sip of alcohol. Or so I thought.

I grabbed a camp stool and sidled up beside him, trying to see if I could get a whiff of booze.

"I'm not drinking. If that's what you're thinking, XO."

I threw another pallet on the fire. "Then what the hell are you doing out here? It's freezing."

"I just couldn't sleep. That's all," Barker said.

"You're not very convincing, Geoff. What's wrong?"

"Nothing," he snapped. "There's nothing wrong!"

"All right," I said. "I know you didn't come out here to get warm, because it certainly isn't any warmer outside the tent." Even by the fire the air was thin and crisp, and a slight breeze brought the frigid air from off the snowbanks to settle right on top of our campsite.

"I'm fine," he said again. "Just fine."

I patted Barker on the back and got up. Sometimes you just

have to let a man deal with his own demons. With one more surge of warmth from the fire, I ran back into my tent, diving into the bag as quickly as possible. The remainder of the night was spent fighting off the cold and a full bladder. It was three hours until sunrise, but as far as I was concerned, morning couldn't come soon enough.

My watch said 0625, but I could tell the other guys were already up and stirring around. I dressed quickly and stepped outside. The scenery, and the altitude, took my breath away.

The sky was almost cloudless and the vibrant colors of nature drew a distinct line between the earth-toned mountains, the deep blue water, the blinding white snow, and the green treetops in the valley miles away.

Barker was just where I had left him several hours earlier. He had never returned to the tent. On the other side of the fire were Carter and Walker. Ellis was down checking out the lake. All three men seemed quietly preoccupied.

I reached down, grabbed the REI coffee pot, and filled up my canteen cup. "What's for chow?" I asked, knowing that all we had were C-rations. No one even looked up from the fire.

Pulling up a camp stool, I grabbed a board from one of the pallets and stoked the fire. "We ready to do some diving?"

No one answered. "Geoff, is the gear ready to go?" I asked.

"Yes sir," Barker answered, struggling to sound motivated.

"Okay," I said, sipping my coffee. "What's wrong with you guys?"

The three men all looked at each other, but no one spoke.

"Come on," I prodded gently. "What's going on here?"

I could see that neither Barker nor Walker were going to open up. But Carter was just waiting for an opportunity to say something.

"Chuck, tell me what's going on."

Carter looked at the other two men, glanced around the campsite as if to see if anyone else was listening, and then asked Barker and Walker, "Did you see it?"

"See what?" Barker said, raising his voice.

"I saw it," Walker offered.

"Saw what? I asked.

Carter hesitated for a few seconds and I leaned across the fire as if to hear a schoolyard secret.

"Yes . . . ?"

"There was someone outside our tent last night," Carter said. "He walked around our campsite."

I scanned the expression on each man's face. There was no twinkle in their eyes, no sly smile around their lips, only a tense sense of bewilderment.

"It was Geoff," I said, laughing. I looked over to get confirmation from Barker. But he remained stoic.

"It wasn't me," Barker said with a tinge in his voice.

"Of course it was," I replied.

"No, it wasn't," Barker said quietly. "That's why I got up and went outside. I saw a man walking around the tent. I thought it was Pat, but when I called out he didn't answer."

I looked at Walker and Carter. "None of us left the tent last night," Carter said. Walker nodded.

"He was there, all right," Carter added. "He must have been over six foot tall and heavyset. He circled our entire tent a couple of times, stopping occasionally like he was looking inside."

Walker jumped in. "When he wouldn't answer, I opened the flap of the tent and looked outside, but there was nobody there."

"Geoff is about six foot tall and heavyset," I countered.

"Yes sir, but not even Geoff can walk on thin air."

"Thin air?" I asked.

Carter got up and motioned me to the side of their tent.

The boulder our campsite sat on was about twelve feet in diameter, and the tent that Ellis, Walker, and Carter shared was butted up against the edge of the rock. Off the back side of their tent was a sharp drop to the ground below, and there was no room between the edge of the tent and the end of the boulder.

"I told you he walked around the *entire* tent," Carter said.

"Might be *just* a little hard for a man Geoff's size to tiptoe around that," Walker said, pointing to the base of their lean-to.

I edged over to see if I could walk the circumference of the tent, but clearly there was no room on the back side for anyone to maneuver safely.

"So what are you guys trying to tell me here? You saw a ghost. Is that it?"

"Look, XO," Barker said. "I know this sounds crazy. When I was drinking a lot it would have made sense. When I drank I would see things that weren't there, hear voices that weren't there, believe things that weren't true. But I wasn't drinking last night and I know what I saw."

Carter and Walker nodded in agreement.

"And there is something else," Barker said.

"Something else?"

"That plane is here. In this crater," Barker said. "It's not in the lake."

"Did the man walking around the tent tell you that?" I said, expecting to get a laugh.

Geoff didn't laugh.

In my years in the Navy many unexplained events would affect my life. I learned to trust my instincts and oftentimes the feelings of others around me. It was clear to me that Barker, Walker, and Carter had seen something, heard something, felt something that in their hearts they believed to be true. While I hadn't seen or heard or felt anything last night, that didn't make the event unreal.

"All right, boys," I said, looking at the ice floe high on the mountainside. "Grab the picks and ropes. Let's go find ourselves an airplane."

The large rocks covering the mountain made movement from our base camp to the ice floe slow going. Additionally, Barker, Ellis,

Carter, and I were weighted down with climbing rope, crampons, ice picks, and lights. After about forty-five minutes we arrived at the base of the ice. The foot of the floe was about fifty yards across and ended abruptly, without the gradual, sloping curvature normally found in these sorts of formations.

From our vantage point on the west side of the mountain we could see the entire basin. The waterfall off the lake into the valley below seemed even more dramatic. While it was difficult to tell the length of the drop, the volume of water spilling over the edge made me worry that any dive in the lake could be more dangerous than I envisioned. The current at that depth could sweep a man away quickly. I mentally made a note of the problem.

Above us the mountains rose steeply. There was no easy route to the top. Reaching the peak would require several hours, even for an experienced climber. With the gear we brought, we were not equipped to go much beyond the middle of the ice floe.

Barker tapped on the outside of the floe with his ice pick. It appeared solid, but with each strike of the pick, there was a change in the pitch.

"Almost sounds hollow," Barker said, trying to peer into the ice.

"If it were hollow it seems the weight of the ice would collapse upon itself," Ellis noted.

Barker took off his gloves to get a better grip and then began to swing the pick with his full force, focusing on a small spot at the end of the floe. Before long, we all joined in.

As each minute of digging passed, the color of the ice at our entry point began to change. It became darker, reflecting not only the outer sunlight, but the absence of light from within.

Suddenly Barker's pick passed through a thin layer of ice.

"It is hollow," he said, struggling to unwedge his axe.

Within thirty minutes we created an opening large enough to get a body through. Poking the flashlight into the hole, I could see that the floe had created an archway extending up for several yards, but it was difficult to see much else from outside the ice. Barker slipped on a climbing harness, attached the rope to his carabiner, grabbed a flashlight, and began to step into the hole.

"Geoff, I don't know about this," I said. "I can't tell how stable this formation is. If the ice collapses, it will be very difficult to get you out. I don't want you doing anything stupid."

Barker looked at me with the confidence of a man who had been in these situations before.

"I'll be fine, XO."

I nodded.

"All right. Move out."

Ellis picked up the slack on the rope and I kept close to the hole, talking to Barker as he moved.

"Everything okay?" I yelled as he faded from view.

"Fine," came the echo.

I watched as the rope paid out farther and farther. Barker was now almost fifty yards into the cavern, when suddenly the rope snapped taut.

Barker began yelling, but I couldn't make out his words. Grabbing my flashlight, I ducked into the opening, latched on to the rope, and began moving in his direction.

The rocks inside the cavern were smaller, but they still made movement difficult. The ice on the ceiling was melting and I could see that certain areas of the ice floe were thicker than others. My heart was pounding from the altitude and adrenaline.

At the edge of my beam, I could see Barker coming down the hill in my direction. We met halfway. The look on his face said it all.

As he turned his flashlight up the mountain, there, smashed into a million pieces—was a 1948 P2V2 Navy airplane.

"Holy shit." I smiled. "Would you look at that!"

As the beams from the flashlight reflected off the ice we could see the outline of the aircraft. It was almost as if it had landed intact and then been pulverized over the years by tons of thawing ice falling from the cavern's roof.

"It looks like our midnight visitor was right after all," Barker said.

"Say what?"

"Never mind, sir."

I could hear Ellis yelling, checking to see if we were okay. I responded back in a calm voice, knowing that he wouldn't understand my words—but he wouldn't move from the opening until he sensed panic and several tugs on the rope.

Barker and I climbed back up the mountain toward the wreckage. I walked up the starboard side of the plane while he took the port. Pieces of metal were strewn everywhere, but in a recognizable pattern. The tail section and the rear fuselage were nothing but fragments, none larger than my fist.

Suddenly, a large chunk of ice dropped from the ceiling, crashing into the midsection of the aircraft. Looking up, I could see the water beginning to cascade from the top of the roof to the sides. The cavern was melting, and more quickly than I realized.

As we approached the wing section, Barker called out, "Sir, over here."

He reached down and pulled a long piece of leather from the wreckage. There on the back side of the worn brown cloth was a circular patch—the squadron's emblem, still intact after all these years.

"One of the crewmen's flight jacket," he said somberly.

I nodded, knowing that the crewman was likely wearing that jacket at the time of impact. "Any signs of remains?" I asked.

Barker picked through the rocks and rubble, but there was nothing to be found. We continued to move up the length of the fuselage.

"Hey, look," Barker said excitedly. "It's a .50 cal!"

Pushing the heavy rocks aside, Barker lifted the barrel of a .50-caliber machine gun, but the receiver section of the weapon was still buried beneath more rubble. Making my way across the center section of the aircraft, I joined in and we pulled the remaining stock of the gun out from under the debris. The weapon was almost completely intact. The barrel was bent slightly, but everything else seemed to be functioning.

"Incredible," Barker said. "The entire plane is crushed into pieces, but the .50 cal survives."

As I put the butt of the gun back on the ground, I noticed a small translucent piece of bone. I was no expert, but it appeared to be part of a hand. Digging further, I found another fragment, and Barker, who was searching as well, picked up a third piece.

By now we were soaked from the melting ice and shaking from the cold. "Hey, boss," Barker said. "I think it's time we got out of here before we join the crew—permanently."

We gathered up the jacket and the bones and returned back down the cavern to the opening. We stepped through the hole, into the bright sunlight.

"Well?" Ellis asked, coiling the rope around his shoulder.

"It's there," Barker answered.

"Hot damn!" Carter yelled.

"I knew it!" Ellis proclaimed.

"Let me have the harness," Ellis said. "I've got to see this!"

"We're not going back in until we have a good plan. It's too dangerous right now," I said.

"Geoff, you and Pat see if we can enter the cavern from the side. Up near the wing section. If we can get in from that angle then we can reduce the distance between the wreckage and our escape if things go bad."

"Roger, sir," Barker acknowledged.

"You going to call this in, XO?" Carter asked.

"Not yet, Chuck. Let's give it a day before we radio in what we've found." Overnight some other naval officers from the Pentagon and Hawaii had flown in to help assist in the identification of remains, if any were found. Additionally, some members of the aircrew's family had come to Tofino. During one of our pre-mission coordination meetings, I had naively agreed that if we found anything at the site, I would radio back to Tofino and those relatives who were fit enough could join us to pay their last respects. But I assumed that if we found the aircraft it would be underwater and most of the elderly folks wouldn't want to make the journey just to look at a picturesque lake—even if their relatives were buried beneath it.

Now that the wreck was accessible, some of the more adventurous men would definitely opt for coming out to see the remains.

Over the course of the next few days, with the help of a small Navy recovery team, we continued to pick through the wreckage, but there wasn't much left of the plane. We salvaged another machine gun and some additional bone fragments, but the cavern became more unstable every day. Finally, I decided to call off the search. I radioed back to Tofino that we had found the plane and any relatives wanting to join us were welcome to fly out.

By that afternoon, we had an additional eight folks on the ground, including Ray Swentek, the brother of the navigator, Edward Swentek. Ray had made it his calling in life to find the plane and have the bodies recovered. Without his efforts none of this would have happened. It was Swentek who had approached the Navy about getting the SEALs to conduct the search. I allowed Ray and several members of the other families to view the wreckage. We roped them in and provided escorts for their safety.

As Ray Swentek walked the length of the plane I could see the pain in his eyes. This frozen metal carcass, twisted and crushed beyond recognition, was the final resting place of the brother he had idolized as a child. Somewhere in the cockpit, now pulverized by ice and rocks, his brother would be buried for eternity.

I watched Swentek scour the area around the cockpit, slowly, deliberately picking through the rubble.

"I was hoping to find it," he said.

"Find what?"

"His Navy ring. He never took it off even when flying."

I knew there wasn't a chance in hell that we would find the ring, but I got down on my knees and began to sift through what was left of the cockpit.

We didn't find the ring, and as the melting ice began to thaw more quickly, I ordered everyone out of the cavern.

Later that day we assembled all the family members and held a small memorial service near our campsite. Half of the bone fragments we buried under a makeshift cross, the other half we would return to Arlington and provide full military honors to our fallen.

As we gathered around the cross it occurred to me that this would be the final time any man would venture to this location. Most of the crew who perished that night had families, children who grew up strong in their absence, but who would never know their fathers except by some old black-and-white photos.

We bowed our heads and I prayed. "Dear heavenly father, we know these men are with you in heaven. We give thanks for their service on earth and we pray that you will continue to bless their families and loved ones. We thank you for your guiding hand that brought us to this site and for allowing us to return these men home where they can rest in peace among others who have paid the same price. God bless them all."

"Amen," came the response.

For a brief moment tears flowed and heads remained bowed.

I glanced up from the gravesite to see Barker staring off into the distance. His head was cocked hard to the right and his mouth was open. Beside him Ellis was wide-eyed and quietly pointing something out to Carter.

Turning around, I looked in the direction of the ice floe, and there, high above the peak, a lone bright object sparkled in the sky.

"It looks like a signal flare," Swentek offered.

It did look like a signal flare, I thought. In fact, it looked like a military-style parachute flare, bright white, almost silver, suspended in the air, possibly caught in an updraft off the side of the mountain.

Suddenly another flare lit the sky, and then another and another and another. As we watched in silence, the entire ridgeline filled with glowing white orbs that hovered just above the mountaintop.

"Boss," Walker stammered. "How many flares do you see up there?"

I began to count, but I knew the answer even before I finished.

"There are nine of them," Carter said.

The orbs hovered for more than fifteen minutes, and then suddenly, one by one, they all rocketed skyward and were gone.

In silence, we packed up the remainder of our gear and shuttled the family members back to Tofino, and as the sun began to set over the mountaintop I boarded the helo for one of the last rides out. As I adjusted the headset the pilot came up on comms.

"You guys are the talk of Tofino, Commander. People have been searching for that plane for years. Now that the lost souls have found their way to heaven, maybe our luck will change."

I adjusted the volume on my headset and unconsciously leaned over to look the pilot in the eye. "What did you say?"

The pilot grinned. "My ancestors believe that the remains of the dead must be visible to heaven so their souls can be guided through the great dome."

Checking his compass setting, he glanced around to make certain we were clear of the mountains. "Legend says that the sky is a great dome and there is a hole in it through which the spirits pass in order to get to heaven. The spirits who live in heaven light torches to guide them through." The pilot craned his helmeted head in my direction and laughed. "It's all just Indian folklore, but I'm sure some local will buy you boys a beer when you get back to Tofino."

Sitting back on the floorboard, I watched as the ice floe disappeared into the distance, the thumping of the rotor blades marking our progress back to Tofino.

I looked skyward, smiled, and rendered a salute. The crew was finally home.

CHAPTER EIGHT

AMERICAN PIRATES

"Fire!"

Whoom! The five-inch round from the destroyer's gun blasted out of the barrel, the concussion wave rolling across the short expanse of ocean and rocking those of us standing nearby on USS *Ogden*. A plume of water exploded twenty yards in front of the Iraqi tanker *Amuriyah*. But still she kept going.

"Fire!"

Another round rocketed from the barrel, the smoke drifting across the port side of the destroyer, the shell landing another twenty yards from the tanker. Over the bridge-to-bridge communications I could hear the master of the *Amuriyah* yelling obscenities at the commanding officer of the Australian destroyer *Brewton*. Even in Arabic, obscenities sound the same.

"Fire!"

The third round flew just over the bow of the *Amuriyah*. The master, just visible on the bridge of the ship, threw the helm hard to port and the nine-hundred-foot supertanker lumbered closer to the American task force.

"Stand by for .50 cal."

"Fire, fire, fire!" The gunner on the destroyer's .50-caliber machine gun opened up with a short burst, barely missing the small Iraqi flag that flew from the forwardmost stanchion.

"Stop! You are crazy! You cannot do this!" the master pleaded in broken English.

"*Amuriyah*, this is United States warship *Ogden*. I say again, under United Nations Resolution 665, you are directed to stop and be boarded." The tone was firm and measured.

"Never, never, never! You are pirates. You cannot board my ship!"

On the horizon I could see a small shape approaching at high speed. It was an F-14 jet screaming across the water just fifty feet above the deck.

"Cease fire!" came the command from the destroyer.

The F-14 was kicking up water behind it and accelerating as it approached the tanker. The crew of the *Amuriyah* could see the aircraft now and they moved to the rails, ready to jump overboard if necessary.

Splitting the seam between the *Amuriyah* and USS *Ogden*, the jet blew past with such velocity that the thundering of the engines brought me to my knees. The crew of the *Ogden*, lining the rails, roared with approval. It was an impressive show of military power, but still the tanker remained defiant and plowed ahead unabated.

Once again, the loudspeaker belted out an order. "Commander McRaven, stand by to board the vessel!"

That was my cue. We'd spent the last eighteen months preparing for something like this. Now it was showtime.

Five months earlier, I had left my wife, Georgeann, and my two boys, Bill and John, on the pier in San Diego as USS *Okinawa* pulled away for a routine six-month deployment to the western Pacific. There are few things more gut-wrenching than watching your family slowly disappear into the distance as your ship sails out of port. While I loved being a SEAL, there was nothing in the world more important to me than my family. My boys were at that age where we were constant companions. I rarely missed a youth basketball or baseball game and we loved spending time on the water in San Diego. Additionally, before I departed we were thrilled to find out Georgeann was pregnant, but that made the farewell even harder. The only saving grace was we knew I would be home in time for the delivery.

After two months underway, we received word that Saddam Hussein had invaded Kuwait. President Bush ordered the commencement of Operation Desert Shield to allow for the buildup of U.S. forces in order to liberate Kuwait and defend Saudi Arabia. USS *Okinawa*, which was the lead ship for Amphibious Squadron Five (PHIBRONFIVE), was ordered to proceed to the Indian Ocean and await further directions. We departed Subic Bay, Philippines, and after a short stop in Hong Kong sailed through the Strait of Malacca, eventually arriving in MODLOC (a naval acronym meaning "modified location," that is, steaming around in circles waiting for the next order) off the southern tip of India.

In addition to the *Okinawa*, there were four other ships in the squadron: USS *Fort McHenry*, USS *Ogden*, USS *Cayuga*, and USS *Durham*, which along with the 13th Marine Expeditionary Unit/Special Operations Capable (MEU/SOC) made up the ARG (Amphibious Ready Group)/MEU Team.

The squadron commodore was a charismatic Navy captain named Mike Coumatos. Coumatos flew Huey helicopters in Vietnam and had that swagger that comes from being a combat pilot. Short, with a large bushy mustache, he was wickedly smart, very professional, with a gambler's streak of boldness. He and I hit it off from the very beginning. He trusted my judgment and I trusted his leadership implicitly.

The MEU/SOC commander, Colonel John Rhodes, was also a Vietnam-era helo pilot with two Silver Stars and four Distinguished Flying Crosses to show for his bravery. Rhodes was vintage Corps: physically fit, disciplined, with a drive for perfection that made his MEU one of the best I had ever seen. He was hard on his staff and his Marines, but they reflected his style in everything they did. It was a superb Navy–Marine Corps team.

As the Naval Special Warfare Task Unit commander and the

senior special operations officer, I was often tasked to command all the elements that were special operations or special operations–like. This included an experienced Marine Force Recon element, the Navy SEAL platoon, and occasionally the Marine boat raid company, the Radio Recon battalion, and a Navy Explosive Ordnance Disposal platoon. We were all well acquainted with each other, having done a nine-month pre-deployment workup prior to leaving San Diego.

While on our way to MODLOC, the ARG/MEU suffered a terrible tragedy when two UH-1N Huey helicopters collided during night operations, killing all eight men aboard. It was a stark reminder that there is no such thing as normal operations when you are at sea. Under the strong leadership of Coumatos and Rhodes, we searched for forty-eight hours, then paid our respects to the fallen and proceeded with the mission. I had witnessed losses before, but it was never easy. Some of the Marines had families back home. Young children like mine. Each time I passed the Marines' empty staterooms I was reminded of just how fragile life is and how fortunate I was to have known such fine men.

MODLOC off India was tiring. Not a cloud in the sky. No wind. No land as far as the eye could see, and the scorching sun made the steel decks so hot we only conducted flight operations during the early morning and evening hours. We had no television, mail took thirty days to reach us, and the only way to find out what was going on in the world was through our ship's Teletype. Every day we anxiously waited for news of the impending war. Saddam Hussein had been warned: Get out of Kuwait or we will force you out. The United Nations issued Resolutions 661 and 665 authorizing a naval blockade to stop any ship providing economic support to the Iraqis.

In October, an Iraqi cargo vessel leaving the Arabian Gulf had been directed by the U.S. Navy to stop. Unfortunately, two Navy destroyers were unable to halt the Iraqi ship from departing the Gulf. The destroyers hailed the vessel, demanding that the master of the ship allow a boarding party to embark. After some verbal exchanges and inappropriate hand gestures, the master kept moving. The destroyers fired .50-caliber automatic weapons across the bow of the Iraqi vessel, but it kept steaming ahead. Finally, the warships attempted to cut off the vessel with several high-speed runs, narrowly avoiding a collision, but to no avail. The master of the Iraqi vessel was determined to continue on, and the only way to stop a ship at sea, short of sinking her, was to board her—underway. And the only underway boarding capability in the vicinity of the gulf was with Amphibious Squadron Five and the 13th MEU/SOC. But we were still seven days away. In a small early victory for Saddam Hussein, the Iraqi cargo vessel fled the Persian Gulf and the Navy broke contact and let the ship proceed on its way.

By that evening, General Colin Powell, the Chairman of the Joint Chiefs, issued an order to the 5th Fleet commander directing PHIBRONFIVE to proceed at once to the northern Arabian Gulf and be prepared to interdict any other Iraqi vessels that might attempt to run the blockade.

We left MODLOC in the Indian Ocean and with a routine speed of approach (SOA) steamed toward the northern Arabian Gulf. Two days into our voyage, another message came over the Teletype. Intelligence revealed that Saddam Hussein had personally relayed a message to the master of an Iraqi supertanker, the *Amuriyah*, that under no circumstance was the *Amuriyah* to stop for the U.S. blockade. The tanker was portside in the city of Aden, Yemen, just a few days' steaming from the Persian Gulf. In order for the Amphibious Ready Group to intercept the tanker before she got to the Strait of Hormuz, we would have to proceed at full steam, which we did.

The following day we received additional intelligence that caused quite a stir aboard the *Okinawa*. Reportedly, the *Amuriyah* was transporting "something" of great value to Saddam. The mysterious

"something" had the analysts spooked. There was speculation rang-
ing from chemical weapons to a small nuclear device. While it
seemed implausible, it nonetheless heightened the anxiety of everyone in the Amphibious Ready Group.

Sitting at the fold-up desk in my stateroom, I heard a light knock
at the door.

"Enter!"

Nothing.

"Enter!" I yelled again.

The door to my cabin slowly opened and a young petty officer
peeked into the room. "Commander McRaven?"

"Yes. Can I help you?"

"Yes sir. The commodore would like to see you in his
stateroom."

"Now?"

"Yes sir. Now."

Dressed in my working khaki uniform, I grabbed my notebook
and headed out the door to the commodore's office. Coumatos had
been my boss now for well over a year and I had become an inte-
gral part of his staff. As the senior SEAL aboard the *Okinawa*, I was
dual-hatted as both a staff officer with the squadron staff and as the
Naval Special Warfare Task Unit commander. As a staff member,
I had spent most of the past eight months living aboard the *Okinawa*. While most SEALs hated spending time on ships, I really
enjoyed it.

Life aboard a Navy ship hadn't changed much in fifty years.
The technology had changed, but as with the ships of World War II,
you still lived in very close quarters, ate together, worked together,
and fought together. There were all the human dynamics of people
crammed into a steel hull, but that's where Navy discipline and a
minimalistic lifestyle were crucial to having a well-oiled crew. The
sailors slept in racks stacked three or four high. The only space for
personal items was underneath your mattress or in a small locker.

The officers' "staterooms" were generally four men to a room, and the more senior officers were two to a room. Racks were made every morning. The sinks were always wiped down after use. Showers were three minutes—no more. You showed up for your watch fifteen minutes prior to turnover. If you showed up fourteen minutes prior, you were late. The brass throughout the ship was polished to prevent corrosion. The passageways were swabbed. Old paint was chipped away and new coats of paint applied every week. Nothing was left unattended. Everything about your day was planned down to the minute. Even your free time was on the calendar. The rigor was tiring at times, but also reassuring and predictable, and in a strange way, comforting.

"Come in," Coumatos yelled from the other side of the door.

Relative to the rest of the officers, the commodore lived well—a large one-room stateroom with his own shower and head. There was a small conference table in a sitting area that served double duty as a dining table. I remember envying the commodore until years later I found myself in command. The old adage "It's lonely at the top" is an old adage for a reason.

To my surprise, the MEU commander, Colonel John Rhodes, was in the room as well. The two men were huddled around the conference table looking at an overhead photo of the *Amuriyah*.

The *Amuriyah* was nine hundred feet long with a seventy-two-foot freeboard (the distance from the water to the first deck). She was riding high in the water and likely had no oil on board. The deck of the tanker was a maze of large pipes running from the pilothouse to just short of the bow. There were only a few open spaces in the maze and they were all quite small.

Coumatos motioned me to the table. "Have you seen this?"

"Yes sir. I've been studying it all day," I answered.

"What do you think?" Rhodes asked.

"Well, sir, it's pretty straightforward." I pulled out a pen and began to outline an initial plan. "We position two Hueys with snipers on the port and starboard sides of the *Amuriyah*. Once we get the all-clear from the snipers we bring in the assault force aboard the CH-46." I circled a spot on the photo.

"The 46 hovers amidships, between the pilothouse and the bow. We do a fifty-foot fast rope onto the deck. Consolidate the men, then split into two teams. One assault element to the engine room to stop the vessel and one to the bridge to take control. Once we have control of the ship we bring the prize crew aboard and steam her wherever you want."

Rhodes nodded. Coumatos asked, "What if they clutter the deck with debris?"

"There is a spot right off the bow that we could maneuver to, but we should have plenty of time to make that decision. We'll know well before boarding her if the primary spot is fouled. If they try to stop us while we're boarding, then the snipers can keep them away."

"Who would you take as your assault element?" Rhodes asked.

Rhodes's question was more than tactical. I was a SEAL, and he likely wondered whether I would take the SEALs over the Marine Force Recon. But the best unit for the mission was the Marines, who were exceptionally well trained in close-quarters battle—the kind of skills we would need for this operation.

"Sir, I'll take the Force Recon as the assault element and the SEALs will be on a second 46 as the Quick Reaction Force."

The two senior officers looked at each and nodded their approval.

"Okay, Bill," the commodore said. "Be ready to brief the CONOP to me and Colonel Rhodes in the next twenty-four hours. I want to know the assets you need for your rehearsal and any additional support required for the mission."

"Sir, what about the R2P2?"

"We don't have time for that. Just get me the brief soonest."

I gave a hearty "Aye-aye, sir," collected my notebook, and left the cabin. Somehow I knew I wasn't going to be popular with the PHIBRON or MEU staff. The R2P2 was the rapid reaction planning process that the Marines and Navy staff had been learning and exercising for the past eighteen months—it was a process intended to develop courses of action for crisis events just like this one. The two staffs prided themselves on their ability to develop a mission statement, identify the specified and implied tasks, outline three courses of action (COAs) and the risks associated with each, and then in a very deliberate and elaborate briefing session advise the Navy and Marine leadership as to the best COA. The R2P2 was ingrained into the PHIBRON and MEU staffs from the beginning, and now we were tossing it out in favor of a more "streamlined" approach—to wit, *McRaven, give us a plan.* For years to come I would question the wisdom of Coumatos and Rhodes to forgo the R2P2, only to find that when I was in command, I did the same thing. Experience matters, and sometimes all the staff work in the world doesn't get you better results than what the experienced officer knows intuitively.

The two staffs did complain about their lack of inclusion in the senior leader planning, but they quickly got over it and we proceeded on with the rehearsals. Within seventy-two hours we were ready.

The loudspeaker on the *Ogden* blared again, "Assault element to spot one!" I knew the Force Recon platoon was already positioned on the helo deck and probably had been for the past thirty minutes. Standing on the bridge, I was getting last-minute instructions from Captain Braden Phillips, the skipper of the *Ogden.* "Time to go," he said, smiling.

"Roger. See you in a bit," I said, slinging my Heckler and Koch MP5 across my back. I walked off the bridge, down the ladder, along the starboard rail, past a number of anxious-looking sailors, and out onto the main flight deck. The Force Recon platoon had already boarded the helo. Gathered around the hangar was a crowd of ship's crew, all smiling and yelling their encouragement. It was the first real "action" of Desert Storm and the historic nature of even this small clash was not lost on the sailors.

The *thump, thump, thump* of the blades began to drown out the crew's cheers as I walked slowly to the ramp of the helo, working hard not to look excited. It was exciting, but inside I was calm. We had a good plan. We had rehearsed extensively. The Marines and SEALs were well trained. We had overwhelming firepower. And I had the confidence in my own abilities to know that under pressure I would make the best decisions possible. Still, on every mission, the unforeseen is always lurking in the shadows.

Looking out the small porthole in the Marine CH-46, I could see the *Amuriyah*, her large bow powering through the water, a massive wave rolling off her port and starboard sides. The master of the Iraqi tanker had turned all the ship's water cannons inward, creating a latticework of high-powered hydraulic projections. The water from the cannons pooled on the tanker's deck, creating pockets three and four feet deep. It would make movement around the vessel difficult for the operators.

Donning my headset, I heard the pilot request permission to launch.

"Launch the assault force," I answered. The ship's tower gave clearance and the helo lifted off, banking hard to starboard and gaining altitude quickly. Inside the aircraft sat twenty-one Marines from 1st Force Reconnaissance out of Camp Pendleton. The platoon was led by Captain Tony Stallings, a six-foot-four, 245-pound former defensive end from Arizona State. Stallings was an imposing figure and had that competitive attitude that made him a formidable Marine and a great platoon commander. His noncommissioned officers were all handpicked and extensively trained in ship takedowns. Each man carried a CAR-15, a .45-caliber pistol, a squad radio, flash-crash grenades, and extra ammo. We didn't expect a firefight, but we were ready if there was one.

Once the helo was off the deck, I moved forward in the cabin to look out the side door. The two Hueys, which came off the *Oki-nawa*, were just arriving on station. I watched as one helo positioned itself on the starboard side of the *Amuriyah* and the other on the port side. Just as planned. I could hear the SEAL snipers in the Hueys talking on the squad radio. They were scanning the ship for any signs of threat.

"There's a lot of movement on deck," the port-side sniper reported.

"Any weapons?" asked the starboard sniper.

"Negative. But some of the crew have axes."

"Roger. Copy." There was a squelch on the radio. "Raven, Raven, this is Hotel Zero One, be advised approximately twenty personnel on the main deck. No weapons. Two crewmen carrying axes. How copy?"

I pushed the talk button and responded. "Roger, Hotel Zero One. Understand approximately twenty pax on deck. No weapons. Two men with axes."

"Raven, this is Hotel Zero One. You are cleared to rope."

"Roger. Raven out."

I switched back to the interhelo comms and raised the pilot. "All right. We're cleared to rope. Take us in."

"Roger, sir," came the reply.

Stallings had been monitoring all the communications and gave his Marines their final instructions. The fast-rope master checked the safety line on the fast rope one final time. The fast rope was a green two-inch-thick heavily woven hawser. What made it special was how it was woven together. The unique weave allowed an operator to squeeze the rope to slow his descent. While you couldn't completely stop, you could slide down a 120-foot rope with a hundred pounds of gear on your back and not hit the ground like a ton of rocks—most of the time. Unlike with a rappelling line, you didn't have to clip in and therefore when inserting a force from a helo you could get more men on the ground much more quickly.

Looking out the hell hole in the middle of the helo, I could see the bow of the *Amuriyah* underneath us as the CH-46 slowed to hover speed. Ripping off the headset, I put on my Pro-Tec helmet, checked my weapons and gear, adjusted my fast-rope gloves, and prepared to exit the helo.

Inside the aircraft the Marines were stacking one behind the other. I was ninth in line. As the helo slowed to a hover the sound of the blades deepened. Out the hell hole I could see the pilot slide right, positioning the CH-46 over a small open space on the tanker. On deck the Iraqis scattered as the downblast from the aircraft created a windstorm, spraying water and oil residue in all directions. The rope master now had control of the helo's positioning.

"Come left five feet," he yelled into his headset. The pilot complied.

"Stand by!"

The rope master pushed the green-coiled rope out the hell hole and watched as it hit the deck, ensuring it was clear of obstacles.

"Go, go, go!" he yelled at the Marines stacked by the opening.

One by one the first four Marines grabbed the rope and slid out of the helo. Within fifteen seconds they were on the deck and had formed a security perimeter. Stallings and the small command element followed. I was right behind them. Grabbing the rope with two hands, I swung my body 180 degrees to the open side of the hole and began the fifty-foot slide down the rope.

Immediately the hot blast from the rotor blades belted the top of my head. The wind off the Gulf was equally oppressive, blowing me sideways, away from the frame of the helo. Gripping the rope with all my strength, I looped my legs around the thick green line and held on tightly. Below me on the rope were two Marines still making their descent. As the first Marine hit the deck his feet slid out from under him and the second Marine piled on top of his buddy. Immediately they rolled away from the rope, sprang to their feet, and cleared the deck as I came quickly in behind.

My gloved hands, burning from the rapid descent, loosened too soon and I hit the *Amuriyah* with a resounding thud. Steel is an unforgiving metal, and as I impacted the ship I could feel a sharp pain shooting up from my heels all the way to my jaw. But adrenaline, and pride, kept me from crumpling in a heap in front of the Marines. Within another thirty seconds the entire Force Recon platoon was on the deck and in position.

The configuration of the *Amuriyah* was typical of a supertanker. While the outer rail of the ship was clear, the inner area was a maze of large pipes, valves, small pumping stations, and circuit boxes. Good for cover if someone started shooting, but difficult to maneuver around. We were somewhat boxed in, but the ship's crewmen had moved back toward the large superstructure that contained the pilothouse.

Stallings got a quick muster of his men and as planned they broke into two elements and began to move. Off to our right and left the Hueys were hovering twenty feet above the deck and just off the ship's railing. I could hear the snipers on the squad radios.

"Port side clear."

"Starboard side clear."

The first sergeant, an experienced noncommissioned officer, took the second element and headed down the port side to an open hatch leading to the engine room. Positioned in the middle of the first element, I swung my weapon into a low port, not threatening, but ready. In front of me, the Recon element began to move, their strides deliberate, slow, but methodical. The point man, in a slight crouch, his weapon swinging from side to side, led the element out of the box and over to the starboard rail. Behind him, the number two man in the stack looked high, watching for possible threats from the outer ladders where most of the crewmen had begun to assemble. The other men in the patrol all had their fields of fire, and with precision honed over years of training, the Marines moved like the professionals they were.

The pilothouse was a five-story structure three-quarters of the way back on the vessel. On the outside of the building were ladders leading to each successive level. As the point man reached the first ladder, several unarmed crewmen blocked his advance.

"Allahu akbar!" screamed a crewman.

Thrusting his weapon a few inches forward, the point man motioned to the crewmen to move.

"Allahu akbar!"

"Fuck you!" came the Marine's response. "I said move!"

Three more crewmen began taunting the Marines, but the two on the ladder stepped aside and we pressed forward up to the next level. Within a minute we were on level five. Stallings quickly stacked the men on the open door and entered as per the standard operating procedures. The point man went first, breaking to the right and sweeping down the front of the pilothouse. The second man through the door broke left and swept through to the rear of the room, and the third and fourth men entered and took up positions at the nearest corners.

"Clear!" came the call from the point man.

I could hear the screaming of the master before I walked through the door.

"Leave my bridge! You have no right to be here. You are American pirates!"

Inside the pilothouse were another six Iraqis. They stood unarmed, but defiant. One man was behind the helm. One man was on the engine order telegraph. One man with binoculars was near the front of the cabin. The navigation officer was at the far end of the room by an old chart table. The first mate was by the master, and the master—all five feet five inches and three hundred pounds of him—stood in the center of the room, flapping his hands and shouting at the top of his lungs.

"You cannot do this! You are pirates!"

I walked to the center of the pilothouse and confronted the

master. "Sir, I am a United States naval officer. In accordance with United Nations Resolution 661 you are directed to stop this vessel and be searched." I motioned to the Marine translator, who repeated the words in Arabic.

"I speak English," the master said, spittle flying off his lips.

"You have one minute to stop this vessel or I will stop it for you," I remarked quietly.

"You cannot stop my ship that quickly. It will destroy the engines."

"I can. And I will."

The red phone on the ship's console rang with a piercing clang. Picking the phone up, the master's eyes widened, and he looked at me and yelled, "You have killed one of my men!" The other Iraqis in the pilothouse began screaming at the Marines.

"If you don't cooperate," I cautioned, "more men will die. You now have thirty seconds to stop your ship." Turning to Stallings, I whispered, "Find out what the hell happened."

Stallings nodded and walked to the bridge wing to make comms with the second element.

Belowdecks the second element had moved from the outer hull of the ship into the vessel's interior. Making their way down five levels, they entered the engine room, which was hot and steamy, the floor slippery with condensation. The element walked along the steel gratings to the engine control room. Hiding behind the giant machinery, a dozen Iraqis watched as the Marines approached the ship's control center.

Walking point, First Sergeant Jones scanned the engine room. The crewmen, peeking around the corners of the immense boilers, seemed to be waiting for something. As Jones stepped forward to enter the control room, an axe-wielding Iraqi leapt from behind a three-foot steam pipe. Jones spun around, leveled his weapon to fire, and then, in an incredible moment of restraint, swung the butt of his CAR-15, catching the crewman on the jaw and sending him sprawling unconscious to the metal floor. Immediately the other Marines fanned out and took up security positions. In the air-conditioned control room an Iraqi who witnessed the action thought his fellow crewman was dead and called the bridge.

Stallings motioned me to the bridge wing. "Sir, no one's dead, but one of their crewmen is going to have a bad headache."

I returned to the master, who was visibly shaken from the news. I decided to let him think the worst. Dictating the tempo of this confrontation was important. Right now I had the upper hand, and it was important to maintain it.

"My men are in the engine room ready to shut down your vessel. So either you can bring it to a stop now or I will. Your choice."

The master grunted, looked around the pilothouse at his senior officers, and then gave the helmsman the order to bring the vessel to all stop.

"It will take some time for the ship to be dead in the water."

"It will take exactly thirteen minutes," I noted. "If the vessel isn't DIW in thirteen minutes, then I will force it into reverse to stop the forward motion."

I had his attention now.

"Master, I will need your ship's manifest and passenger information. I assume you have it locked in your stateroom cabin. Please go with my Marine and bring it to me."

The master looked at Captain Stallings, whose six-foot-four-inch frame would be intimidating under any circumstances, but when you cover it with camouflage and give it a weapon it takes on a whole different level of fear. Stallings grabbed the master by the elbow and directed him to the passageway leading to the cabin. I motioned to another Marine to buddy up and follow Stallings and the master.

After a few minutes the ship began to slow markedly. I'm not sure it was really thirteen minutes, but in short order the vessel was dead in the water. From inside the bridge, I could see that we were surrounded by warships: the *Brewton*, the *Ogden*, and in the distance the *Okinawa*.

My radio squelched and I could hear Stallings on the other end.

"Sir, we're having some difficulty down here. The master is playing games. Says he can't open the safe. Forgot the combination." Before I could answer I heard a voice over the radio yell, "Look out!" The radio went silent.

"Stallings? Stallings? Can you hear me?" Nothing. The Marines on the bridge monitoring the radio heard the commotion as well. Pointing at the two Marines outside on the bridge wing, I said, "Go down to the master's cabin and find out what's going on."

"Raven. This is Wildcat."

"Roger, Tony. What's going on down there?"

"Nothing, sir. Everything's fine now. The master has decided to open the safe. We should be up in a few minutes."

The two Marines on the bridge wing looked at me and I nodded for them to stay put. A few minutes later the door to the pilothouse opened and in walked Stallings. Behind him came a flex-cuffed and bruised master. There was a large welt over his left eye, and his lip was swollen and bleeding slightly.

I looked at Stallings. He shrugged his shoulders and with a look of complete astonishment said softly, "Sir, the son of a bitch jumped me. I tried to push him off, but he came at me again. He's built like Jabba the Hutt. Finally I just popped him a couple of times and he stopped fighting."

Glancing over at the master, I could see him smiling beneath his bulging lip. His fellow Iraqis were happy. Their captain had resisted the Americans and he had the scars to show for it. I began to hear reports over the net of similar confrontations around the ship. The last thing I wanted was to kill or injure a merchant seaman, but without reinforcements, we were not going to be able to control the ship and contain the large number of crewmen.

I approached the master. "Sir, please request your crew to cooperate. If they fail to do so, they may be injured or killed."

Standing by the ship's public address system, the first mate grabbed the microphone and yelled in Arabic, "Resist, resist! Do not let them take the ship!"

The Marine point man ripped the mic away from the first mate.

"Asshole!" the mate yelled.

On deck now I could see the crewmen grabbing crowbars, brooms, anything that made a weapon. I was losing control and needed to regain the upper hand. Walking out on the bridge wing, I squeezed the push-to-talk button and called the SEAL reserve force.

"X-ray Two Zero, this is Raven Zero One."

"Roger, Raven Zero One. Two Zero."

"Two Zero. Insert the Quick Reaction Force and link up with assault element."

"Roger, Zero One. On final now."

Within two minutes the fourteen-man SEAL element, under the command of Lieutenant Dave Kauffman, was on the ship and corralling the belligerent crewmen. It took another hour or so and several fisticuffs before we finally policed up all the Iraqi sailors and detained them in the crew's lounge. After ninety minutes on the *Amuriyah*, the ship was secure without any major injuries to either the Americans or the Iraqis. A Law Enforcement Detachment (LEDET) consisting of a Coast Guard officer and several other naval officers from the U.S. task force boarded the ship and began a thorough search of the cargo. Six hours later, I extracted the Marines and the SEALs and we returned to the *Ogden*. A few hours after that the *Amuriyah* was cleared to proceed to Iraq. Nothing unusual was ever found, but considering the size of the massive tanker, it's conceivable that "something" was carefully hidden in the ship's hold.

The *Amuriyah* returned to Iraq. On January 17, the United

States and its allies began Operation Desert Storm. During the opening days of the war, intelligence revealed that Saddam was preparing to create an ecological disaster by filling Iraqi ships with oil and then sinking them in the Arabian Gulf. One of those ships was the *Amuriyah*. On January 23, an A-6 from the carrier USS *Midway* dropped two five-hundred-pound bombs into the hull of the *Amuriyah*, sinking her off the coast of Bubiyan Island, well before she could take on any oil.

During Desert Storm, PHIBRONFIVE and the 13th MEU would go on to liberate a number of small Gulf islands seized by the Iraqis, participate in the amphibious deception operation, and secure the Kuwaiti island of Failaka, detaining over twelve hundred Iraqi soldiers. It had taken me fifteen years since SEAL training, but I had finally gotten to serve my country in a meaningful way.

As terrible as it sounds, every SEAL longs for a worthy fight, a battle of convictions, and an honorable war. War challenges your manhood. It reaffirms your courage. It sets you apart from the timid souls and the bench sitters. It builds unbreakable bonds among your fellow warriors. *It gives your life meaning.* Over time, I would get more than my fair share of war. Men would be lost. Innocents would be killed. Families would be forever changed. But somehow, inexplicably, war would never lose its allure. To the warrior, peace has no memories, no milestones, no adventures, no heroic deaths, no gut-wrenching sorrow, no jubilation, no remorse, no repentance, and no salvation. Peace was meant for some people, but probably not for me.

Ten months after I left San Diego I returned home and was met by Georgeann, Bill, John, and my new daughter, Kelly Marie. A few weeks later I visited my father in San Antonio. He hugged me tightly, told me how proud he was of me and that he hoped I would never have to go to war again. But twelve years later I would return to Iraq to help finish the job of defeating Saddam Hussein.

CHAPTER NINE

SECOND CHANCES

MORRO BAY, CALIFORNIA
February 1995

Second chances. They are noble intentions that come with expectations and obligations. They can heal or they can cut. They can result in an uplifting hymn or a Greek tragedy. The outcome of second chances is never preordained. Some people will make the most of them and the giver of the chance will be proud, and some will squander them and the world will say, "I told you so." Giving second chances can be risky.

"Guilty."

At my words, Lieutenant Jeremy Carter, dressed in his summer white uniform, seemed crushed by the decision. He was a young SEAL who had a good career behind him and a lot of potential for promotion. Now his career was finished.

As the commanding officer of SEAL Team Three, I had reviewed the charges against him and found that he had violated article 133, conduct unbecoming an officer, and article 92, failure to obey a lawful order. He had been caught driving under the influence and evading a police officer, and I knew that I had to hold him accountable for his actions. He was a SEAL officer and we had high standards for conduct.

After everyone left my office, my command master chief, a seasoned Vietnam veteran named Billy Hill, returned to talk with me.

"You were a little hard on him, sir."

"I know, Billy, but I can't bust the enlisted guys for a DUI and then not hold the officers accountable as well."

"Yes sir, but the enlisted guys can survive a bust. The officer's career is over."

Billy was right, but in my mind the expectations were higher for officers and therefore their performance needed to be higher as well.

"Maybe you should give him another chance."

I just nodded.

Commanding a SEAL Team was the best job in the Navy, but the proverbial Sword of Damocles always hung precariously over your head. Every day you had to choose between being a hard disciplinarian, making the tough decisions necessary for running a SEAL Team, and being compassionate when someone made a mistake, looking beyond their failure to an alternate future—a future where they excelled and made a positive difference in the lives of your sailors. Of all people, I knew the value of a second chance.

Since graduating from training, I had done just about everything expected of a SEAL officer. I had served two tours with our SEAL Delivery Vehicles, commanded a SEAL platoon in South America, deployed to Desert Shield and Desert Storm as a SEAL Task Unit commander, and worked in the Pentagon, overseas in the Philippines, and on various SEAL staffs. I was married with three wonderful kids. But not everything in my career had gone perfectly. In 1983, while serving as a squadron commander at our elite East Coast SEAL Team, I was fired. Relieved of my command. It was a jarring, confidence-crushing, hard-to-swallow moment, and I seriously considered leaving the Navy. There seemed little chance of being promoted after losing my job. But, as she would do several times in my career, when I stumbled or circumstances turned against me, Georgeann reminded me that I had never quit at anything in my life—and now was not the time to start. Fortunately, several senior officers still saw potential in me. They gave me another opportunity, and over the years that followed the firing, I tried to redeem myself, proving to the doubters that I was good enough to lead a SEAL Team.

The master chief changed the subject.

"Sir, are you going up to Morro Bay to watch Echo Platoon's final pre-deployment exercise?"

SEAL Team Three's Echo Platoon was scheduled to deploy to the western Pacific in about forty-five days, and this was their last training exercise before leaving. As usual, the scenario called for an over-the-beach infiltration by the platoon. The fourteen-man SEAL element would depart from Morro Bay, in central California, aboard two thirty-three-foot Rigid Hull Inflatable Boats (RHIBs). They would transit about thirty miles up the coast to a point off the beach where we had constructed a simulated target. From there, the platoon would swim through the surf, hit the target, swim back through the surf, rendezvous with the RHIBs, and return to Morro Bay. Standard stuff.

"I'm scheduled to be down in Tampa next week to brief the SOCOM operations officer, but I think I'll stop by the exercise for a day and see how things are going."

The master chief had other commitments and couldn't make the trip, but the following week, as planned, I drove up the coast to Morro Bay and linked up with Echo Platoon as they were planning a final day of rehearsals.

Morro Bay is as picturesque a coastal town as there is in California. The entrance to the bay passes by a huge rock formation, appropriately called Morro Rock, and then snakes around, first to the north and then to the south, opening up into a placid harbor where hundreds of yachts of all sizes find refuge. For most of the year the surf rolls gently over the beach in perfect waves, making the coastline a favorite spot for surfers. But during the winter months, that same surf builds to enormous heights, and when funneled by the breakwaters off Morro Rock, they can reach fifty feet.

Driving into town around sunset, I could see ten-foot waves rolling off the beach, a result of a storm system centered about a hundred miles to the west. However, the funnel effect of Morro Rock and the breakwater was creating a more dangerous situation with a series of plunging twenty-five- to thirty-foot waves right at the entrance to the harbor.

We had set up our command center at the local Coast Guard station, and as I pulled up to the entrance, Master Chief "Tip" Ammen came out to meet me. The master chief was in charge of the SEAL Team Three training cell and was responsible for the conduct of the exercise. Ammen was older and more experienced than most of the senior enlisted at the command. He was always upbeat, with a good sense of humor and an unflappable personality.

"The platoon is briefing now, sir. Do you want to sit in on that or take a quick break?" Ammen asked.

"I'm ready, Tip, let's go hear what they have to say."

The master chief ushered me into the conference room and I sat at the head of a long felt-covered table. On the wall were pictures of Coast Guard cutters, rescue helicopters, and citations for Coast Guard heroism on the Pacific coast. The Coast Guard certainly earned their pay on this dangerous stretch of shoreline.

The entire platoon was in attendance. The platoon commander, a Naval Academy graduate, was heading his second SEAL platoon, and having watched them for the past six months, the experienced leadership showed in the discipline of the men and the professionalism of their planning.

Seated along the walls around the room, the members of the platoon were dressed in a mixture of sweats and camouflage utilities. They had been in the bay most of the day, and with the water temperature in the low fifties, many of the men were still red-eyed and shivering from the cold.

The platoon commander did a quick recap of the brief for the following day's events. "Sir, we will be conducting our final daylight rehearsals." He pointed to the nautical chart tacked to the wall. "There is a small island inside the protected jetty of the harbor. While there is no surf to contend with, I think it's a good place for us to do our contact drills."

I looked at the chart, and the patch of sand that passed for an island was in sight of the entrance, but well beyond the booming breakers.

"As you know, sir, the waves at the entrance of the harbor are too large to get past right now. My guess is we may be delayed a couple of days before the waves settle down enough for the boat guys to get through."

"Have we talked to the boat officer-in-charge?" I asked.

"Yes sir. Lieutenant Jones said he is going to take the RHIBs out into the bay tomorrow to see what it looks like at the edge of the surf zone."

The chief petty officer of the platoon piped up. "The Coasties warned the boat guys not to get too close to the surf. They showed Lieutenant Jones an old picture of a fifty-foot wave crushing some large pleasure boat." The chief smiled. "That seemed to get Lieutenant Jones's attention."

The platoon commander continued. "I'm going to let the guys get a good night's sleep tonight, so we won't begin the rehearsals until about 0800. Once we complete the daylight drills we will break for lunch, prep our gear, and then start our evening rehearsals as soon as the sun goes down."

The platoon commander finished summarizing the brief and we broke for chow. In the mess hall I spent time chatting with the young SEALs. It was the best part of the job. Being a commanding officer was like being the coach of a football team. You knew all the players, their strengths and their weaknesses. Some were quarterbacks, some linemen, and some safeties. Some loved the two-minute drill, the pressure to make a tough decision when the game was on the line. Some were grinders: No matter what you threw at them, they just kept coming at you. Some were risk takers, always trying to jump the route. But all of them loved to play the game, to be where the action was. But beneath the pads, and the helmets, and the bright lights, they were just men, and men made mistakes, they needed guidance. My job was always to find the balance between letting them play hard and keeping them between the lines.

"Rise and shine, boss! It's another day in which to excel."

I rolled over in my sleeping bag, checked my watch, and slowly climbed out of my Army-style cot. It was 0600 and Ammen was already up and brewing coffee. The weather outside was overcast and, looking out the windows of the Coast Guard station, I could see the American flag flapping violently in the wind.

I threw on my camouflage utilities, grabbed breakfast, and by 0700 the master chief and I were motoring out to the island in our Zodiac. The platoon was fully kitted up. The swimmer scouts, the two-man element that surveys the beach before the main force comes ashore, were dressed in wet suits and carrying CAR-15s. The main assault force was dressed in dry suits, each man armed with a CAR-15 and three hundred rounds of ammo.

The platoon went through several contact drills, exercising their fire and maneuver in the event they were engaged by the "enemy" while crossing the beach. The SEALs moved well. The swimmer scouts established flank security. The point man of the main element directed his squad to form a semicircle around the two Zodiacs while the second squad hauled the Zodiacs up past the high-water mark and into the sand dunes. Once the boats were camouflaged, the platoon formed up in a single file and patrolled off the beach. After several renditions of this tactic the platoon commander called for a quick break to review their actions on the beach.

As the short debrief was occurring on the island, I looked out toward Morro Rock and saw the two thirty-three-foot RHIBs loitering just inside the harbor, their bows pointed toward the plunging surf. As each giant wave crested and then crashed, the sound rolled across the harbor like the proverbial thundering herd—then a moment, just a moment, of silence, followed by another deafening crash and then another and another. Mother Nature was not happy.

"Tip, do we have comms with the RHIB OIC?" I asked.

"No sir," the master chief replied.

"Grab one of those Zodiacs. I want to find out what this guy is up to."

The master chief quickly commandeered one of the zodiacs from the SEAL platoon and we headed over to the RHIB to talk with the crew. As we approached the entrance of the harbor I could see the waves much more clearly now. It was worse than I thought. There was a line of three plunging waves. Each would build from outside the entrance, its massive face growing as it gained speed and power. Then, when it hit its peak, the wave crashed violently upon itself, erupting in a volcanic display of white foam and dark blue water. The surge from the first wave was sucked immediately into the oncoming wave behind it, causing each successive wave to grow to new heights until the set of three waves exhausted themselves just long enough for the new set to begin.

The master chief slowed the Zodiac and pulled alongside the RHIB. A crewman reached out his arm. I grabbed it and scrambled over the large rubber gunnels that encircled the inflatable boat. After dropping me off, the master chief pulled away from the RHIB and motored back to the island.

The RHIB was a relatively new boat in the Naval Special Warfare inventory. It was built specifically to carry a SEAL squad of seven men and was crewed by sailors from the Special Boat Squadron. These sailors were all trained as Special Warfare Combatant-Craft Crewmen (SWCCs), and the officer-in-charge was a Navy Surface Warfare Officer, schooled and qualified to pilot a Navy ship.

The RHIB had a crew of four: a coxswain, who was the most experienced member of the crew and was in charge of driving the boat; an engineer, who ensured that the inboard motors were well maintained; a boatswain mate, who manned the .50-caliber machine gun; and an officer-in-charge. The RHIB had all the latest technology: high-end Furuno surface search radar; GPS; a full instrument panel for long-range night navigation. At half a million dollars, it was the most combat-capable inflatable on the market.

The swells from the surf zone were causing the RHIB to roll slowly to port and starboard. Grabbing the instrument console, I steadied myself and looked around the boat.

"Hey, skipper," came a familiar voice. I turned to the aft part of the RHIB and there, strapped into an upright bolster seat, was SEAL lieutenant Geno Paluso. Paluso was the Special Boat Squadron operations officer and a damn good SEAL. Unbeknownst to me, he had also come along to observe the training. Alongside Paluso was Lieutenant Tom Rainville, another SEAL platoon commander, who was watching the exercise as well.

"Sir, is something wrong?" the RHIB officer-in-charge asked.

"No, Mr. Jones. Nothing's wrong. I just wanted to find out what you were planning," I said with a clear tone of concern in my voice.

"Sir, my senior chief is positioned on the jetty at the entrance to Morro Bay. He's timing the waves and radioing the results to me. I think we can get out between the sets."

The RHIB OIC pointed out that once the third wave passed he had two minutes to scurry around the jetty and out into open water before the next set of waves came crashing in.

"Sir, my boat crew has been training in Kodiak, Alaska, for the past three months," Jones said. "Petty Officer Smith is the best coxswain in Special Boat Unit 20 and I have no doubt we can make it through the surf if we just time it right."

I looked at the booming surf again and then into the eyes of the boat crew. I wasn't so sure they shared their lieutenant's enthusiasm.

The hardest part of commanding SEALs and special operations forces is finding that right balance between building confidence in their capability, so that during wartime they will be ready for the most difficult situations—and risking their lives doing so.

I went to each sailor in the crew and asked, "Is this within the capability of your craft and your crew?"

"Yes sir," came the response from each man.

"Lieutenant?"

"Yes sir. We can do this."

"Okay, then get me a life jacket. I'm going with you."

"What?"

"I said, get me a life jacket."

The lieutenant continued to object. "Sir, it's not just the life jacket. You need a dry suit. The water is fifty degrees and if we capsize you'll freeze your ass off."

"Then don't capsize."

In the back of the boat Paluso and Rainville were laughing. "Good advice," Rainville offered sarcastically.

Paluso patted the empty bolster seat next to him. "Strap in, boss, this is going to be a fun ride."

The bolster seat had a three-point harness and was intended to keep the passengers firmly attached to the RHIB in heavy seas. As I began to strap in I realized I had two Cuban cigars in my pocket. I knew that later that night we would be sitting around the fire, and it never hurt to have a good cigar handy.

I pulled out the cigars and waved them at Paluso. "If you guys get me wet, you'll have to buy me new cigars."

Paluso laughed. "Don't worry, sir. These guys are really good. We'll be toasty warm throughout the ride."

I looked out toward the Coast Guard station and saw that Master Chief Ammen had gotten word about my intent to ride along and subsequently headed back to the base camp.

The waves continued to build and plunge, build and plunge. With a plunging wave you have no ability to ride over it. As quickly as it builds, it crashes. There is no subtle rising, peaking, and then curling—just a large wall of water that falls on top of itself in a deadly whirlpool that sucks you under and spits you out, only to have the next wave do the same.

The lieutenant gave the order and the coxswain inched closer to the first wave, waiting for the three-wave set to complete, with the intent to make a mad dash to the edge of the wave and out into open water.

Paluso, Rainville, and I were all experienced SEALs who understood the nature of waves and the need for good timing. Together we watched as the first set seemed to peter out, waiting for the next set to build.

Now was the time! We needed to go now! There was an opening to the side. *Gun it! Go now!* The three of us were all thinking the same thing: *Go! Go! Go!*

But we waited.

Okay, he was just checking the timing. We'd wait until the next set was over.

Suddenly, the coxswain gunned the engines to full throttle.

No! No! This was the worst possible time! The first wave of the set was peaking. Paluso looked at me with wide eyes and murmured, "Oh shit!"

We were making thirty knots when the RHIB reached the base of the first wave. The bow knifed through the water and the engines propelled us straight up the face, shooting us over the top and into the air.

I clenched my teeth and began to count. It was a natural instinct from jumping out of planes. We were airborne and falling fast. "One thousand, two thousand, three thousand, four thousand!"

We slammed into the trough, the impact tossing the sailor on the bow out of the boat and jamming bodies into the hard aluminum floorboard.

"Man overboard! Man overboard!"

Before anyone could react, another thirty-foot wall of water was upon us.

The coxswain looked up and gunned the engines, trying to get his bow around into the fast-moving wave.

I looked over and Paluso and Rainville were wincing in pain, holding their ribs, which had been driven into the side of the bolster seat.

We hit the next wave much like the first, driving up the face and over the edge. "One thousand, two thousand, three thousand, four thousand, holy shit ... five thousand!"

The impact left me breathless as we hit with such force that the bow cracked, the engines stalled, and the RHIB was now dead in the water. Looking up, all we could see was the next wave. The wave of the day: a forty-foot monster that was about to eat our lunch.

"Hold on!" I yelled.

The wave picked the boat up, stood it on end, and then with an angry roar crushed us beneath the foam.

As the RHIB tumbled underwater I was trapped in the bolster seat, rolling over and over again as the force of the wave pushed me along the bottom. Shotline, that thin nylon cord that SEALs use to tie down loose gear, had somehow gotten wrapped around my neck and my arms. It was like a wire garrote, strangling me as I cartwheeled over and over. Grabbing the line, I tried to pull it away from my neck, but the tension was too tight and the more I pulled the tighter it got.

There had been several times in my SEAL career when I faced the possibility of dying, but the events happened so quickly that I only had time to react. It was over before I could think about it. Now, trapped under the RHIB, a noose around my neck and no air to breathe, I thought this was finally it.

A quietness came over me. Shades of dark and light seemed to flash before my eyes as the surging water changed color. This was how I would die. My thoughts were slow and methodical. Tugging hopelessly against the shotline, I said to myself, *I will never see Georgeann, Bill, John, or Kelly again. Dear God, take care of them.*

As I struggled for air, my lungs began to convulse. Deep throaty sounds echoed in my ears and everything began to fade to black. One final tug at the shotline. One final grasp for survival. *Please let me live.*

In my life in the Teams, there have been several times when the inexplicable happens. When all that was set against you suddenly resolves itself and you come out from the darkness into the light. And when, in the quieter moments that follow, you reflect on the event with no logical conclusion other than that the hand of God played a role in keeping you alive. This was one of those moments. Suddenly, inexplicably, I was free! Free from the bolster seat, free from the shotline, free from the tumbling boat.

Shooting upward toward the sunlight, I broke the surface with a gasp. Looking up, I realized that I was still in the surf zone, and as I turned around the next big wave was almost on me. The old life jacket I wore had lost its buoyancy and my utilities were heavy with water. I couldn't survive another hit.

In the roar of the surf I could hear a faint yell. "Skipper! Skipper!"

Turning toward the shore, I saw a Zodiac screaming in my direction. On board were two SEALs dressed in only their swim trunks, one steering the outboard motor, the other positioned to snatch me from the water. The SEAL on the bow was pointing. Pointing at the next wave. They weren't going to make it, and I knew that if they capsized in this surf, with this water temperature, it would likely mean their lives. Still, they kept coming.

The first wave was building to a crescendo as the SEALs rushed to grab me. Right at the base of the wave, the SEAL coxswain cranked the prop over hard, did a U-turn, and drove right for my bobbing head. With no time to pull me in, the SEAL on the bow held me tight against the rubber sponson, the blades of the outboard motor nipping at the soles of my jungle boots.

"Hang on, skipper!" he yelled.

Face up and dangling from the side of the Zodiac, all I could see was a wall of blue-green ocean about to crush the tiny boat. The outboard motor whined as the coxswain cranked the throttle to full just as the torrent of water broke from the top of the wave, impacting inches from the fleeing Zodiac. The cauldron of churning foam pushed us forward at twice the normal speed, propelling the small boat into calmer waters.

Looking back, I could now see that we were out of the surf zone and into the safety of the harbor. Slowing the Zodiac, the SEAL on the bow pulled me into the boat.

"Are you all right, skipper?" he asked as I rolled onto the floorboard.

Shaking from the cold, it took me a second or two to answer. "I'm fine. What about the rest of the crew?"

"They were thrown free of the boat when the RHIB capsized. The surge pushed them into the harbor. I think the other RHIB picked them up."

"Get me over to the other RHIB. I need to make sure we have a full head count."

Moments later I arrived at the second RHIB and on board was Lieutenant Jones trying to ensure he had all his men accounted for. For a man who had just lost his boat and was clearly injured from the impact of the wave, he was doing exactly what I would have expected—he was taking command of the accident scene and trying his very best to salvage a bad situation. With my rescue, he now had all men accounted for.

There was a look on his face that I knew well. Fear. Fear that he had failed in his duties. Fear that his future as a naval officer was over. Fear that his fellow sailors would lose respect for him.

Worst of all, fear that he had almost cost men their lives. Deep fear.

"You okay?" I asked.

"Yes sir," came the stoic reply.

I put my arm around him and pulled him close. "Listen to me," I said gently. "No matter what happens from here, everyone is alive. It will be okay."

He nodded, but that didn't seem to console him. Losing a boat in the Navy, even a small boat, is never a good thing.

But near death has a way of putting things in perspective. There would be no funerals—his, mine, or our fellow SEALs and boat guys. There would be no mourning wives and orphaned kids. There would be no memorial dedicated to the lost lives of valiant sailors. There would only be happiness that everyone had returned alive.

Slapping Jones on the back, I said laughing, "Well, you boat guys sure know how to have a good time."

"Sir?" came the startled response.

"Do what you can to raise the boat and get things back in order and I will go make the reports to our seniors."

Jones smiled, still trembling from the cold. "Thanks, sir." He paused, looked out at the waves still pounding and threatening the narrow channel. "I thought I was going to die."

I laughed. "Yeah. Me too," I admitted. "But we didn't. So let's make the best of it."

Hopping back in the small Zodiac, I headed to the pier.

Back on the shore, the five injured men were laid out on the floor of the Coast Guard station awaiting an ambulance. The corpsmen were attending to their injuries as best they could.

Paluso, who suffered a broken left foot and cracked ribs, was clutching his side, trying to find a comfortable position, his face contorted in pain, his breathing quick and labored.

Walking up to him, I bent down and pulled out the two cigars, now mangled and soaked with saltwater. "Geno, you got my cigars wet."

Paluso cracked a smile and rubbed his head with the universal sign of the solitary finger. "I guess I owe you."

"We'll take it off the price of the RHIB," I replied. "That should get us under a half a million."

Paluso moaned, either from the pain or the sudden recognition that we had indeed lost a five-hundred-thousand-dollar boat.

The ambulances arrived and I began notifying my bosses of the accident. With each phone call I was reminded of why I chose the military as a way of life. Every senior officer, upon hearing about the loss of the pricey boat, had only one question: "Are you and the men okay?"

Of the seven men aboard the RHIB, five ended up in the hospital with broken ribs, fractured legs, contusions, and mild hypothermia. Also that day, another Zodiac crew had charged into the surf to rescue Lieutenant Tom Rainville, whose dry suit filled with water, almost drowning him. The RHIB was eventually raised from the bottom, but it was a total loss. An investigation ensued, and over the next ninety days depositions were taken, interviews were recorded, reports were made. The final report concluded that in spite of the loss of a high-value craft, there was a critical need for such challenging training. And while the decision to attempt the surf passage was unwise, the review board recognized that taking risks is part of what makes us a special operations force. We would all be given a second chance.

For their actions that day in saving my life and that of Tom Rainville, Petty Officers Dan Mero, Nate Johnson, Scotty Stearns, and Chief Brad Lucas received the Navy and Marine Corps Medal—the highest award for heroism during time of peace. In November 1995, with my wife, Georgeann, standing beside me, we were honored to pin the award on each man's chest.

A few years later, I served on the promotion board for Lieutenant Jeremy Carter, the officer I had found guilty of a DUI. *A good man who had made a mistake.* Carter was promoted to lieutenant commander and would eventually go on to serve in Iraq and Afghanistan, earning the Bronze Star for valor and saving the lives of several of his fellow SEALs. SEALs who also got a second chance.

CHAPTER TEN

AIRBORNE FROGGY

SAN DIEGO, CALIFORNIA
2001

S ix minutes! Six minutes!"
     The SEAL jumpmaster motioned to the aircrewman and the ramp of the C-130 slowly lowered, roaring like some giant mechanical beast.

It was mid-July in San Diego, and the sky outside the plane was a cloudless blue, just a few shades lighter than the Pacific Ocean, which stretched from the ramp of the aircraft to the horizon.

I was a Navy captain, the commodore of Naval Special Warfare Group One and in charge of all the SEALs on the West Coast. We were based out of the Naval Amphibious Base (NAB) Coronado, in California. NAB was a small man-made peninsula that jutted out into San Diego Bay and was by far the best place in the Navy to be stationed. Thirty minutes earlier, fifteen other SEALs and I had boarded the C-130 aircraft out of North Island Naval Air Station and were preparing for a freefall training jump over Brown Field, located just south of San Diego, on the Mexican border.

"Stand up!" came the next command.

The jumpers unhooked their seat belts, rose from the nylon benches, and turned and faced the ramp. The roar of the four Allison turboprops was deafening.

"Check equipment!" the jumpmaster yelled.

"Check equipment!" came the response from every jumper.

There was no one in front of me as I faced the rear of the aircraft, but the man behind me began to check my MT-1X freefall parachute to ensure the ripcord pin was properly in place and the automatic opening device was set to the right altitude.

Once the rigs were checked, starting at the end of the line, each man patted the jumper in front of him on the rear, indicating the rig was good to jump. As the last man in the line, I received a strong pat on the butt and announced to the jumpmaster that we were all good to go.

Returning to the ramp, the jumpmaster got to his knees and took one final look out the side of the aircraft. Communicating with the pilot, he aligned the C-130 along the right course to ensure that when the SEALs exited the aircraft at 12,999 feet we would be in the right position to reach the drop zone.

"One minute!"

"One minute!"

The jumpmaster motioned for me to move to the edge of the ramp. In a straight line behind me, the other jumpers fell into place. Approaching the ramp, I looked out over the terrain below me. From almost thirteen thousand feet I could see the sprawling city of Tijuana, Mexico, the border crossing leading to South San Diego, and the tall untended fields of grass. We were on a northbound heading and everything to the south came into view.

Under my breath, I began to sing, "*Happy Anniversary, baby, got you on my miiiind,*" over and over. It was one of those silly superstitions that started in Army jump school more than twenty-five years earlier. Before every jump, I sang the words, certain that they would keep me from harm. It had worked up until now. There must be some magic in those words.

The jumpmaster grabbed me by the front of my rig and pulled me to the very edge of the ramp. He looked me in the eye, smiled, and yelled, "Go, go, go!"

Thrusting my arms forward and tucking my legs beneath me, I dove off the back of the ramp, tipping over slightly before the prop blast and the speed of my descent began to level me out. The wind rushed by me, a loud whistling noise in my ear. My heart pounded and my breathing matched the beats in my chest. As I gained speed I pulled my arms parallel to my ears and allowed my legs to jut out a bit farther. My breathing began to slow. My pulse settled down.

At 12,500 feet, I was stable now. No drifting or spinning or tumbling. While many of the guys in the Teams were exceptional jumpers who could maneuver easily around the sky, I was not one of them. But I still loved jumping. There was something special about being untethered and falling through the air at 120 miles an hour while the earth below rushed up to meet you. It was both exhilarating and terrifying at the same time. Skydiving was one of the great thrills of being a SEAL, and each time out of the aircraft was memorable.

As I looked out across the Pacific Ocean and the beautiful hills that surrounded South San Diego, I could tell today was another jump I would never forget.

Ten thousand feet.

The other freefallers began to come into view. We were all wearing standard green Navy flight suits, black Pro-Tec helmets, goggles, and on our back a 270-square-foot parachute with a smaller reserve chute capable of being deployed if the main chute failed.

Off to my right, I saw a few of the better jumpers forming a four-way—four jumpers with arms linked, dropping together until the time to pull their ripcords. I envied them. Relative work, the ability to maneuver smoothly in the air, was something I had never mastered. Oh, I could link up with one or two others if they were in close proximity, but sailing across the sky to a specific point and stopping your relative motion on a dime—that was skydiving.

Six thousand feet.

Off to my right I could see one jumper below me. About two hundred feet away and five hundred feet down, he was spinning slightly counterclockwise, because his arms were not symmetrical and the force of the air was pushing him to the left.

To my other side were two jumpers. One was well off to my left, but the second SEAL was about a hundred feet away and two hundred feet down. Shifting my hands slightly, I maneuvered farther to the right to ensure I was out of his way. The spinning SEAL on my right had corrected his body position and was tracking away from me, preparing to open his chute.

Below me, the ocean seemed flat and tranquil. The air was clean and a little cool for a July day. The sun was bright but not blinding. It was just perfect.

Fifty-five hundred feet.

"Holy shit!"

Below me, the close-in SEAL was waving his arms, a signal that he was about to pull his ripcord. Our paths had converged in the sky and he was directly beneath me. Instantly, the pilot chute came off his back, jerking him upright as the main chute began to deploy. Throwing my arms to my side, I tried to track away from the man and his chute as we rocketed toward each other, his descent slowing while I still fell at 120 mph.

Suddenly I was enveloped by the light blue main canopy of the man below me. As his nylon parachute opened, it hit me with the force of a heavyweight boxer, sending me tumbling through the sky. Stunned by the initial impact of the deploying canopy, I struggled to understand what was happening. Although I had slid through the jumper's opening parachute, I was now falling out of control, unaware of my altitude or whether I had been momentarily knocked unconscious.

Spinning head over heels, all I could see was ground, sky, ground, sky, ground, sky. Where was my altimeter? How much time before impact? Time to get stable? Screw it. *Pull the ripcord. Pull the ripcord!*

Grabbing the aluminum handle, I pulled hard and felt the pilot chute begin to deploy. *Ground, sky, ground, sky, ground, sky.* Springing off my back, the small chute wrapped around my legs, flapping against my ankle as I tried to shake it loose.

Ground, ground, ground. All I could see now was the ground, and it was rushing toward me. I was in a completely head-down angle, tangled in a mess of pilot chute, half-deployed main parachute, and risers. With each hundred feet I fell, I could feel the main chute slowly inching its way out of the pack, further encircling me with more nylon.

Craning my neck toward the sky, I could see that my legs were bound by two sets of risers, the long nylon straps that connected the main parachute to the harness on my back. One riser had wrapped around one leg, the other riser around the other leg. The main parachute was fully out of the backpack but hung up somewhere on my body.

As I struggled to break free of the entanglement, suddenly I felt the canopy lift off my body and begin to open. Looking toward my legs, I knew what was coming next.

"Mother..."

Within seconds, the canopy caught air. The two risers, one wrapped around each leg, suddenly and violently pulled apart, taking my legs with them. My pelvis separated instantly as the force of the opening ripped my lower torso. The thousand small muscles that connect the pelvis to the body were torn from their hinges.

My mouth dropped open and I let out a scream that could be heard in Mexico. Searing pain arched through my body, sending waves pulsating downward to my pelvis and upward to my head. Violent muscular convulsions racked my upper torso, shooting more pain through my arms and legs. Now, like an out-of-body experience, I became aware of my screaming and tried to control it, but the pain was too intense.

Still head down and falling too fast, I turned myself upright in the harness, relieving some of the pressure on my pelvis and back.

Fifteen hundred feet.

I had fallen more than four thousand feet before the parachute deployed. The good news: I had a full canopy over my head. The bad news: I was two miles from the drop zone, broken apart by the impact of the opening and heading into a field of eight-foot-high tomato stakes.

Shock was setting in. My breathing was erratic. My body was numb, but my mind was still clear. Looking over the tomato field, I found an area of tall grass that looked unencumbered by pointy sticks.

The chute was inverted and the toggles that controlled the direction of flight were backward. Pulling hard on the left toggle, I maneuvered the square parachute toward the right, trying to set up for a landing. A small patch of tall grass looked inviting, but there was no way to know what was hidden beneath it. Too late. I was committed now.

Leveling the parachute for a short approach, I waited until I was just about ten feet off the ground and jerked downward on the two toggles simultaneously. The parachute flared upward, easing me onto my backside and sliding me gently into the soft field.

Well, I thought, laughing, *I may be shitty in the air, but I do know how to land a parachute.*

The pain was gone. Shock had set in. I was on my back with the parachute strung out behind me draped over the top of the tall grass.

"Oh, that's not good," I said, looking down at my pelvis. The bones were protruding off to one side, causing my jumpsuit to bulge awkwardly to the right. I couldn't sit up. The muscles in my abdomen were no longer connected. I was unable to move in any direction.

"Shit."

Looking around, I thought that no one knew where I was. The tall grass hid my location, and unless someone on the drop zone had noticed my descent, it could be an hour before they found me.

Strapped to my side was a Mark 13 flare, a signaling device that puts out a high-intensity flame that can be seen for miles. Great idea, except for one minor problem—I was in a field of tall dry grass. Oh, they would find me all right, but only after the fire department scraped my charred body from the tomatoes.

Minutes went by as I tried to think through my options.

"Billy! Billy Mac!"

I heard a voice in the distance.

"Over here! Over here!" I yelled.

Men were making their way through the tall grass.

"Billy!"

I knew the voice. It was Bill Reed—a hard-as-nails Vietnam vet who had been on the jump.

"Here!" My voice was fading.

They were circling my position.

"Billy!"

"Here..."

Through my fogged-up goggles, I could see the blond hair and stern face of Bill Reed.

"Billy. Are you all right?"

I didn't let many men call me Billy, but I had great respect for Bill Reed and we had known each other for over twenty years.

"I think I'm broken up pretty bad, Bill."

"We have an ambulance on the way," Reed answered.

I nodded.

"Man, that must have been one hell of a landing."

"It didn't happen on the landing. It happened in the air."

More men began to come into my view. Leaning over me was the drop zone corpsman.

"Sir, I'm Doc Smith. We have EMTs on the way. Can you tell me where you're injured?"

Smith was a Navy SEAL corpsman. While not qualified MDs, the corpsmen in the Teams were great at trauma care.

"Pelvis, back, legs."

Reaching into his kit bag, he pulled out a pair of large surgical scissors and began to cut my jumpsuit away from my body. Two other SEALs helped as Smith began to survey the extent of my injuries. At my feet, someone else was removing my boots.

In the distance I could hear the sound of the ambulance. Around me now there was a lot of activity, with Smith and Reed directing the action.

"Are you in pain?" Smith asked.

"No, Doc. I'm feeling okay."

We both knew that was not a good sign.

"I can wiggle my toes," I said with great joy. I knew that if my spine had been severed, I wouldn't be able to feel my toes.

Doc didn't smile.

"Holy shit," came a muffled voice in the back.

My jumpsuit was off and the extent of my injury was now apparent to those around me.

"Commodore, we're going to take your helmet and goggles off. Let me know if you're in any pain," Smith said.

"I got it, Doc," came the voice of Steve Chamberlain, my command master chief. Chambo was my senior enlisted at Naval Special Warfare Group One and the finest enlisted man I had ever worked with. Personally tough, professionally demanding, and loyal beyond words, Chambo was always there for me.

Lifting my head, Chamberlain gently removed my helmet and goggles.

"Chambo."

"Yes sir. I'm here."

"Chambo. Call Georgeann and let her know I'm all right."

"Yes sir. Will do."

But I knew it was a request he couldn't honor. There were procedures. Someone would contact Georgeann and let her know there had been an accident. But no one would give her my status until the real doctors had done their assessment.

The whine of the siren got closer and closer. I could hear the guys directing the ambulance through the tomato fields and to my location.

Soon I was strapped to a backboard and hoisted into the ambulance. Doc Smith jumped in beside me and we drove off bumping across the field until we hit a dirt road. Within a few minutes we were on the highway heading to Sharp Memorial Hospital in downtown San Diego.

The EMT wired me up to several machines and reached into his bag, drawing out a syringe.

"Sir, I'm going to give you some morphine for the pain."

"No. No morphine," I said.

"Sir, you don't have to be tough. The pain must be excruciating. Let me give you a shot of morphine."

"No. No morphine!"

Admittedly, I wasn't in my right mind, but many years ago I read a spy novel in which the main character refuses morphine so he can feel the pain and not mask his injuries. Okay, I know it sounds stupid, but...

"Sir, I'm required to give you morphine unless you specifically tell me no. And you must tell me three times."

"Okay."

"Sir, do you understand?"

"Yes."

"Do you want morphine?"

"No."

"Do you want morphine?"

"No."

"Do you want morphine?"

"No."

The EMT just shook his head.

Doc Smith leaned over. "Sir, are you sure?" He smiled.

"Yeah, Doc, I'm sure."

Within twenty minutes we were pulling into the emergency

entrance at Sharp Memorial. A flurry of activity ensued as doctors, nurses, and medics all surrounded me and began to move me into the ER. Secured onto the gurney and rolling through the halls of the hospital, all I could see was the acoustic tile of the ceilings and the occasional nurse who leaned over to ask me how I was.

Then a booming voice penetrated the sounds of the orchestrated chaos.

"Man, you look fucked up, Commodore!"

"Well, I have had better days," I offered.

Lieutenant Mark Gould was a Navy surgeon who was assigned to Sharp to undergo additional training. A former Army Special Forces medic, Gould finished his Army enlistment, got his degree, joined the Navy, and received his medical degree from the military medical school in Maryland. Grabbing the clipboard at the bottom of the gurney, he walked briskly along with the crew that was wheeling me into the ER.

"What's my status, Doc?"

"Well, it looks like you have a separated pelvis, back and legs are screwed up. The real concern is whether you have any internal injuries."

I nodded.

"They're going to roll you into the ER. Take some pictures and we'll have a better idea of what to do after that."

Inside the ER, the doctors began to administer a radioactive dye designed to identify internal damage. Suddenly, I began to lose consciousness. I could see the concern on Doc Gould's face.

"You okay, sir?"

My breathing was erratic and I tried to settle it down. "I'm fading, Doc."

A nurse unceremoniously pushed Gould out of the way and began to call my readings. "Blood pressure is dropping," she announced loudly. "Pulse is dropping!"

I was having a bad reaction to the dye.

Grabbing my hand, she gently squeezed it and said, "Stay with me." Above her surgical mask all I could see were her eyes. But they were good eyes: blue, middle-aged, mature, caring, professional. There was a certain confidence about her eyes that gave me comfort.

Gasping for breath, I tried to calm myself, but I could feel my mind slipping away.

"We're losing him!" the blue-eyed nurse shouted.

"I need epinephrine now!"

Stay awake. Stay awake. Got to stay awake.

Masked faces came in and out of view.

"Stay with me, honey," blue-eyes exhorted.

In my mind I nodded.

She patted me gently on the arm. "That's right. Just stay with me."

I'm not going anywhere, I thought. But maybe I was wrong.

"Come on!" she yelled. "He's still dropping!"

She squeezed my hand tightly and I could see her eyes watching the monitor. "Come on. Come on," she whispered to herself.

"Pressure's coming back up," someone yelled.

Her eyes never moved from the monitor, but she patted my hand gently as if trying to coax my blood pressure back to normal.

After a few minutes she leaned over and gave my hand a good squeeze. "Okay, honey, you're going to be fine," she said. "You did good." She smiled, the surgical mask lifting high on her cheekbones.

My breathing was slowly returning to normal. It seemed like several minutes passed before blue-eyes came back into view.

"Okay, dear. We're going to give you something to help you sleep."

"No!" I protested. "I don't want to sleep!"

The mind does funny things when your body is torn apart. Sleep meant death. I was certain of it. No morphine. No sleep. I needed to be awake. Feel the pain. Stay conscious.

"It's okay. We're not going to operate on you right now. But we need to do some scans and make sure you're not bleeding inside. It will be easier if you're asleep."

"No," I repeated. "I'm okay."

Blue-eyes shook her head and left my view. I could hear her talking with Gould. Moments later she returned.

"Okay, sir. We're going to keep you conscious, but if you get too irritated or can't deal with the pain we're going to have to put you under."

"I understand."

The imposing face of Doc Gould popped back into view. "You're going to make them think all SEALs are fucking superhuman."

"No, just afraid of losing control, Doc."

"All right, Commodore. We're going for a ride."

Over the course of the next hour I was X-rayed, scanned, probed, and then wheeled back into the ICU. Blue-eyes had removed my neck brace and I could see more of what was around me now.

Through the glass window, Georgeann, my son John, a college freshman now, and my good friend and fellow SEAL Joe Maguire huddled outside waiting to hear from the attending physician. A few minutes later Joe entered the room.

Joe and I had known each other for twenty years, since our early days in the Philippines. He, his wife, Kathy, and their two children, Daniel and Catherine, were our closest friends. Joe had broken his back during a fast-rope accident many years earlier. Georgeann and I had been the first to the hospital then. This is what good friends do.

Joe was always upbeat, never lacking a joke or a good story to make one feel better. "Man, what some guys will do to get out of work!"

"Yeah, I was getting a little tired of the daily staff meetings."

"You doing okay?"

"I don't know. What did the doc tell you?"

"Not sure I'm supposed to tell you just yet."

Joe looked around the room and then whispered, "You're pretty screwed up, but the good news is there is no internal damage and your spine is okay."

"What's the bad news?"

"Your pelvis is separated by about five inches. All of the muscles in your abdomen and legs have been separated from the bone and your back is slightly fractured."

"No big deal, then." I laughed.

"Naw, you'll be fine," Joe said without conviction.

Outside I could see the doctors conferring with Georgeann. She nodded stoically as they gave her the news. "Of course," the doctor mouthed as Georgeann asked if she could see me.

Georgeann and John entered the room and came to the gurney. John, a tall, broad-shouldered young man, who would later go on to get his PhD in theoretical physics, was our brilliant child. But he also had a very sensitive side and I could see that as much as he wanted to approach my accident as something to study—logically, scientifically—it was hard when it was his dad lying in the ER.

"Hey, Dad. How you feeling?"

"I'm fine." I smiled. "Really, no big deal. Look, I can wiggle my toes."

John cocked his head and furrowed his brow as he thought about my statement. He seemed to immediately understand the connection between my toes and my well-being. He forced a smile and touched me on the shoulder.

Georgeann moved beside me and held my hand. Her fingers fit perfectly between mine. To me there was nothing in the world more comforting than holding her hand. She kissed me on the forehead.

"Are you in much pain?" she asked.

"No, no. I feel fine," I lied.

"Well, the doctor says they may try to operate tomorrow."

"Sure, sure. They'll patch me up and I'll be out of here in no time."

She nodded, trying to maintain her composure.

Being the wife of a Team guy was never easy. It took a certain kind of woman to say, "I do." SEALs were overseas constantly, gone for months at a time. Every day was filled with anxious moments—wondering if and when we would return home. Every man who was married for long knew who was the toughest member of the family—and it wasn't us.

Joe stood by quietly as John, Georgeann, and I made small talk to convince us that everything was in fact going to be all right. Later that night, my two other children, Bill, the oldest, and Kelly, who was ten at the time, showed up at my bedside. Bill, always the caring older brother, made sure Kelly was not too upset and good-naturedly ribbed me about the accident's effect on my basketball game. Kelly, with tears rolling down her cheeks, didn't want to leave my bedside as they rolled me off to another room.

Hours later Doc Gould showed up to discuss my options.

"Sir, I have a friend in L.A. who is the best back guy in the nation. He thinks that we will need to plate you in the front and run a long screw across your backside to stabilize the pelvis."

"Okay," I said. It sounded good, but what the hell did I know?

"Now . . ." Doc paused. "There is some risk here."

Doc thought for a second, as if to decide whether to outline the full extent of the procedure.

"That screw will be placed very near your spine. Obviously, if the doctor makes a mistake inserting the screw, it could have serious implications."

I took a deep breath.

"But," Doc continued, "this guy is the best, and if we can get that screw in place the chances that you will have a full recovery are much better."

A full recovery? I hadn't thought about it until that moment.

What if I couldn't be a SEAL anymore? What if the damage was so bad that I couldn't run or jump out of airplanes or scuba dive? What if my career was over and I was the only one who didn't realize it?

No, that was not going to happen! As long as I could wiggle my toes (again that fixation), I was going to stay a SEAL.

"Let's do it, Doc."

"You're sure?"

"I'm sure."

That evening, the doctor arrived from L.A. My confidence waned momentarily when he appeared to be no more than twenty-five years old. As it turned out, he was a bit of a surgeon savant, and the next morning he managed to pin me and plate me back together with great success.

After recovery, the first visitor I had was Moki Martin. Moki, a Vietnam-era SEAL and one of my SEAL instructors, had been in a bicycle accident years earlier. The head-on collision with another cyclist left him paralyzed from the waist down, with limited use of his arms. In a wheelchair now, Moki was one of the most inspirational men I knew.

He rolled up beside my bed, reached out, and grabbed my hand. "Well, clearly I need to give you some parachute lessons."

"Clearly," I replied, laughing.

"I talked with Gould. He said you're going to be okay, but it could be a long recovery."

"No sweat. I didn't have anything on my calendar for the next year."

He moved his wheelchair closer so we could be eye to eye. "Bill, never forget that you're a SEAL. You got to this point in your life because you're tough. I watched you go through training. You were tough then. You're tough now. You'll get through this just fine. But no matter what happens." He paused. "Don't ring the bell."

Don't ring the bell. Don't ring the bell. It was the call to continue no matter what obstacles lay ahead. No man wearing a SEAL Trident ever rang the bell. Ringing the bell was for those who couldn't make it. Ringing the bell was for those who weren't up to the challenge of SEAL training. Ringing the bell was an admittance of defeat. Moki Martin never rang the bell. I wouldn't either.

For a week after the operation I struggled with "Sundowners Syndrome"—hallucinating wildly, screaming at night, fighting the nurses, and unable to maintain any sense of sanity. Finally I told my military doctors that I had to escape the hospital. I truly feared for my long-term sanity.

After a contentious discussion with the hospital staff, they reluctantly agreed to let me go as long as the military doctors promised to check up on me throughout the day. That night the ambulance took me back to my house at the Naval Amphibious Base. My command surgeon had equipped the living room with a hospital bed.

For the first week, my military doctors were checking on me every several hours. As my sanity returned and my health got better, Georgeann took on the nursing duties. Every day she gave me a series of shots to keep my blood from clotting. She changed my bedpan, cleaned my surgical wounds, checked my vitals, fed me, and, most important, told me everything was going to be okay. I believed her, even if she didn't believe it herself.

As the days went by dozens of well-wishers came from all around to check up on me. Within three weeks, I was able to sit in a wheelchair, and even attended a traditional SEAL gala event, much to the dismay of my doctor—who was not invited on grounds that he would prevent me from drinking.

I remained worried that in spite of my quick recovery, weeks after the accident I was still in and out of a wheelchair. Occasionally I wheeled myself over to the office, which was minutes away from my house. One day, Admiral Eric Olson, the commander of Naval Special Warfare Command and my boss, came by to talk about my future.

Olson was a Naval Academy graduate and one of the toughest

SEALs I had ever known. He received the Silver Star for his actions in Mogadishu during the famed Black Hawk Down incident. He was a serious man, hard to read, but universally respected and admired by all the SEAL community. Olson would go on to be the first three-star and the first four-star SEAL in Navy history, but was now a one-star admiral. My fate rested in his hands.

Navy regulations required that an officer have a full medical examination after a serious accident. Subsequent to the examination, a Navy medical board must meet to determine the officer's fitness to continue to serve. I knew that the board would never find me fit to continue as a Navy SEAL. I was barely fit to get out of bed.

"How are you feeling?" Olson asked.

"Great, sir! Just great!" I lied. *It was getting to be a bad habit.*

"Bill." He hesitated. "You know that I'm required to have your record reviewed by a medical board."

"Yes sir. I'm aware of that."

Olson continued, "I called the Navy staff and they are okay with delaying your arrival at the Pentagon for a few weeks."

Olson had personally arranged for my next assignment to be on the Navy staff. He was positioning me to make admiral, and he knew that a job in the Pentagon would get me some much-needed recognition with the Navy leadership.

"The problem is, if the med board doesn't approve you for continued service, then the Navy is unlikely to accept you for the position in the Pentagon."

"Yes sir. I understand," I said, with a certain sense of resignation. "Sir, Bob Harward and I are scheduled to have our change of command next week. After that, I have a couple of weeks' leave before I have to report to the Pentagon. If I can get out of my wheelchair and make the change of command on my crutches, is there any way we can waive the med board requirements?"

I was putting Olson in a tough position. There were rules to be followed. People to be notified. Forms to be filled out.

Olson nodded. "If you can do your change of command, on crutches, then I will see what I can do."

A week later, dressed in my finest "choker" white uniform, I stepped out of the military sedan, grabbed my crutches, and hobbled my way to the outdoor stage. With a band playing, flags flying, and bells ringing, I passed command of the West Coast SEALs to Captain Bob Harward. As per tradition, we both turned and saluted the senior officer, Admiral Eric Olson. By then I knew that the paperwork had never made it to Washington. Rarely had a salute to a senior officer come with more appreciation.

That evening I returned to my house and collapsed back into my bed. I knew that the road ahead was going to be long and painful. I would need a lot of rest in order to get strong again. Admiral Olson had graciously granted me thirty days' leave to help with my rehab. The extra leave delayed my arrival at the Pentagon by a few weeks, but the Navy staff never complained and never questioned the reason.

Thirty days later, as I lay in my living room, Georgeann and I watched in horror as American Airlines Flight 11 and United Airlines Flight 175 struck the World Trade Center towers. Moments later, pictures of the Pentagon, smoke pouring out of the E-Ring, came across the screen. Georgeann looked at me, but we never said a word—only a silent prayer for the families who had lost loved ones in New York, Pennsylvania, and Washington.

Within a few days, my orders to the Pentagon had been changed. I would now join retired General Wayne A. Downing in the Office of Combatting Terrorism, a newly formed directorate on the National Security Council staff. Our job was coordinating the counterterrorism activities of the nation. The two years that followed gave me time to fully recuperate. By October 2003, I was in combat in Iraq and Afghanistan.

As the casualties mounted and my daily routine involved visits to the combat hospital, I never forgot the kindness of those who helped me through the tough times after my accident. Not a week went by without some wounded soldier pleading with me to keep them in special operations. *They didn't need that second leg. They could see fine out of just one eye. They shot better with a prosthetic hand.*

But as the commander I had a job to do. There were rules to be followed. People to be notified. Forms to be filled out. I had to follow the regulations. But somehow my damn staff kept losing the paperwork.

One of these days, I need to check into that...

CHAPTER ELEVEN

1600 PENNSYLVANIA AVENUE

THE WHITE HOUSE
October 2001

The Pope?"

"Yes. The Pope."

"You want me to draft a letter from the President to the Pope justifying the war in Afghanistan?"

"That's right."

"You do know that scholars, philosophers, and theologians have been trying to justify war for . . . oh . . . like since the beginning of mankind."

"Well, you've got a week."

"Oh, well a week . . . should be plenty of time."

The voice on the other end of the phone didn't seem to appreciate my sarcasm. "Can you get this done or not?"

"Yes sir, of course. I'll have it to you in a week."

He hung up abruptly.

I had arrived at the White House just five days earlier assigned to my new position as the Director of Strategy and Military Affairs in the Office of Combatting Terrorism. My boss, retired four-star General Wayne Downing, had persuaded Admiral Olson that my services would be better utilized in the White House, helping orchestrate the war on terrorism, than on the Navy staff in the Pentagon. Georgeann and I had moved across the country, and along with my ten-year-old daughter, Kelly, we were temporarily living at Fort Belvoir in northern Virginia.

The days had a sense of purpose. The United States had just

suffered the worst attack on its soil since Pearl Harbor. The nation was mobilizing. Flags were everywhere. You could feel the patriotism. You could feel the fear. Young soldiers were preparing for war. The news was a constant drumbeat of urgency. A spirit of revenge filled the American heart, and it felt justified. Nothing seemed ordinary. We were living history.

Downing glared at his phone.

"I'm sorry I won't be here, Congressman, but something's come up. My Director of Military Affairs, Captain Bill McRaven, will be in the office. He's a Navy SEAL. He can help you."

Me! I pointed to myself.

Downing glared again, this time in my direction. "No sir. I don't think I'll be back." Downing looked at me and rolled his eyes. "Yes sir. One o'clock. Bill will be ready."

Downing put down the phone and shook his head. "Rohrabacher is coming by," he said, referring to the California Congressman. "He wants us to help out some warlord named Dostum. I've got to head out. You handle it."

"Where are you going, sir?"

"I've got a meeting with Condi." He grinned, knowing I knew better.

"Rohrabacher is a very influential Congressman," Downing said. "He's got the phone numbers of every mujahedeen leader in Afghanistan and thinks he has the authority to direct the war from Congress. Just hear him out and don't promise anything."

He laughed. "Well, is this what you expected the White House to be like?"

"I don't know what I expected, sir. But if I can't be on the ground in Afghanistan, I guess being at the White House is the next best thing."

Downing rose from his desk, smiled, slapped me on the back, and headed out the door.

I liked Downing a lot. General Wayne A. Downing, referred to as "the WAD" by junior officers, was a legend in special operations.

A 1962 West Point graduate, he had served in the Vietnam War and Desert Storm. A recipient of two Silver Stars for valor and a Purple Heart, he was as tough a soldier as the Army had ever seen. Downing had commanded the famed Ranger Regiment, the Joint Special Operations Command, the U.S. Army's Special Operations Command, and eventually, all U.S. special operations. Now he was the President's point man on the war on terrorism. With dusty blond hair, short in stature, but strong around the edges, he was a physical fitness machine. Even in his sixties, he could outrun and out-PT most younger men. He had a dry sense of humor, and when in the Army he loved to test his junior officers' mettle. Could they keep up with him on the long runs? Did they understand Clausewitz, Sun Tzu, and Liddell Hart? Were they afraid of a thirty-thousand-foot night parachute jump? Did they lead from the front in combat or training? He seemed to see everything and judge every man's fitness to command.

Somewhere along the way, I had measured up.

It was a quarter past one and I was hoping the Congressman wouldn't show. Sitting in Downing's office, I looked out the window onto the South Lawn. Our spaces in the Old Executive Office Building were small, but it's all about location, and we were a two-minute walk into the Oval Office. The third-floor offices had once been home to Marine Lieutenant Colonel Oliver North. North had infamously been involved in the Iran-Contra scandal, using his position at the White House to move arms to the Contras. Although it was fifteen years later, the specter of Ollie North hung over every thing we did. The White House was supposed to do policy, not operations. With New York City, Washington, and a field in Pennsylvania still smoldering, I sensed that was about to change.

There was a pounding on the door. I opened it and in barged Congressman Dana Rohrabacher and his assistant Al Santoli.

"Where's the general?" Rohrabacher demanded, moving quickly from room to room.

"Sir, General Downing's out of the office. I'm Bill McRaven," I said, extending my hand. "He asked me to help, if I could."

"You're the SEAL?"

"Yes sir."

"Damn it! I really need to talk with Downing."

No offense taken, I thought.

I moved into the small office and offered Rohrabacher the one extra chair. Nicely attired in a blue suit and maroon tie, Rohrabacher could have been mistaken for a retired general. He was clean-shaven, his hair was closely cropped, and he had a confidence and a swagger about him that came from years of being in a position of authority.

Santoli leaned against the wall and Rohrabacher began talking fast.

"Look, I got a call from General Dostum. He needs supplies fast—and airstrikes. Lots of airstrikes. His men are under attack, and unless we help them there is no way they are going to survive."

Rohrabacher got up from his chair and started pacing. "You need to call George Tenet right now and get the Agency birds to start providing supplies. Or call the Pentagon. Call somebody and get those Afghans some help!"

A phone suddenly rang. I turned to pick it up and realized it wasn't Downing's phone.

"Sir, it's Dostum," Santoli said, pulling a satellite phone from his attaché.

Rohrabacher grabbed the large black Iridium phone. "Yes! Yes! I know! I know!" he yelled into the receiver. "I'm working it as fast as I can. Can you give me some coordinates for the drop?" He motioned for a piece of paper. "Okay. I've got it. I'll get back to you as soon as I have it confirmed."

Santoli gave me a look that seemed to imply this was routine business for the California Congressman.

"Okay, SEAL. Here's the coordinates for the drop. Call Tenet and let's get this thing moving."

I stared at the eight-digit grid numbers on the paper. Somehow

I thought calling the Director of the CIA and asking him to resupply an Afghan warlord was just a bit above my pay grade.

"Sir, I know this is urgent."

"Damn right it is. Our allies are going to die if they don't get supplies soon."

"Yes sir, but I don't think Director Tenet will take my word for it. As soon as General Downing gets back I'll run this by him and have him give you a call."

"Give me a call! Give me a call! Son, I need this done now. Can you do it or not?"

I looked down at the numbers on the paper again. Was this the way we were going to run the war on terrorism? Congressmen calling directly to the front lines? Was I just too naïve about how things happened in Washington?

"No sir," I said, somewhat reluctantly. "General Downing will have to take care of this."

"I knew it!" he fumed. "This was a wasted trip. You tell Downing to call me the moment he gets back."

Rohrabacher shook his head again for effect and he and Santoli left the office in a hurry.

Downing returned an hour later and I relayed the details of the visit, adding color commentary where I thought appropriate. He muttered under his breath, called Tenet, and a day later supplies were airdropped into the mountains of Afghanistan. Three days after that I finished my letter to the Pope, and in a meeting the following week, President Bush presented the letter to the papal nuncio for delivery to His Holiness.

This job was clearly not going to be what I expected.

The document on my desk was marked SECRET. It read like an action novel.

"Gunfire erupted in the early morning of May 27, 2001, at the Dos Palmas resort on the island of Palawan in the Philippine

archipelago. Fanatics from the Al Qaeda affiliate Abu Sayyaf screaming *Allahu akbar, Allahu akbar* stormed through the peaceful hotel
complex and within minutes captured twenty hostages, forcing
them aboard a thirty-five-foot speedboat. Among the hostages
were two American missionaries, Martin and Gracia Burnham.
The Burnhams are members of the New Tribes Mission, an evan-
gelical Christian organization that ministers to people around the
world. Martin is a qualified pilot who ferries supplies to those in
need around the Philippine islands and Gracia helps with everything from monitoring his flight routes to teaching English to
the locals. They came to Dos Palmas to celebrate their wedding
anniversary."

I read the document a second time: "May 27, 2001." It was now
November 27, 2001.

"WTF," I said. "You mean these Americans have been hostages for
six months and nobody's doing anything?"

There was uneasiness among the members of the Interagency
Hostage Coordination Group. The senior FBI representative spoke up.

"Well, we can't get DoD's support, and with everything going
on in Afghanistan the Agency just doesn't have the resources. The
Bureau is also shorthanded, and the Philippine government just
doesn't have the capability to rescue them."

"This is bullshit!" I said. "These are Americans. We can't just let
them rot in the jungle. What's the process for getting someone to
take action?"

I looked around the room at the other members. The Interagency
Hostage Coordination Group was a committee of representatives
from around D.C. It included all the three-letter agencies—CIA,
FBI, DoD, NSA—as well as Treasury and State. Good people, but we
were all mid-level managers with no real authority.

State spoke up. "We will have to develop a plan and then take that plan to the deputies, the principals, and then get POTUS approval."

"Okay! So what's the holdup?"

A lot of eyes danced around the room. As the new head of the Hostage Coordination Group, my responsibility was to track Americans in trouble around the world and coordinate the activities of the interagency to try and get our citizens home safely. The HCG had been around for some time, but the reality was, the government rarely did much to help. The United States had a "no ransom" policy, and consequently, negotiating the release of hostages invariably fell to the private company or the family of the victims. While the FBI and State provided advice and assistance, the U.S government was not allowed to intervene directly with the delivery of payment.

But this was different, I thought. Abu Sayyaf was a terrorist organization and their leader, Khadaffy Janjalani, was a certifiable extremist. Abu Sayyaf and Janjalani had proclaimed their allegiance to Osama bin Laden well before 9/11. Hiding in the jungles of the southern Philippines, they were notorious for kidnappings, beheadings, and political murders. The Philippine Army had been hunting them for years without much success. With just a little effort from the United States, I was convinced we could rescue the Burnhams and destroy Abu Sayyaf. Not everyone shared my optimism, but some did.

The CIA representative, an experienced field agent named Tom, smiled at my new-guy enthusiasm. "You know." He paused. "Maybe I can get some aerial reconnaissance assets and see if we can spot them from above."

"Great." I nodded. "Anybody else?"

State took a deep breath and then chimed in. "Okay ... let me reach out to the embassy in Manila and see what they can tell us. I know they have been tracking this from the beginning."

The Bureau guy lifted his hand slightly off the table to get my attention. "Yeah. I'll also reach out to the LEGAT in Manila and see what negotiations are taking place between the New Tribes Mission and the hostage takers."

"Treasury will see what we can find out about Abu Sayyaf's assets. Maybe we can leverage something there."

I looked around the table and smiled. "Thanks, guys. We've got some work to do. I'll pull together some ideas and send them around for comment. We can get together next week and plot a course forward."

As the meeting broke up, CIA Tom approached me. "I like your style," he said. "I'm all in."

"Well, be careful what you agree to." I smiled. "We SEALs aren't exactly known for our shy, retiring ways. It's gotten me into trouble before."

"Good." He laughed. "We're going to get along just fine."

Martin looked thin, Gracia pale and drawn. The three terrorists behind them, faces covered, brandishing AK-47s, had the classic menacing pose. The proof-of-life photo did nothing to ease my concerns about the Burnhams' welfare.

The Burnhams and their fellow hostages had been constantly on the move from the time of their capture, each evening at a new jungle hideout. Each day hiking miles to avoid capture. From my time as a young SEAL in the Philippines, I knew what the jungle was like. Nothing about surviving in the jungle was easy.

The Armed Forces of the Philippines (AFP), while enthusiastic, weren't helping much either. They had aggressively and clumsily pursued the Janjalani group, engaging in a series of running firefights and dropping bombs on the small band of hostage takers. I didn't know how long the Burnhams could survive either the jungle or the AFP assaults.

*   *   *

Downing grabbed me by the arm as we rushed into the Oval Office. "Just be brief," he whispered. "Give the high points of your plan and let's try to get a decision out of him."

I nodded without saying a word.

The President stood chatting with Dick Cheney as we entered. Also in the room was General Colin Powell, the Secretary of State, and Dr. Condoleezza Rice, the National Security Advisor. Downing walked me over to the President and made some quick introductions.

Bush sized me up, gave me a firm handshake, and in his Texas drawl said, "So, you're a Navy SEAL?"

"Yes sir," I responded, coming to a modified attention in my Brooks Brothers suit.

He looked me over again. "Can you run a six-minute mile?"

"Well, sir." I paused, realizing the President knew nothing about my parachute accident. "I used to be able to."

"Hell, Bill." Powell laughed. "We all *used* to be able to."

The President smiled broadly and everyone else in the room laughed along with Powell.

"Mr. President, Bill would like to give you a quick brief on our plan to rescue the Burnhams," Rice said. "We just finished a Principals Committee meeting, and I have to tell you Don Rumsfeld was not at all supportive. He says DoD is just too busy with everything going on in Afghanistan. However, Colin, George Tenet, and Bob Mueller all think it has merit."

Powell waded in. "Mr. President, I don't think we can just stand by and do nothing when we have Americans being held hostage by an Al Qaeda affiliate."

"I agree," Cheney offered.

"Okay, so what do you have?" Bush asked.

Downing gave me the look to proceed.

"Sir, the Hostage Coordination Group has developed a three-pronged approach. First, we believe the Philippine Army needs a lot of help with tactics, logistics, and equipment, and we are proposing sending a hundred or so Green Berets to provide training and, if necessary, go along on the missions to help the Filipinos."

"What else?"

"Sir, the Agency is willing to provide clandestine air assets to help locate the Burnhams and provide intelligence to the Filipinos."

Bush paced in front of the fireplace as I laid out my recommendations.

"Finally, Director Mueller has agreed to provide an FBI negotiator to work with the New Tribes Mission and the embassy in an attempt to get Abu Sayyaf to release the hostages."

"We're not making deals with the terrorists, are we?" the President asked.

"No sir, absolutely not. But that's not to say we're going to be absolutely truthful with Abu Sayyaf either. Hopefully, we can lead them on and gather some intelligence that may help guide the Filipino rescue force."

Rice spoke up. "Mr. President, President Arroyo is arriving for a short visit in a few weeks. We can use that opportunity to encourage her and the Philippine government to accept our help and get more aggressive against Abu Sayyaf."

Bush looked around the room. Everyone seemed to be nodding in agreement.

"Okay. Let's get this done."

That was it, I thought. It took months to get agreement from the interagency, but only minutes for the President of the United States to make a decision. This was why I had come to the White House.

I thanked the President and walked out of the room by myself. Downing stayed behind to talk with Rice and the President. I knew there were still some concessions to be brokered between Defense, State, and the Bureau, but after three months of haggling with the interagency, we finally had a breakthrough. The Burnhams were on the White House radar.

I pushed the phone closer to my ear. Our office in the Old Executive Office Building was a Sensitive Compartmented Intelligence Facility (SCIF), which meant acoustics were terrible.

"The triple canopy jungle in Basilan is difficult to penetrate. We catch glimpses of them in the pictures, but there isn't enough time to process the intelligence and get it to the Filipinos," CIA Tom said.

"What about your sources?" I asked. "Are they telling us anything?"

"We think Martin has malaria. Some of the Filipino hostages who were released last month say he has lost a lot of weight and is very weak. Candidly, Bill, I don't know how long either he or Gracia can survive in the jungle. They are moving every day. The AFP is chasing them. They eat maybe once a day." He paused. "They're missionaries, for God's sake, not Navy SEALs."

"They may not be SEALs, but what I do know is that their faith is strong."

"I got it," Tom said angrily. "Man shall not live by bread alone, but this is taking it to the extreme."

There was a rap on my cubicle window. It was Nick Rasmussen, my closest friend in the White House and the smartest guy on our staff.

"Bill, the SITROOM called. They need you immediately."

"Is this about the Burnhams?"

"Don't know. But they seemed pretty anxious."

I finished the conversation with Tom and headed over to the White House Situation Room.

The Situation Room, or SITROOM as it was commonly referred to, was underwhelming. You entered the space through a door across from the White House Dining Room. Once inside, there was a bank of telephones answered by six or seven young officers from the military, State Department, or CIA. An Air Force colonel and a senior civil servant supervised the SITROOM, ensuring all telephone and facsimile message traffic coming in were properly handled. All crisis management for the U.S. government began in the SITROOM. Off to one side was a small conference room. The only thing that distinguished it from a thousand other small conference rooms around Washington, D.C., was the chair at the head of the table. Embossed on the back side of the leather were the words *President of the United States.*

I waved my badge and entered the room.

"Hey sir. Glad you're here. We've got a problem!" The Army major, dressed in his class "A" uniform with full ribbons, held out a piece of paper. "I just got a call from the FAA ops center and then they faxed this over."

I looked over the WASHFAX as the major continued.

"They are reporting that some nutcase aboard an American Airlines flight from Paris to Miami just tried to blow up the plane by setting off a bomb in his shoe."

"In his shoe?"

"Yes sir. The guy's name is Richard Reid. We are running the traps on him right now. I guess he had a fuse sticking out from some sort of plastic explosive in his shoe and when he tried to light it the passengers jumped him."

"Yeah, I don't know that you could put enough plastic explosive in your shoe to make much of a bomb. Besides, it's really difficult to ignite C-4 or PETN with a match," I said.

"Sir, the FAA sent over this schematic of what they think the bomb looks like."

I glanced over the crude drawing. Based on my experience, it certainly didn't look like a workable bomb, but I thought I would call just to confirm my suspicions. I picked up the phone and contacted the operations center at the FAA.

"Ed Kittel," came the voice on the other end.

"I'll be damned. Ed Kittel!" I said, drawing out the last name.

Kittel and I had worked together in the Pentagon almost fifteen years earlier. Ed was a former Navy Explosive Ordnance Disposal officer and really knew demolitions.

"Ed, it's Bill McRaven over at the White House. We'll have to catch up later, but for now I need to know whether you think this shoe bomb is a real threat?"

"It is," he said without hesitation.

"Really?"

"Really!"

Ed walked me through his assessment, and while I had some reservations about his conclusions, he was *the* expert.

"If Al Qaeda can put explosives in a shoe, what else could they make a bomb out of?" I said, thinking out loud.

"Well, provided they're not using a time fuse, they would have to have an electrical impulse to initiate a blasting cap of some sort," Ed offered.

My heart began to race a bit. "What if they got a hold of a thin roll of plastic explosives and slipped it inside a laptop and then used the power from the battery. Could they initiate the explosive train?" I asked.

I could hear the wheels grinding in Ed's encyclopedic brain.

"Holy shit!" he said. "Yeah. It's possible. But I would have to run some tests to determine if it's really feasible."

"Yeah, not sure we have time for tests right now," I responded. "Downing is with the President on Air Force One. I need to call him ASAP and give him an update. Work the problem for me, Ed, and then get back to me."

I thanked Ed, hung up, and immediately had the SITROOM patch me through to General Downing on Air Force One.

"Yes sir, the FAA thinks the threat is legit," I said, yelling through the static of the ground-to-air communications.

I could hear Downing dropping F-bombs on the other end. What if this attempt to bring down an airliner was a coordinated attack by Al Qaeda? What if there were more Richard Reids in the air right now? What if more Richard Reids were, at this very moment, preparing to board planes somewhere around the world?

And then I said it—words that I would regret for the rest of my traveling days.

"Sir." I paused. "I think we need to have everyone boarding a plane bound for the U.S. take their shoes off and have them inspected. Also, we need security to check every laptop. The battery on a laptop could be used to initiate a bomb."

Downing didn't hesitate. "Yes! Yes!" he shouted, clearly having the same difficulty with the air-to-ground communications. "I'll talk to the President and get him to order it right away."

(In my defense, I only thought the order would be in place for a few weeks. Sorry...)

Downing hung up, and within minutes the FAA had been ordered to upgrade their security protocols. An hour later, Richard Reid was apprehended upon landing at Boston's Logan Airport, and within days the world of airline travel was never the same again.

I went back to trying to rescue the Burnhams.

By early in the new year, the plan we had briefed the President on was beginning to take shape. U.S. special operations forces had deployed to the Philippines and established a base of operations on the southern island of Zamboanga. The media coverage about the plight of the Burnhams was gaining traction and people were paying attention. The effort to eliminate Abu Sayyaf and Janjalani was now being called "the second front." The State Department, FBI, and the intelligence community were in full swing trying to locate and recover the Burnhams.

But, tragically, with every war effort, there are always consequences. In February, an Army Chinook helicopter returning from a resupply run to U.S. Special Forces on Basilan crashed off the coast near Zamboanga, killing the eight crew members and two Air Force pararescuemen.

Throughout history, there have always been warriors who understood the risks of serving. They understood that there was a chance their lives could be lost in the pursuit of a greater goal. They understood that they could perish while trying to protect others. To some outside the military, this belief may seem like naïve patriotism, misguided loyalty, or foolish enthusiasm—reasons given to young men and women by those in power to cover for adventurism or empire building. But I have learned many times over that those who serve do so with their eyes wide open. Young and old soldiers alike are not fooled by the political rhetoric. On the contrary, they question the cause every day, but they overcome their doubts and concerns because they are inspired by their fellow soldiers who serve nobly and not for some political agenda. Those who serve are serving for their hometown, their high school football team, their girlfriends and their boyfriends. They are serving and sacrificing because they believe in the America they grew up in. They know that America and the people who live in its big cities and small towns are worth the sacrifice, sometimes the ultimate sacrifice. I can guarantee you that the men aboard that helicopter never once doubted why they were serving.

By late February, intelligence indicated that Martin was thinner than ever. Handcuffed throughout the day, he was suffering from diarrhea, dehydration, and bouts of malaria. He was physically struggling to keep up with the young fighters fleeing the Philippine Army. Gracia, battling severe diarrhea as well, also had to deal with the constant indignity of no privacy for her illness. Bombs from the Philippine Air Force routinely and indiscriminately rained down on the small band of Abu Sayyaf, forcing them and their hostages to stay incessantly on the run. It had been nine months since the Burnhams were captured. Nine long, excruciating months.

In March, an anonymous donor paid $300,000 hoping to gain the release of the Burnhams. While the payment didn't achieve its goal, some intelligence was derived from tracking the dispersal of the cash. Still, even with the added information, the group of hostage takers proved very elusive in the jungles of Basilan.

Later that month, the Director of the FBI, Bob Mueller, flew to the Philippines to ensure that the Bureau was doing everything possible to gain the Burnhams' release. Back at Langley, the CIA continued to coordinate the intelligence activities in the Philippines, keeping the White House and the Hostage Coordination Group advised. From my cubicle on the third floor of the Old Executive Office Building, I continued to push for more U.S. involvement and less reliance on the Philippine forces.

"Look, Bill," CIA Tom said. "The Filipinos are doing their best, but they aren't the SEALs and they are never going to let U.S. Special Forces take the lead. This is their country and they see it as their problem. All we can do at this time is give them some training, provide them the best intelligence possible, and then point them in the general direction of the Burnhams. We can hope they get lucky."

I knew he was right, but that didn't make it any less frustrating. As Tom spoke, I couldn't help but think of an old military adage: "Hope is not a strategy." But I knew I didn't need to lecture Tom. He and the CIA were doing everything they could to help.

March became April, April became May, and May became June. On June 7, I managed to escape the White House for twenty-four hours and was giving a lecture at West Point. That evening after my talk, I returned to the Thayer Hotel on the campus. It was a beautiful night, and from my window I could see the moon cresting over the Hudson River.

On Basilan Island in the southern Philippines it was beginning to rain. Peering through the thick jungle canopy, the Filipino sergeant could barely discern the outline of the small band of armed men and their hostages. The Filipino Special Forces had been tracking the insurgent group all night, just waiting for an opportunity to attack. Camped on a steep hillside, the Janjalani group settled in for the night, hoping the rain had covered their tracks.

As the commandos fanned out from the edge of the jungle, the captain in charge maneuvered his men into firing position.

On the hillside, Martin and Gracia Burnham were just unrolling their hammocks.

"I love you," she whispered.

Martin smiled.

Suddenly the tree line erupted with the sound of automatic weapons. "Fire! Fire! Fire!" screamed the Filipino captain.

Falling from her hammock, Gracia tumbled down the hillside, struck in the leg by a large-caliber round. As she rolled to a stop, the body of Martin Burnham lay next to her, dead from the first volley. All around her, soldiers and captors were shooting wildly, men screaming in pain from their wounds. Screaming in fear for their lives.

Bullets continued to fly both ways, killing another hostage and wounding several Filipino soldiers. Within minutes the Filipino soldiers had swept through the campsite and chased the remaining Abu Sayyaf into the jungle.

In the Thayer Hotel my phone rang. It was the SITROOM. The voice of the young officer on the other end was tense. He was talking fast, breathing quickly. Reports of the "rescue" were coming in. Martin was dead, but Gracia had survived. I was immediately connected to Downing and Condi Rice. We were briefed that the Filipinos were moving Gracia to Zamboanga for medical attention and then back to Manila. The U.S. ambassador, Frank Ricciardone, would meet Gracia planeside and then make the calls to Martin's parents, informing them of their son's death. In the chaos of their fight, the Filipinos had left Martin's body in the jungle, but they pledged to retrieve it at first light—which they later did.

Over the course of the next few days, Gracia was reunited by phone with her children, and while in the Manila hospital she received a visit from President Arroyo. On June 17, after a long flight from the Philippines, she arrived back in Kansas City.

Within a few weeks, I returned to the daily grind. Downing

had put me in charge of drafting the National Strategy for Combating Terrorism. It was to be the first comprehensive, interagency, presidentially directed strategy for taking the fight to terrorists worldwide. I went about the work with a sense of purpose, hoping to make a difference in the war on terrorism, a difference that seemed to have eluded me up to this point.

As I sat in my cubicle pounding away on the computer, the phone rang.

"McRaven," I answered promptly.

"Is this Bill McRaven?" came the man's voice on the other end.

"Yes sir," I said, recognizing the distinct drawl of the wealthy donor who had sought the Burnhams' release.

"I have someone here who would like to talk to you."

The phone went quiet for a moment and then a soft, almost angelic voice spoke up. "Captain McRaven. This is Gracia Burnham."

I took a deep breath. It was a voice I thought I would never hear. "Yes ma'am."

"Mr. McRaven, I just wanted to thank you for all that you did for Martin and me."

My eyes began to well up. "I am so very sorry that we weren't able to save Martin," I said, stumbling a bit with my words.

"It's all right," she said sweetly. "I know you tried your best. God has a plan for all of us, and I pray that something good will come from Martin's death."

We talked for bit longer and then hung up.

A year later I would leave the White House. Over the course of the next decade, as I took command of the nation's hostage rescue and counterterrorist forces, I did everything I could to ensure that something good came from Martin's death. I promised myself that as long as I had the authority to act, we would try to rescue every hostage, and as long as I had the forces to strike, no terrorist would go unpunished.

In her book *In the Presence of My Enemies*, Gracia would write that the only way to overcome the hatred in the world is to have "genuine love in our hearts."

But I must confess, as I hunted bad men around the world, I did not always have love in my heart. To each man God has given special talents. Mine seemed better suited to exacting justice than to offering mercy. I hope Martin would understand.

CHAPTER TWELVE

THE ACE OF SPADES

BAGHDAD, IRAQ
December 2003

I squinted to get a better look at the video screen. Two MH-47 Chinook helicopters were streaking across the western Iraqi desert, bound for a small Arab compound north of Fallujah. Inside the helos were twenty-four Army special operations soldiers from our special operations task force. Their objective: Saddam Hussein.

The grainy black-and-white pictures were being broadcast from a Black Hawk helicopter flying above the Chinooks.

"Two minutes out," came the call from the Joint Operations Center (JOC) noncommissioned officer.

"Roger. Two minutes out," I acknowledged.

Around the JOC, fifty men, headsets on, eyes fixed on the screen, quietly talking into their microphones, were helping coordinate the mission.

"Little Birds on target, sir."

Small black shadows jetted across the screen as the AH-6 Little Bird gunships, acting as fire support, took up positions on the north and south sides of the compound.

"Taking fire from the compound, sir."

"Roger," I said, adjusting my headset and leaning in to get a better look.

A steady stream of gunfire erupted from inside one of the small structures, aimed at the hovering Little Birds. The mini-guns on the Little Bird whirled in response, sending a burst of 7.62 rounds into the building, silencing the shooter.

Adventure was in my DNA. Dad with his Spitfire in North Africa; 1943.

My cousin Paul and me looking cool. Paul drove. Grapeland, Texas; 1963.

Football was a way of life in Texas. With my dad in San Antonio, Texas; 1966.

Anna and Claude McRaven. Two fabulous parents.

A Gravel Gertie ammunition storage facility. *Amarillo Globe-News*

Coach Jerry Turnbow as an assistant at Roosevelt High School San Antonio, Texas; 1972.

SEAL training with my swim buddy Marc Thomas. Coronado, California; 1977.

Class 95 upon SEAL graduation. I am at the far right with Lt(jg) Dan'l Steward. Coronado, California; February 1978.

Our wedding was the start of a 41-year love story. Dallas, Texas; May 6, 1978.

A SEAL Delivery Vehicle (SDV) landing on a submarine. *US Navy via Getty Images*

Hanging off the lock-out chamber of the USS *Grayback*. Philippines; 1979.

Iraqi tanker. *RAED QUTEINA/AFP/Getty Images*

Fast-roping onto a moving ship. *Stocktrek Images via Getty Images*

Lieutenant Colonel George Flinn and me on Faylaka Island, Kuwait; February 1991.

Rigid-Hulled Inflatable Boats (RHIBs) in action. *U.S. Navy via Getty Images*

Saluting Admiral Eric Olson at my Change of Command from Naval Special Warfare Group ONE. Coronado, California; 2001. He saved my career.

Martin and Gracia Burnham were held captive by the terrorist group Abu Sayaf. Philippines; 2001. *AFP/Getty Images*

I had the honor of working in the Bush 43 White House after 9/11. Washington, DC; 2003.

Dr. Condoleezza Rice promoting me to Rear Admiral. With my daughter Kelly and Georgeann. The White House; June 2003.

The Ace of Spades, Saddam Hussein, after his capture by Army Special Operations forces. Baghdad, Iraq; December 2003. *U.S. Army via Getty Images*

MH-60 Black Hawks in action. *Justin Sullivan/Getty Images*

The lifeboat that held Captain Richard Phillips. Indian Ocean; April 2009.
Megan E. Sindelar/U.S. Navy via Getty Images

Captain Richard Phillips after the SEAL rescue. *Darren McCollester/Getty Images*

Osama bin Laden.
Universal History Archive/
Getty Images

After a mission with Command Sergeant Major Chris Faris and several of my men. Afghanistan; 2009.

After a mission with Command Sergeant Major Chris Faris and several of our allies. Iraq; 2010.

Things didn't look so good at that moment. The White House; May 1, 2011. *Pete Souza/ The White House/MCT via Getty Images*

Bill – The country owes you a great debt for your extraordinary service and superb leadership. Thank you, on behalf of all Americans. (And next time, use the tape!)

President Obama presenting me with a tape measure. The White House; May 4, 2011. *The White House*

Briefing President Obama in the Oval Office with Command Sergeant Major Chris Faris. May 4, 2011.

As the SOCOM Commander, I'm sharing a laugh with General Lloyd Austin and King Abdullah II of Jordan. Tampa, Florida; 2013.

My final salute. Tampa, Florida; August 2014.

I have been blessed.
John, Kelly, me,
Georgeann, and Bill.

After retirement I served
as the Chancellor of the
University of Texas System.
January 2015. *Holly Reed*

"Birds on the ground."

Dust enveloped the two Chinooks as they landed, one beside the other, just outside the walled compound. The SOF operators sprinted off the ramp of the helos, running full speed toward the metal gate on the outside of the wall.

"Sir, we have activity inside the compound."

Onscreen I could see multiple Iraqi men moving in the courtyard. The operators had breached the outside gate and were flowing into the first building.

"Shots fired. Shots fired."

There was a brief pause from the NCO.

"Two Tangos EKIA."

"Roger." I breathed a little easier. *Two enemies killed in action.*

I watched as the operators systematically cleared each building. Lining up outside the building entrances, the first man in the stack would toss a flash-crash grenade, stunning the occupants inside, followed by a bull rush of armed soldiers. Within ten minutes the fight was over.

My radio squelched. The squadron commander came on the line. "Raven Zero One, this is November Zero One."

"Roger, Bill," I answered.

"Sir, it's a dry hole," he said, sounding exasperated.

"No worries, Bill. Everyone okay?"

"Yes sir, everyone's fine. We have a couple of EKIAs, but no Jackpot. It looks like these guys were building car bombs."

Car bombs. VBIEDs. Vehicle-borne improvised explosive devices. They had killed hundreds in the markets of Baghdad and were one of the most lethal and effective weapons in Al Qaeda's inventory.

"Well, someone is going to live because of your boys. Nicely done."

"Sir, we've got another hour or so on site exploitation. Who knows, maybe someone will talk or we'll find some pocket litter, but I don't really think anyone here knows where Saddam is."

"All right, Bill. Tell the boys thanks. We'll reset and try another target tomorrow."

"Roger, sir. Out here."

Another night. Another dry hole. It was beginning to get old.

I had arrived in Baghdad three months earlier, in October 2003, to replace the outgoing Task Force 714 commander, Air Force Brigadier General Lyle Koenig. Our special operations task force was garrisoned at a small camp off the Baghdad International Airport (BIAP). When Task Force 714 first arrived in Baghdad in March 2003, the commander at the time, Major General Dell Dailey, named the small garrison Camp NAMA, for "Nasty-Ass Military Area." While it certainly wasn't as bad as some places I had bedded down, Camp NAMA wasn't Saddam's Al-Faw Palace either. Most of us lived in tents or dilapidated buildings where the stench from broken sewer pipes and the smell of burning trash wafted over the entire camp. But I didn't care. I was finally out of the White House and helping with the fight.

We set up our joint operations center in one of the few buildings not destroyed during the U.S. invasion. The camp housed about eight hundred soldiers, including a company of Army Rangers; a company from the 1st Cavalry Division, which provided our Abrams tanks, Bradley Fighting Vehicles, and M113s; a support company; the task force headquarters element; and a twelve-man intelligence element that ran our small jailhouse. The jail contained about five to twelve detainees who were held under very strict DoD guidelines. The intelligence we received from these detainees was providing invaluable leads to other Baath Party leaders.

As a way to motivate the American troops, some enterprising young public affairs officer came up with the idea of creating playing cards with the names and faces of Iraqi's most wanted emblazoned on the cards. Saddam was the Ace of Spades.

Our Army special operations unit was given the job of hunting down the Top 50 High Value Targets. One by one, over the course of the past eight months, task force operators had captured or killed some of the more notorious Baath regime members. Most notably, just a few months before I arrived in Baghdad, Lieutenant Colonel Mark Erwin's A-Squadron located Saddam's sons, Uday and Qusay, in a barricaded hideout near Mosul. The two sons were well known for their abhorrent behavior. Uday kept women as sex slaves in his villa on the Euphrates River, and Qusay, whose villa was right next door to Uday's, loved to torture innocent Iraqis for their disloyalty to Saddam. When we finally seized the villas after the fall of Baghdad, they reeked of blood, urine, and fear. Behind the barricades in Mosul, Uday and Qusay fought to the death, wounding several A-Squadron members in the fight and killing a military working dog. It finally took a TOW missile from a unit of the 101st Airborne Division to seal the bastards' fate forever.

But while locating the top-tier Baathists came quickly, Saddam still eluded us nine months after the fall of Iraq.

I was having one of those feelings again. Inexplicable. Powerful. Eerie. One I couldn't shake and certainly couldn't rationalize. But it wasn't the first time I had a "premonition," and as I would find out later, it wouldn't be the last time.

"Turn the plane around!" I shouted over the sound of the C-130's engines.

"What?"

"I said, tell the pilot to turn the plane around and return to Baghdad."

My military aide, Army Captain "Hank" Henry, pulled off his Bose headset and moved across the aisle to sit next to me.

"What did you say, sir?"

"Hank, we need to get back to Baghdad. Tonight's the night we get Saddam Hussein."

Hank looked around the sparsely filled airplane and asked quizzically, "Did someone call you?"

"No," I continued to yell above the noise. "We just need to get back to Baghdad—and now."

Hank was a Special Forces officer—a Green Beret. A former linebacker, he was big, strong, with a great sense of humor and an infectious smile. We had connected from day one. He was loyal to me and I was loyal to him.

"Roger, sir. Let me go talk to the pilot."

Moments later Hank returned to tell me that we couldn't divert the plane in Iraqi airspace. We would have to wait until we got on the ground in Al Udeid, Qatar, before we could hitch a ride back to our task force camp at Baghdad International Airport. This would delay our return by two hours, but it was the only option we had.

Once on the ground in Al Udeid, Hank managed to arm-twist some Air Force pilot and got us on the very next plane returning to Baghdad. Unbeknownst to me, Hank also called back to our Joint Operations Center and they assured him that nothing was going on. Certainly there were no leads on the whereabouts of Saddam Hussein.

"I hate this part," Hank said as the C-130 pilot began his combat spiral into BIAP, dropping precipitously to avoid possible insurgent missiles. The landing at Baghdad International went without incident, but the passengers, a mixture of military, contractors, and Foreign Service types, seemed relieved to be on the ground.

Waiting for me on the tarmac was my sergeant major, Ed Certain. "Boss, what are you doing back?"

Hank flashed the sergeant major a look begging him not to encourage my eccentricity.

"Tonight's the night," I said. "What is the JOC tracking?"

The sergeant major grinned and looked at Hank. "Well, Admiral, funny you should ask. C-Squadron pulled al-Muslit out of the jailhouse a few hours ago and they think he can lead them to Saddam's driver and possibly Saddam himself."

Mohammad Ibrahim Omar al-Muslit, whom C-Squadron had

been hunting for two months, had just been captured earlier that morning. He was the closest associate to Saddam that we had in custody.

We jumped into the waiting Toyota Hilux for the short drive back to Camp NAMA.

"Sir, for all we know, al-Muslit could be just another Beacon Boy. I wouldn't put a lot of stock in this lead either," Certain said.

Beacon Boy. It was all I'd heard since arriving in Iraq. Beacon Boy was supposed to be the golden source. The guy who would lead us to Saddam. He was so named because our tech guys had given him a tracking device, a beacon, that he would initiate if he were colocated with Saddam. Our Army special operations task force was always on standby to immediately react if Beacon Boy signaled the force. The signal never came, but somehow we hung on, desperate for anything that would lead us to Saddam. We all knew Beacon Boy was crooked, but he always gave us just enough intelligence to keep us interested. We were being played. We knew it, but we had no choice. He was our only lead—until now.

"I think this time is different," I told the sergeant major.

"What's different about it?"

"Just call it a hunch," I said, smiling.

"Okay, sir," the sergeant major said, shaking his head. "But didn't you have some important meeting with General Abizaid in Al Udeid?"

"Well, if I'm right about tonight, Abizaid won't mind me missing the meeting."

"And if you're wrong?" Certain asked.

"If I'm wrong...I'm sure he'll understand."

During my time as the commander of the task force in Iraq, I reported to General John Abizaid, who was in charge of Central Command. Abizaid was an exceptional leader. He was strong-willed, tactically minded, understood the Arab culture, and had a dry sense of humor that surfaced in the toughest moments. As a new admiral living in an Army world, learning from officers like John Abizaid set me up for success later in my career.

We pulled up to the JOC and offloaded our gear. It was about 1930 local when I walked inside and immediately looked up to the massive screen that displayed our feed from the surveillance helicopter that the task force owned. On the screen was a small one-room mud building, the kind that was prevalent throughout Iraq. A few palm trees dotted the landscape around it, but there were no other houses visible in the area. At the bottom of the picture our JOC chief had overlaid the words "Objective Wolverine One." It was tonight's mission.

Navy SEAL Captain Lee Snell, my deputy commander, was on the radio headset talking to someone in the field. I sat down next to Snell and he immediately got up to give me the command seat. I waved him off.

"You've got it, Lee. What's going on?"

"Sir, C-Squadron thinks they have a lead on Saddam's cook, Qais. We moved al-Muslit from the jailhouse to Tikrit early this afternoon, and al-Muslit says he will lead them to Qais, and supposedly Qais is hiding Saddam. We're monitoring Qais's house, Objective Wolverine One."

The picture from the WESTCAM optical sensor on the helicopter was grainy and occasionally the sensor would slew outward, going from a close-in look to five thousand feet.

Putting on the headset, I listened to the radio communications on C-Squadron's tactical frequency.

As the chatter on the net increased, it was clear that we had captured Qais, but as usual with all detainees, he denied having any knowledge of the whereabouts of Saddam. Unbeknownst to me, at the urging of al-Muslit, who was with a second SOF troop, Lieutenant Colonel Bill Coultrup, the C-Squadron commander, and Colonel Jim Hickey, from 1st Brigade, 4th Infantry Division, had maneuvered farther up the dirt road from Wolverine One to another small house, designated Wolverine Two.

As I watched the ISR feed from the WESTCAM and listened

to the radios, the visual and the verbal didn't match up. Wolverine One appeared reasonably quiet, but the radio calls from Coultrup sounded like they were moving rapidly on a target.

"It sounds like they're on target, Lee. I don't see any movement outside the house."

I motioned to the JOC noncommissioned officer, who sat at the end of the long wooden table that made a horseshoe around the ISR screen. He was also on the headset, seeing what I was seeing—which was nothing. I raised my hands in the universal sign of "WTF," and he shrugged and called back, "ISR is on the target. I don't know where the squadron is, sir."

I hated to call the squadron in the middle of an operation. It's the last thing any tactical guy on the ground wants—a call from his boss sitting warm and comfortable in a JOC fifty miles away from the action. Still, it was our responsibility to manage the Quick Reaction Force and the medical evacuation if something went wrong on target. That was hard to do if you didn't have good situational awareness of the mission. And the truth was, I was curious as to whether this new lead was panning out.

Somewhat reluctantly I pushed the talk button and reached out to Coultrup. "Bill, are you on target?"

"Yes sir," Coultrup responded somewhat excitedly.

"We don't see you on ISR."

There was a pause on Coultrup's end. "Sir, we are on Wolverine Two. Just down the road from the original target, and we have Jackpot."

Jackpot? Jackpot?

Jackpot was the code word meaning they had captured the objective. At first I assumed Coultrup meant Qais, but suddenly it occurred to me that the tone of Coultrup's voice indicated something more significant.

"Jackpot? Do you mean *Little* Jackpot or—*Big* Jackpot?"

"Big Jackpot!" Coultrup answered.

Around the JOC floor, where everyone was listening in, there was a strange sense of quiet, as though no one believed what we were hearing. I didn't want to appear too anxious. Over the course of the past several months the operators on the ground had called Jackpot on other targets, only to find out that we were mistaken. A lot of the Iraqi names and faces were similar—easy to make the mistake. But this was Saddam Hussein, one of the most recognizable men in the world. Surely they couldn't be wrong this time.

"Call me on the land line when you get back to Tikrit," I told Coultrup. If this was Saddam, Coultrup didn't need me asking a lot of questions while he was still on target. We could talk when he got back to the squadron's base in Tikrit.

Behind me in the JOC, I could feel the sense of excitement building. I turned to Snell and told him to secure all outside lines. No communications were to leave Camp NAMA without my approval. No persons were to leave Camp NAMA without my approval. Until we could verify that the Jackpot was indeed Saddam Hussein, no one was going to go off half-cocked and tell the outside world the news. This would be strictly by the book.

Thirty minutes later, Bill Coultrup called me from Tikrit.

"Well, what do think, Bill? Is it him?"

"Yes sir, I think it's him."

"Bill, before I call Abizaid, McChrystal, and Sanchez, I have to know for certain. How certain are you?"

Over the phone, I could hear other SOF operators talking loudly, taking off their kit, the post-mission clatter that accompanied every operation.

"Sir, I'm about 98 percent certain," Coultrup responded. In the background one SOF operator yelled out, "Bullshit! It's 100 percent."

Coultrup laughed. "Sir, it's him. We pulled him out of a spider hole on Wolverine Two and the first thing he said was, 'I'm Saddam Hussein, the President of Iraq and I am willing to negotiate.'"

As it turned out, al Muslit had indeed led the assault force to the right target. On Wolverine Two was Qais's brother, who also denied knowing where Saddam was located. While on target, al-Muslit, trying not to be too obvious, tapped his foot on the floorboards around the small house, indicating that there just might be something underneath. After a few minutes, and with the help of a troop K-9, the SOF soldiers unearthed the spider hole. Saddam, who had a gun by his side, almost didn't make it out of the hole alive, but the assaulters quickly disarmed him and dragged him out. After he announced that he was Saddam Hussein, President of Iraq, one of the operators responded, "President Bush sends his regards!"

Lee Snell was listening over my shoulder. I smiled and nodded to Lee. "Coultrup says it's him."

I directed Coultrup to put Saddam on the first helo available and get him down to Camp NAMA. Then I started making my calls to Abizaid and McChrystal, my new boss at Fort Bragg. During the calls both men wanted assurances that it was Saddam, which I didn't have at the time. I briefed them on the plan to get Jackpot here within the hour and then I could verify with my own eyes that it was Saddam. However, if there *was* any doubt, we would get blood samples and send them back for a DNA match.

As I was completing my calls, a young sergeant approached me and said that Lieutenant General Sanchez was out in the lobby.

Rick Sanchez was the military commander in Iraq. He and I had met only briefly in General Abizaid's office months earlier, but I liked the man. His leadership in Iraq had been heavily scrutinized, mostly by those who weren't in the fight. During my time with him I found him to be competent, hardworking, poised, and approachable. Still, I was quite surprised by Sanchez's arrival. His headquarters at the Al-Faw Palace was a good thirty-minute drive from Camp NAMA. Had he gotten the word on tonight's mission? I was still on the phone coordinating our detainee's arrival to Baghdad when Sanchez and Major General Barb Fast, the senior intelligence officer in Iraq, walked up to my table.

Sanchez pulled up a folding chair and sat down beside me. "Well, I understand you got Saddam," he said matter-of-factly.

"Sir, I don't know just yet. The man we captured should be on the ground in ten minutes. You can see for yourself when he lands."

"Well, I got a call from the CIA. They think you have him, and I'm told George Tenet has already notified President Bush."

I shook my head in exasperation. Someone in the intelligence community had called Buzzy Krongard, the Executive Director at CIA, who had notified Tenet, who had called Bush—all in a matter of minutes after the capture.

"Well, I hope they're right," I said, with some sense of frustration.

Fifteen minutes later, the jailhouse called in to tell Captain Snell that the detainee had arrived. I was still working with the CENTCOM staff to develop a follow on plan for the movement of Saddam, if it was him. Additionally, I was coordinating with the military holding facility across the street to get Chemical Ali transferred to me for the evening so I could have another eyewitness verify the identity of our detainee. I knew that millions of Iraqis and Americans alike would need proof positive before they accepted that Saddam was alive and in custody.

Sanchez, Fast, and Snell went to the jailhouse to verify our detainee's identity, while I continued my coordination. Minutes later, Snell called me to confirm that we had captured the President of Iraq, Saddam Hussein.

Snell returned from the jail and I headed over to see our newest prisoner. The jailhouse was a one-story, eight-room concrete building, which we had turned into a temporary holding facility. The hallways were short and narrow. The smell of sweat and dust permeated the building. The room's air conditioners spewed out lukewarm air and only added to the musty, humid atmosphere. Inside was a small cadre of intelligence officers, military policemen, interrogators, and medics whose only focus was to get intelligence from Iraqi detainees.

As I arrived, there were more than the usual personnel scurrying about, all wanting to help, and all hoping to get a peek at our prisoner. I gently pushed my way through the crowd and found Sanchez talking with Bill Coultrup.

"This is a historic moment," Sanchez said.

Coultrup was beaming from ear to ear, and rightfully so. Coultrup had been an Army Special Forces operator most of his adult life. He was in Mogadishu during Black Hawk Down. He fought in Bosnia, Kosovo, and was part of the initial invasion of Iraq. He was a bit eccentric, but Bill Coultup was a warrior through and through. I worked with him many times over the next few years, and few men I knew were as professionally aggressive and talented.

Coultrup turned to me and said with a smile, "Okay, boss, I've done my job. He's all yours now."

I thanked Coultrup for a good night's work, and then Sanchez and I got down to discussing the next steps. A press release was drafted, but it still needed some adjustments. In anticipation of this day, we had also developed an interrogation plan to see if we could find out the truth about the WMD and the whereabouts of Navy Captain Scott Speicher, a pilot who was shot down during Desert Storm in 1991. But the plan still needed approval from Abizaid. The new Iraqi leadership in Baghdad would also want a say in Saddam's ultimate disposition.

But first of all, we had to show the Iraqis and the world that Saddam Hussein had indeed been captured. At the time of capture, Saddam was wearing a long, full beard that hid some of his features. While it was still obvious to me that it was Saddam Hussein behind the whiskers, I felt it was necessary to shave him so there was no doubt in the average Iraqi's mind that this was their former President.

Turning to Sanchez, I said, "Sir, I'm going to have one of my medics shave Saddam so we have a good picture for the press."

"Shave him?"

"Yes sir. Clean him up for the photo."

"Do we have the authority to shave him?" Sanchez asked seriously.

"Sir." I laughed. "We had the authority to shoot him if he was a threat. I think I have the authority to shave him."

Sanchez smiled. "I guess you do."

We got a good before-and-after photo. Sanchez and I personally wrote the press release, and by early the following morning things had settled down.

At 1000 hours on December 14, 2003, with cameras rolling, Ambassador Paul Bremer, with Sanchez at his side, stood before the media and announced, "We got him!"

The world press went crazy. All the television channels broadcast our before-and-after photos of Saddam around the globe. In the press release, we gave full credit to the 4th Infantry Division for the capture. The 4th ID was an invaluable part of the pursuit, and in an attempt to protect the identity of our special operators, we shaped the story accordingly.

Later that same day, Bremer and Sanchez flew into Baghdad International with Ahmed Chalabi, the leader of the Iraqi National Congress, and three other Iraqi resistance leaders. I met Bremer's party at the airfield and escorted them to our holding facility. Along with Bremer and Sanchez were several Foreign Service officers from the embassy and a couple of press folks.

Upon arrival at the holding facility, I ensured that each man was searched and made it clear that no photos were to be taken. Once inside, we walked down the passageway to the room where Saddam was being held. Bremer moved with a cool sense of accomplishment and confidence, selectively ignoring the stench and rawness that accompanied a battlefield jail. Sanchez seemed somewhat annoyed at the circus-like atmosphere that surrounded Bremer. I could tell that Sanchez would have preferred not to be there. As we got closer to the room, I could see by the looks on the faces of the resistance leaders that they were nervous. Their fear ran deep and they believed that even a captured Saddam was a threat to their lives.

As I nodded to the guard outside the room, he opened the door. Inside, Saddam, dressed in an orange jumpsuit, was sitting on an Army cot looking very much in control. As Bremer and Sanchez entered the room, Saddam remained seated, his arrogance still unchanged by his capture. Chalabi and the other Iraqis pushed past Sanchez and immediately began to yell profanities at Saddam.

Saddam smiled like a Mafia boss caught by the police, but who somehow knew that eventually he would get the last laugh. Screaming, shaking their fists, and spitting in Saddam's direction, the Iraqis seemed to be releasing decades of hatred in an outburst of emotion.

Saddam motioned to them to quiet down. He was still the *President of Iraq* and they were his subjects. After purging their anger, they moved to the back of the room as though the prisoner in the orange jumpsuit still had some mystical power to cause their demise. Only Chalabi seemed unfazed by Saddam's show of authority. In what was clearly a surreptitious preplanned photo opportunity, he moved forward from the back of the room and sat directly across from Saddam. I saw the flash, but couldn't identify who took the photo. By the next morning, a picture of a confident-looking Chalabi "lecturing" a captured Saddam Hussein hit the press.

The meet lasted about thirty minutes, and Bremer and his party departed Camp NAMA. As word of the meeting leaked out, speculation about the treatment of Saddam, his whereabouts, and his final disposition were all subjects of banter on the news stations.

One commentator implied that we were likely torturing Saddam and using drugs to get vital information on the location of the WMD. At one point, the hype got so out of control that the commander of U.S. Special Operations Command, General Doug Brown, called me directly to confirm that we were not using drugs to elicit information. I reassured Brown that no drugs were being used and that in fact, Saddam was living better than most of the soldiers at Camp NAMA. He remained isolated in the small room and I kept a doctor and an Army Ranger in attendance at all times. Saddam received a medical checkup every day and we delivered food from the dining facility for each meal. Initially, I expected to hold him for only a day or two before we moved him to Basra and then out to a Navy ship in international waters. That plan was quickly scuttled by General Abizaid, who subsequently directed me to hold Saddam until further notice.

I had three overarching concerns with respect to Saddam's detention and protection. Would he commit suicide? Would one of our Iraqi colleagues try to kill him (the Jack Ruby scenario)? Would the Iraqi insurgents attempt to storm the facility and break him out? Camp NAMA was only a few hundred yards from a main road in which hundreds of Iraqi trucks moved every day to supply U.S. troops. While I thought most Americans wouldn't care if Saddam was assassinated or committed suicide, he was now my prisoner and therefore I had an obligation, both morally and legally, to keep him safe until the chain of command or the Iraqis could decide his fate.

In an effort to ensure Saddam's safety, I directed that all Iraqis be barred from entering the jailhouse. This was difficult for many of our staunch Iraqi allies who saw my order as an affront to their loyalty. *It was*, but the consequences of failure outweighed their sensitivities. Additionally, I reinforced our small jail facility by establishing exterior fighting positions and placing Rangers and some of our great 1st Cavalry soldiers along the main avenues of approach. Within forty-eight hours I felt comfortable that I had all the right precautions in place to ensure Saddam's safety.

On day three of Saddam's incarceration, Abizaid called to tell me that "another government agency" was taking over the questioning of our prisoner. I wasn't happy, but the topic was not open for discussion. I "requested" that General Abizaid send me a written order directing me to hand over the prisoner. He completely understood my concerns and was kind enough to oblige.

I expected that the other government agency would take Saddam to an undisclosed location and question him there, but as it turned out, they wanted to keep Saddam at Camp NAMA and continue with the dialogue at our location. Additionally, they knew that our translator, an intelligence officer who worked for me at Camp NAMA, had developed a relationship with Saddam, which would be beneficial to their efforts.

When the other government agency's team arrived, I made it clear that Saddam's health and welfare remained my responsibility. Concerned that their techniques might be more aggressive than the established military procedures, I wanted to ensure that I had a vote in anything that occurred at Camp NAMA. As it turned out, my fears about the team were completely unfounded. They were professional, courteous, followed the rules to the letter, and complied with every one of my requests.

The questioning was more like an interview than an interrogation. The team spent four to six hours a day talking with Saddam, trying to build rapport in hopes of finding the WMD or the whereabouts of Captain Speicher. Saddam was surprisingly chatty and seemed to enjoy the banter that went on between the team and him. It was obvious from the start that he had no idea of the location of Captain Speicher. While the Navy MIA was of great concern to the United States, to Saddam he was just another pilot lost during the first Gulf War. Whatever happened to Speicher was below Saddam's level of oversight.

There were also no weapons of mass destruction, and no matter how many times the team reengaged Saddam on the issue, the answer was always the same. Iraq didn't have nuclear WMD. It was not the answer we were hoping for.

When asked about the Kurdish genocide, sarin gas that killed tens of thousands of Kurds in the north of Iraq, Saddam was dismissive and replied with a shrug of his shoulders, "That was Ali, not me." Chemical Ali, Saddam's closest friend, had been placed in charge of the Kurd situation up north and resorted to unspeakable atrocities to wipe out the population. It was only through the U.S. imposition of the Northern No-Fly Zone in 1992 that the Kurds survived.

When questioned about the murder of his two sons-in-law who fled to Jordan with Saddam's daughters and then naively returned thinking all was forgiven, like a Mafia don, Saddam replied, "It was family business."

Over the course of the next ten days, the team continued their questioning, but it was becoming clear that the interaction was giving Saddam a source of pride that wasn't helpful. From his vantage point, he had the upper hand in the discussions, and as such, he felt empowered. The team was aware of the dynamic and eventually decided that nothing more would be gained from their continued dialogue. After two weeks they departed, without having obtained much insight into the critical questions, which we had hoped to have answered.

During Saddam's stay, I visited the small room once a day to talk with the doctor and the guard to ensure everything was okay. Each time I entered, Saddam would stand up and attempt to engage me in a conversation. I would motion for him to sit down and never addressed him directly. I had given a standing order that no one was to talk with Saddam unless I granted approval. As the days went by, Saddam's haughtiness and confidence began to wane, and with every visit I made, *and every conversation I didn't have*, his frustration grew and his sense of power diminished. Over time, the change in his personality was dramatic.

About three weeks into Saddam's imprisonment, General Abizaid came by the holding facility to meet with the military intelligence team and to thank them for their efforts in capturing Saddam. At one point I asked Abizaid if he wanted to meet Saddam. Without hesitation Abizaid said, "Why in the world would I want to meet with that megalomaniac?"

In a strange way, the starkness of his answer surprised all of us. The Saddam we saw every day was a broken old man in an orange jumpsuit who sat quietly on his cot hoping to talk with anyone who would listen. But the real Saddam was indeed a megalomaniac. On his hands was the blood of tens of thousands of his own citizens. He had gassed another ten thousand Iranians during the ten-year Iran-Iraq War. His sons and his close friends were deranged human beings who took perverse pleasure in the pain of others. His secret police protected Saddam with a degree of ruthlessness not seen since Stalin's era. Saddam viewed himself as a historic Arab figure who ruled like the pharaohs of old with godlike authority over the lives of his subjects, but in reality he was just evil.

After thirty days of holding Saddam at Camp NAMA, I received orders to move him to a military police facility where the former President of Iraq would be interned until his trial. By early January 2004, we were in the midst of a growing insurgency. Al Qaeda in Iraq was becoming a real threat to stability. Car bombs and suicide bombers were commonplace. The rise of Abu Musab al-Zarqawi and his Sunni extremists was creating untold problems for an American military that had come to dislodge Saddam's army and now found itself fighting a shadow force of Iraqi insurgents.

On his final day at Camp NAMA, I decided to gamble and ask Saddam to go on television and order the insurgents to surrender. I developed a plan with my translator and rehearsed my remarks so the translator knew exactly what I wanted to say and how. While I had no illusions as to the potential for success, I also felt I had nothing to lose.

As I entered the small room, Saddam stood up, smiled, and began to engage me in conversation. I remained stoic and asked him to sit. He attempted to maneuver me to the cot and himself to a nearby chair. I grabbed him by the shoulders and gently but forcefully placed him back on the cot. His demeanor immediately changed. He did not like being told what to do.

I began my pitch by telling him that the war was over and that U.S. forces were fully in control. While nine months after the invasion that fact might have seemed obvious, but during the interrogations it was clear that Saddam didn't know the current status of the fight. A small grin appeared on his face. It was a smile of satisfaction. He knew there was something else I wasn't telling him just yet.

I continued by saying that there were many Iraqis who had not yet laid down their arms, and as such, we were killing a number of his citizens who didn't need to die—the war was over. He remained silent, waiting for my offer, which he seemed to know was coming.

To save his people the anguish and to help rebuild Iraq to the great nation it could become, I offered Saddam the opportunity to make a video asking for the remaining fighters to lay down their weapons and begin the reconstruction.

He looked directly at me and said in Arabic, "Would you ask your men to surrender?"

It was a question I knew was coming. "If it meant saving my countrymen, yes. I would ask them to surrender."

It was a lie and Saddam knew it. He responded, "I don't think so."

"You will undoubtedly hang for your crimes," I continued. "Do you want to be remembered as a petty dictator like Mussolini, or do you want to be remembered as a patriotic Iraqi who tried to save his country."

"We shall see if I hang for my crimes," he said, his arrogance back on full display.

"Then this is the last time we will see each other. I will be transferring you to another facility tonight." Saddam seemed shaken by my final comment. I stood up and promptly left the room.

Later that night, under tight security, I handed over my prisoner to the commanding officer of the military detention facility on the Baghdad airport. I would never see Saddam Hussein again, but I would continue to fight in Iraq for another six years until U.S. forces departed in December 2010.

On December 30, 2006, after a lengthy trial, Saddam Hussein was hanged for crimes against the Iraqi people. Thirteen years later, as Iraq remains a troubled nation, haunted by ISIS and Al Qaeda, and often on the verge of sectarian war, some may ask whether the U.S. effort was worth it. There were no WMD, and the fracture of Iraqi society caused the death of thousands of innocent people and the loss of over three thousand American and allied lives. I have no good answer. I have only hope. I hope that someday from the ashes of this war will arise a stronger, more representative, more inclusive Iraqi government. I hope that from the broken pieces of countless Iraqi lives will come a man or woman who will change the course of history: develop a cure for cancer, bring peace to the Middle East, or lighten the darkness. I hope that the families of the fallen warriors will find peace in knowing that their loved ones died serving valiantly, protecting their fellow soldiers and halting the spread of Saddam's evil.

I can only hope.

CHAPTER THIRTEEN

WANTED DEAD OR ALIVE

BAGHDAD, IRAQ
2008

Allahu akbar! Allahu akbar!" screamed the young Algerian man. The women in the crowded market grabbed their children and began to run. But it was too late. Looking down at his suicide vest, his face ashen and covered in sweat, the wide-eyed boy reached for the handle to ignite the blocks of explosives wrapped around his waist. According to later reports, there was no hesitation; his reward awaited him in heaven, and the sooner he martyred himself, the sooner he would be with Allah. And in his mind, the twenty-one men, women, and children who died that day would all be sacrifices for the cause of Islam. It was the eightieth suicide bombing that year. Over two hundred Iraqi civilians had perished so far, and one man, *one man* who remained untouchable, was responsible for all the carnage.

I was tired, bone tired. The kind of tired that was so exhausting you have trouble breathing. The kind of tired that makes you wonder whether you will ever be strong again. The kind of tired that makes you realize you're not nineteen anymore.

It was early October 2008 and I had just returned from a combat mission in Baghdad with the Army Rangers. At fifty-three years old, lugging around an M-4 rifle, with body armor back and front, a Kevlar helmet, and three hundred rounds of ammo was just hard on the old body. But nothing gave me more satisfaction than spending time in the field with the soldiers.

However, I hadn't planned to be fifty-three when that opportunity finally came around. Now, as Stan McChrystal used to say, I was just a "battlefield tourist," a three-star admiral who occasionally rode along on combat missions. But in my own defense, riding along also gave me a much better understanding of what my troops had to deal with every night.

The mission ended around 0200. I had returned to my headquarters at Balad Air Base, dumped my gear, and fallen into my rack completely wasted. The temperature outside hovered around a hundred degrees, but the small one-room air conditioner pumped wonderfully cold air into my stark white aluminum sleeping unit. I bit an Ambien in half and quickly fell asleep.

"Sir, wake up."

"What?"

"Sir, wake up! Colonel Erwin is on the phone. He needs to talk with you immediately."

I sat up and looked at the clock. Three o'clock in the morning.

"I know, sir," whispered my aide, Major Pat Lange, with only a bit of regret. "But he said it's really important."

Colonel Mark Erwin was the Army special operations task force commander. He was a magnificent officer, and we had worked together off and on for the past five years. Mark was tall and lean, with the build of an All-American soccer player—which he had been at Wake Forest. Years earlier, when Erwin was a squadron commander and I was a new one-star admiral, we had become friends. As a Navy guy in an Army world, I appreciated the friendship, and Mark taught me a lot about how his task force worked. He was a tough disciplinarian, and now as the Army task force commander, he expected a lot from his men. His task force had without a doubt some of the finest soldiers in the world.

I grabbed the phone, cleared my throat, and tried to shake off the effects of the Ambien.

"Mark. What's up?" I said, trying to sound completely awake.

"Sir," he answered, with a tinge of panic in his voice, "my guys crossed the Iraqi border and went into Syria."

"I'm sorry," I responded. "Say that again."

I could hear the exasperation on the other end.

"Sir, the sergeant major and five other guys are in Syria."

"When you say, 'in Syria,' what exactly do you mean?"

"Sir, they're about fifteen kilometers inside Syria, heading toward Abu Ghadiya's hideout."

Abu Ghadiya. Damn . . .

Abu Ghadiya was the most wanted man outside Iraq. No one had facilitated more suicide bombers or been responsible for more American and Iraqi deaths than him. For years he had been operating from across the border in Syria, facilitating the flow of hundreds of terrorists into Iraq, young radicalized men from around the Middle East and North Africa.

Syria was technically our ally at the time. We had an embassy in Damascus and we routinely shared intelligence on Al Qaeda high-value targets. But for some reason, the Syrians seemed to turn a blind eye toward Ghadiya. It was reported that a Syrian intelligence officer had been running him for years, helping him hide from the Americans and other Syrian officials.

Ghadiya always operated within close proximity of the Iraqi border, but not so close that we could just stroll across and grab him. He frequently visited a town called Abu Kamal, but rarely stayed there longer than twenty-four hours.

After taking command of Task Force 714, I reviewed the existing plan to capture or kill Ghadiya and wasn't satisfied that anyone would approve it. The plan called for a large helicopter assault force with fifty Army Rangers and twenty Army task force operators. Five helicopters carrying the assaulters would fly from Iraq across the border, avoiding Syrian air defenses, land en masse,

SEA STORIES 203

surround the compound, capture or kill Ghadiya, and then return to Iraq. The plan also required an overhead combat air patrol and even on-call artillery. In my mind, it was way too conventional and much too large a footprint for anyone to support. Nevertheless, soon after taking command, I had timidly presented it to General Dave Petraeus, in hopes that we could garner some support for trying to get Ghadiya. Petraeus had appropriately scoffed at the plan and we went back to the drawing board.

After the Petraeus briefing, I called Mark Erwin into my office and challenged him to come up with a small package, something unconventional, something worthy of his task force. Within two weeks he came back with a plan. But there was one strange request...he wanted to procure high-end mountain bikes so his men could ride across the desert, allowing them to move much faster without being detected. I think he assumed I would laugh him out of the office, but I loved the idea—until now.

"Okay, Mark," I said, trying to sound calm. "Let's get them back to Iraq as quickly as possible."

"Yes sir. I have already recalled them, but it's going to take them a few hours to get back across the border."

"Well, I'm meeting with Petraeus at 0700, will they be back by then?"

There was a slight pause. "Sir, if everything goes okay, we should have them back by around 0800."

"All right, Mark. No worries. Do what you need to do to get them back safely and let me know immediately if anything goes south."

"Roger, sir, understand."

I could tell Mark wanted to say something else. "What is it, Mark?"

"Sir, I'm sorry," he said painfully. "I have been pushing the guys hard, maybe way too hard. We have been working for weeks trying to find a way to breach the border undetected and get into Syria. Tonight the sergeant major found a way and decided to keep going."

Contrary to what most people thought, the Iraqi border in this area was not just a line in the sand. It was layered with wire, patrolled by both sides, and likely covered by Syrian radar.

"Mark, don't sweat it. Just get the boys back safely and we'll figure out the next steps."

"Roger, sir. Will do."

After I hung up I just knew a serious ass chewing was in my future. Crossing the Syrian border required presidential approval, State Department approval, U.S. Embassy Syria approval, U.S. Embassy Iraq approval, CENTCOM approval, and General Petraeus's approval—none of which we had. If for some reason the operators got into trouble, I would immediately call in air support and artillery to ensure their safe return—without anyone's approval.

Later that morning I flew from Balad to the Al-Faw Palace in Baghdad to meet with Petraeus. The meeting was one of those moments when you realize what separates the great generals from merely the good ones.

Standing at a modified attention in front of his desk, I began to explain the situation. "Sir, I received a call from Mark Erwin a few hours ago."

Before I could continue, Petraeus asked, "How is Mark doing? He's a terrific officer."

"Yes sir," I acknowledged. "Absolutely superb."

Petraeus glanced at his daily calendar to see what was next on his schedule.

"Well sir, we have a bit of a problem and I wanted to ensure you were aware of it."

"What is it?"

"Sir, six of my operators crossed the border into Syria last night heading toward Abu Kamal to get Abu Ghadiya."

Petraeus nodded as if to say, *Go on*.

"They were supposed to be doing a recon, but decided, on their own, to continue to Ghadiya's hideout. As soon as Mark found out about it, he ordered them to return."

"Are they back yet?" he asked.

I looked at my watch. "No sir, I expect them back by 0800."

Petraeus got up from behind his desk. He stared out his window and asked, "How far into Syria did they get?"

"Sir, they were about fifteen kilometers in when we recalled them."

He turned from the window, came and stood directly in front of me. He looked up at me, smiled, and said, "Well, you probably should have let them continue on." It was not the response I was expecting, but in the years to come I would realize that the greatness of Dave Petraeus was his ability to shoulder the missteps and even the failures of his subordinates: to build loyalty through his personal sense of command responsibility. He knew that both Erwin and I were doing our best. We had made a mistake, one that he knew we would correct and learn from. But now was not the time for an ass chewing, but the time for understanding.

Petraeus continued, "I'll give Ryan a call and let him know, but if the boys get back safely, I think we can leave this between you and me."

Ryan was Ryan Crocker, the U.S. Ambassador to Iraq. Another great American with whom I would serve many times over the ensuing years.

"Bill, I want to get Ghadiya as bad as you guys do. Bring me a plan, a workable plan that we can take to the President. You will have my support."

I thanked Petraeus and left the palace. By eight o'clock the operators were back in Iraq and we were already planning the next steps.

Even though moving the small force by mountain bikes was somewhat faster than walking, it was still not fast enough to get us across the desert, onto the target, and back into Iraq before the sun came up. No matter what infiltration approach we used, invariably we were going to have to have helicopters to bring us back from the mission. Consequently, we settled on a very straightforward plan. First, we knew that there was no way we could ever get Ghadiya in the small town of Abu Kamal. The town was just too congested and a firefight would likely kill innocent civilians. So the only window for action was when Ghadiya returned to his compound well outside the city limits. If and when that happened, a small force of operators would fly in two Black Hawk helicopters right to the target. They would be supported by two other MH-60 helicopter gunships that could provide fire support if needed. The most difficult part of the plan would be getting all the approvals quickly enough to be able to react when Ghadiya was on target. But in reality, we needed only one yes vote, and that was the President of the United States, George W. Bush.

Over the course of the next few months, the intelligence community doubled their efforts to locate and track Ghadiya. On several occasions he returned to Abu Kamal, but that remained a nonstarter and so we waited and hoped that the right moment would come.

While Ghadiya was important, he wasn't the only bad guy we were chasing. At the time, the Army task force, the Rangers, and the SEALs were conducting around twenty-five missions a night in Iraq, all of them targeting some high-value individual.

On October 20, my deputy commanding general, Major General Joe Votel, came over to Iraq to relieve me for a few weeks. Joe was a superb officer. Tall, wiry, with close-cropped black hair, he was an Army Ranger through and through. Having commanded the Ranger Regiment as a colonel, he was tactically brilliant and incredibly hardworking. Votel also had extensive combat experience in Iraq and Afghanistan, and with a dry sense of humor he was the perfect fit to be my deputy. I trusted him implicitly.

Right before Votel's arrival, intelligence indicated that Ghadiya might be moving to his compound in the next few days or weeks. These kinds of warnings had become routine, even though they rarely panned out. Nevertheless, with each potential opportunity, we moved the assault force to a small combat outpost near the border so they could be ready to launch on a moment's notice.

I always felt completely comfortable leaving the forward command in Votel's hands. He would make as good, if not better, decisions than I would.

It was a long flight back to the States from Baghdad, one I had made numerous times aboard the command's military jet. While our transatlantic communications were sometimes spotty, it was clear from Votel's reports to me that the intelligence on Ghadiya was building. The opportunity for a mission was growing by the hour.

I arrived at Fort Bragg, North Carolina, around 2000 hours on the evening of October 25. The driver picked me up at the airfield and handed me the latest update on Ghadiya. Human intelligence (HUMINT) indicated that Ghadiya would be moving to his compound the next day. Votel had already given a warning order to the operators and he had notified Petraeus, the Joint Chiefs, and CENTCOM that we were postured for the mission.

The transition from Iraq to Fort Bragg was always a little surreal. One night you're in a combat zone with nonstop action and soldiers' lives on the line, and by the next morning you're surrounded by the tranquil pine trees, red clay, and bright blue skies of North Carolina. Coming home after time in combat or on a long deployment was something every soldier, sailor, airman, and

Marine longed for. Home was meant to be a safe place, away from the stress, away from the loneliness, away from bad people trying to kill you. Georgeann always made coming home special. My first day back, she never burdened me with the challenges of family life. Somehow the kids were all doing great, the finances were strong, and all was well. In the days to come, we would get back to dealing with life, but not the first day home. However, when you are in command, home is never completely isolated from work. No sooner had I dropped my bags, kissed Georgeann, and wrestled with the dog than the secure phone in my upstairs office began to ring.

Dashing up the flight of stairs, I grabbed the phone. "McRaven!" I announced, a bit out of breath.

"Bill, Hoss Cartwright here."

General James "Hoss" Cartwright was the Vice Chairman of the Joint Chiefs of Staff. A Marine officer, he was the second most senior officer in the military and the primary military liaison to the White House.

"Are you tracking the Ghadiya movements?"

"Yes sir, of course."

"I understand you want to get POTUS approval if Ghadiya moves to this compound of his." Before I could answer, he said, "I have asked for an NSC meeting tomorrow at 0700. Can you be ready?"

"Yes sir. We'll get you the briefing package tonight."

"Okay, see you at seven."

Cartwright abruptly hung up the phone and I called Votel. He and Colonel Jim Jarrett, Mark Erwin's second in command, were working on the briefing slides and would have them to me within a few hours. All indications were that Ghadiya would indeed be at the compound tomorrow.

The next morning I arrived at my headquarters on Fort Bragg at 0600. Ghadiya had entered his compound earlier that day and appeared to be staying awhile. Votel had passed me the briefing slides and all we needed now was POTUS approval.

My headquarters at Fort Bragg had the most technically sophisticated command center in the world. From there I could communicate with all my units around the globe, watch the real-time video from every unmanned aerial vehicle (UAV), and have full situational awareness of each ongoing mission. But this morning I just wanted to make sure I could connect with the White House Situation Room.

Grabbing a cup of coffee, I sat down in the commander's chair and received the first update. The video teleconference (VTC) was already connected with Votel, Petraeus, CENTCOM, the U.S. Embassy in Iraq, the Joint Staff, and the White House. The briefing slides were on my desk. The plan remained basically unchanged. Four helicopters with a small assault force would cross the Iraqi border, flying just feet off the ground to avoid Syrian radar. Once in sight of the compound, the helicopter gunships would take up positions above the high walls and be prepared to provide fire support for the assaulters. The two remaining helos would land inside the compound. Once on the ground, the assaulters would exit the helos, engage the enemy, and capture or kill Ghadiya. Either way, Ghadiya would be returned to Iraq for questioning or burial.

Precisely at 0700, the White House Situation Room came on the screen. At the head of the table was the National Security Advisor, Steve Hadley. Hadley and I had worked together years earlier when I was a Navy captain on the NSC staff. He and I had always gotten along well, but I knew he thought I was a bit reckless and that I took too many risks: *maybe a fair criticism.*

Around the rest of the table sat the remaining members of the National Security Council: Bob Gates, the Secretary of Defense; Admiral Mike Mullen, the Chairman of the Joint Chiefs; Hoss Cartwright; Condoleezza Rice, the Secretary of State; Mike Hayden, the Director of the CIA; and numerous backbenchers. Also on the screen, linking in from Wyoming, was Vice President Dick Cheney.

"Good morning, Bill," Hadley began.

"Good morning, sir. Good to see you again."

Turing to the assembled group, Hadley said, "I expect the President to arrive in a few minutes, but before he does, Bob, if you can give us a quick update."

Gates made a few quick comments and turned the discussion back over to me. I briefed the NSC on the most recent intelligence and then turned it over to Votel and Jim Jarrett to give an operational update. About the time they completed their portion of the brief, the President walked into the room. Everyone stood and Hadley moved aside so the President could take his place at the head of the table.

The President seemed to be in an unusually good mood. He made some quick small talk with Gates and then got down to business.

"So, Bob. What do we have here?"

"Well, Mr. President, I have Bill McRaven on the line, he's going to brief you on this mission to get Abu Ghadiya."

"All right, Admiral, brief away," he said in that familiar Texas drawl.

I looked down at the slides and began my prepared remarks. At one point in the brief the President stopped me and asked, "Why are we sending the SOF guys in? Can't we just drop a GBU-31 on this guy?"

The question was telling in so many ways. Here was a President who had been intimately involved in fighting this war for the past seven years. He was so well versed on the missions and the nomenclature of the specific ordnance that he understood that using a precision-guided five-hundred-pound GBU-31 was in fact the right munition for the job. I was momentarily taken aback by the question.

"Well, sir, we did look at that option. Unfortunately, there is a small tentlike structure in the middle of the compound. We aren't certain, but there is the possibility that a woman and a few kids could be inside the tent. We think the woman helps with the cooking and cleaning."

"Okay," he responded, but I could tell he wasn't completely satisfied with my answer.

I continued, "Additionally, sir, while it's unlikely we will be able to keep this raid a secret, we are hoping that a quick in-and-out might reduce the Syrian backlash." The President immediately agreed.

I finished the brief and then asked Votel and Jarrett if there was anything additional to add from Iraq. They were good on their end.

The President looked around the long table and said, "Okay, let's vote." He stuck out his right hand with his thumb protruding upward and said, "Here's my vote. Bob, how about you?" Secretary Gates smiled and gave a thumbs-up. As the President went from person to person they all extended their arms and gave a hearty thumbs-up. Last, he turned to Vice President Cheney at his remote location in Wyoming. "Dick, what's your vote?" My video at Fort Bragg had multiple pictures onscreen. In the upper corner I could see Cheney. His face filled the screen. He raised his hands in front of the camera and extended double thumbs-up.

"Okay," said the President with some sense of delight. He looked directly into the camera and announced, "Admiral, go get him!"

I gave an informal salute, signed off with, "Yes sir. Will do," and the video from the White House went blank.

Minutes later I gave the official order to Votel that he was cleared to proceed when he felt the operational conditions were right. The mission was now in his hands.

"Assault force is airborne. Time 1630 local."

"Roger," Votel answered, his voice carrying the calmness of a man who had done these missions thousands of times before.

In a cloud of dust the helos lifted off from an airfield in west-ern Iraq and within minutes were in a tight formation, screaming across the desert just fifty feet off the ground.

Two minutes later came the next call. "Crossing the border."

A drone flying high overhead captured the scene as the four helos crested the large berm separating Iraq from Syria. It was broad daylight and there was no hiding from view. If the Syrian air defense detected the helos, either visually or on radar, they would immediately open fire with surface-to-air missiles or antiaircraft guns. The Syrians were our allies, but not our friends.

"One minute to touchdown."

From above, the two Black Hawk gunships took the lead and immediately began to separate, one taking the north side of Ghadiya's compound, the other the south. They would provide gunfire support for the assaulters.

The view from the drone shifted away from the approaching helos and onto the compound. In the large courtyard seven men, hearing the noise of the inbound helos, began to run excitedly, looking for cover, grabbing their guns, ready to fight.

"Onscreen!"

"Roger," Votel responded, watching as the helos came into view.

Barely missing the outside wall, the lead helo flared, its nose arching upward, tail rotor down as it stopped in midair and landed hard on the ground inside the courtyard.

"Shots fired. Shots fired," came the familiar refrain.

The operators poured out of the first helo and immediately were engaged by Ghadiya and his men. The next helo was seconds behind, executing the same aerial maneuver, landing just feet from the first aircraft. Outside the wall the last two helos set down, the soldiers rushing off the aircraft and taking up security positions to ensure that none of Ghadiya's men escaped the assault.

"Shots fired. Shots fired."

The operators inside the courtyard spread out, sweeping forward toward Ghadiya, the rounds flying both ways. There was no way out. One by one Ghadiya's men fell, and within minutes the fight was over. Cowering unharmed in the small tent in the middle of the compound were several young children and a woman.

The drone overhead watched as the operators went from dead man to dead man, looking for their target. Minutes later came the call. "Jackpot. I say again, jackpot."

"Roger," Votel answered, a smile coming across his face. This mission had been a long time in coming.

On target the chaos was subsiding. The gunfire had stopped, but the clock was ticking. By now the Syrians were aware the Americans had crossed the border. It was time to go.

Picking up the body of Abu Ghadiya, the assaulters exited the compound, boarded the helos, and within three minutes were back in Iraq. The total time of the mission was seventeen minutes.

I made my reports to the White House and Petraeus, and then I went back to focusing on the rest of the war.

Later that evening, in accordance with Islamic tradition, Ghadiya's body was cleaned, wrapped in white linen, prayed over by an imam, and buried facing Mecca. The grave, somewhere in the Iraqi desert, was left unmarked so his followers could not turn his burial site into a shrine.

Through the courage of the Army task force operators and the decisiveness of the President of the United States, one of the greatest threats to U.S. and Iraqi lives had been eliminated. As we approached the 2008 presidential elections, I wondered how the new man in the Oval Office would respond to such a challenge. Would he have the same level of commitment against our enemies? Would he take the same level of tactical and strategic risks? Would he put his reputation and that of the nation in the hands of his special operations forces? Would he allow us to continue our global manhunt?

As fortune would have it, it wouldn't take long for me to find out.

CHAPTER FOURTEEN

HIGH SEAS HOSTAGE

BAGRAM, AFGHANISTAN
April 8, 2009

I t was out of place in the world of tents, sprung shelters, and single-story berthing huts, but it was possibly the most important building in the war on terrorism. The Plywood Palace, built in 2004 by Navy Seabees, was a two-story wooden structure and the Afghanistan headquarters of my task force. The building had twenty or so rooms, nothing fancy, just plywood and framing, but over the years the Plywood Palace had been upgraded with state-of-the-art technology.

The main command center on the first floor, referred to as the Joint Operations Center, was a large open room with over 150 people working behind computers, controlling aircraft, calling in medevacs, monitoring and directing drones, coordinating with the regional commanders, and orchestrating the thousand little decisions that go into a successful mission.

The wall on the far end of the command center was thirty feet high and covered from top to bottom with flat-screen monitors. Every mission was observed. Every soldier was tracked. Every radio call was monitored. Every round fired was noticed. There was not a moment during any evening when real-life drama was not unfolding in front of your eyes.

In the center of the large room, the Ranger Regimental Commander, an Army colonel, sat in a swivel chair, headphones on, coffee in hand, calling out commands as he directed the task force's tactical fight in Afghanistan. With him was a small army of majors, captains, and noncommissioned officers all helping to ensure success on the battlefield.

By 2009, we were conducting five to ten missions a night, from the Hindu Kush in northeast Afghanistan to Helmand Province in the south. As the task force commander, I reviewed and approved all the daily missions in Afghanistan, but my main job was to look at the fight from a global perspective. We had ongoing missions in Iraq, Yemen, Somalia, North Africa, and the Philippines. Already this year, we had taken the fight to Al Qaeda in Yemen and Somalia and chased terrorists across Mali and Nigeria.

On the second floor of the Plywood Palace was my office and a smaller command center referred to as the Situational Awareness Room (SAR). The name was misleading. We didn't just keep aware of the global situation; from my plywood desk, with an array of video feeds, secure communications, and an unending supply of energy drinks and peanut M&M's, I could command forces anywhere in the world—and did so routinely.

"Never too early for a Rip It, is it, sir?"

I popped the top on my highly caffeinated, chemically infused fizzy orange-flavored energy drink and nodded toward the SAR NCO, who was just starting the morning shift. "The breakfast of champions," I said, downing my first gulp.

I wasn't a morning guy. When I joined the SEAL Teams they told me that we would be working at night. I like the nights. The mornings—not so much. Although in truth, it wasn't really morning anymore. The bright red LED clock showed 1000 hours, Zulu time, or Greenwich Mean Time. Everyone in the task force worked on a common time zone: Zulu time. That way, no matter where you were in the world, from Somalia to Washington, D.C., we all had the same reference point when it came to the clock.

The night before had been fairly routine. The Rangers and SEALs hit five different targets across Afghanistan, from a Taliban compound in Kandahar, to a suspected Al Qaeda hideout in Konar, to a predator strike in Wardak. In Iraq, our Army task force elements and our British colleagues were continuing their nightly raids on Al Qaeda forces from Baghdad to Basra. Several of the boys had been wounded, but nothing too serious.

I had departed the SAR around 2300. Some missions were still in progress, but as usual, unless something critical was going on—a hostage rescue, a mass casualty, a missile strike, or an assault on a politically sensitive target—I generally left the tactical fight to the colonels. I knew that the Ranger regimental commander, who was as good a warfighter as anyone in the task force, would make all the right decisions. The same was true for the Army task force commander running the fight in Iraq.

I was in my rack by midnight. By 0600, I was rolling out of bed and on my way to the gym. Even at that hour, the large sprung shelter, filled with weights and cardio equipment, was packed. After a quick shower and breakfast, I headed off to my office, checked my emails, and then shuffled over to the SAR.

On the video screens were the results of last night's missions. I reviewed the casualty reports and got an update on the wounded. It looked to be just another day in the war zone.

"Good morning, sir," came the familiar voice of my chief of staff.

"Morning, Randy," I said, downing my last sip of Rip It. "How'd your Red Sox fare last night?"

"Good, sir. They beat the Rays 5 to 3. Their bats were strong and the bullpen looked sharp. But it's a long season."

As my chief of staff, Colonel Randy Copeland was in charge of running the camp in Afghanistan. He handled all the administrative and logistics issues that go with managing a large deployed force. Copeland was a former infantry officer, older than most of my colonels and a bit stocky. He had a dry sense of humor and he used it to great effect in keeping morale high during the tough times. He loved to harass everyone in the SAR, myself included.

Copeland pulled up a chair beside me, looked me in the eye, and didn't say a word. He just stared for a few seconds.

"What...?" I asked.

Copeland dropped his head to his chest. "Sir, the gate guards are at it again."

"You've got to be kidding me!"

"They stopped General Khan and his men at the gate. They won't let them in."

Ali Khan was a general in the Afghan Army and my liaison to the Afghan senior staff. Every day he traveled an hour from Kabul to be at our command center. He and his officers helped coordinate our combat missions with the Afghans in the various districts. They were indispensable in the fight. However, the American guards at the main gate to Bagram Air Base always stopped Khan and questioned him for hours.

"Get the base commander on the phone! I'm really getting tired of this shit," I said.

"Sir, I've already sent the sergeant major down to get General Khan. We'll have him here in a few minutes."

"We can't keep doing this every day, Randy. Get this damn thing solved."

"Yes sir," Copeland responded.

"I'm rounding up all the gate guards. I have the firing squad standing by and I intend to have them shot at dawn. I assume you're okay with that?"

"Absolutely!" I said. "And just to make the point, don't give them blindfolds!"

Copeland hopped up from the chair, gave me a crisp salute and a wry smile, and left the SAR. Somehow I knew he would get the problem solved and no executions would be required.

As Copeland departed, the SAR NCO leaned over from the back row to get my attention. "Sir, the Joint Staff just called. They are requesting a video teleconference in one hour."

"What's the subject?" I asked.

"Apparently an American ship has been boarded by pirates off the coast of Somalia. They don't have a lot of details right now."

"Roger. Let's get the usual suspects assembled and see if Fort Bragg has any additional information."

"Roger, sir. Will do."

For years, Somalia had been a breeding ground for pirates. Thousands of ships passed through the Gulf of Aden every year, and a huge volume of merchant traffic came through the Red Sea. This year alone, Somali pirates had attacked more than two hundred ships, with 263 crewmen being taken hostage. Most of the ships and their crew were taken to an anchorage point off the Somali coast where they waited, sometimes for years, before the shipping company negotiated their release. I never understood why the shipping companies didn't hire a bunch of "good ol' boys" with deer rifles to stave off pirate attacks or just sail farther away from shore. When I asked the obvious question, I was told that ships weren't allowed to enter port if they were carrying firearms and that it was more cost-effective to pay the ransom than to sail several hundred miles off the planned course. Still, none of it made sense to me.

Within the hour, my entire staff was gathered in the SAR for the VTC.

"Good afternoon, sir," came the voice over the video screen.

"Scotty, how are you?"

"Just another day in paradise, sir."

Colonel Scott Miller was the Deputy Director for Special Operations and the former commander of the Army task force element. Stan McChrystal had brought him to the Pentagon when McChrystal became the Joint Staff Director of Operations. Miller was exceptionally talented. A seasoned operator, he was on the ground as a young officer during the fight in Mogadishu in 1993, and since then he had been in constant combat in all the hot spots around the world. In 2004, I had pinned a Purple Heart on his chest after he sustained wounds during an ambush in Iraq. He was as good as they came.

"What do we have, Scotty?"

"Sir, here's what we know." Miller paused and looked down at his briefing notes. "Early this morning, a large U.S.-flagged cargo ship, the *Maersk Alabama*, was taken over by Somali pirates."

On the video screen to the left of Miller's picture, my SAR NCO brought up a recent photo of the *Maersk Alabama*.

"From what we understand, the crew attempted to resist, but the pirates were able to board anyway. We don't have the exact details, but the captain, a guy named Richard Phillips, has been taken hostage."

"Hostage aboard the ship?" I asked.

"No sir. The pirates left the *Maersk Alabama* in a lifeboat and took Phillips with them."

"What kind of lifeboat?"

The SAR NCO spoke up. "Sir, I've got a picture right here." Onscreen was a small twenty-eight-foot orange vessel with an enclosed top. It was the standard lifeboat found on most merchant ships.

"How many pirates do we think there are?"

"Sir, the crew reports there are four pirates and the captain in that lifeboat," Miller responded.

"How far is the nearest U.S. naval vessel?"

"Sir, the *Bainbridge*, the *Halyburton*, and the *Boxer* are in the Gulf. The Chairman has directed them to start moving toward the coast of Somalia."

"What's their ETA?"

"It will take them about twenty-four hours to be on station."

I turned to the SAR NCO. "Do we have Captain Moore on the line?"

The SAR NCO nodded.

"Scott, are you up?" I asked, speaking into virtual space.

"Sir, I'm here," said Moore, his face appearing on the screen.

Captain Scott Moore was the commanding officer of our Navy SEAL task force. Known as "Go to War Moore," he was professionally aggressive and loved to be in the fight. He was a world-class mountain climber, incredibly fit, and tactically very sound. He had recently turned over the Afghanistan task force commander position to a Ranger colonel after two years of a long, tough fight. Under his command, his SEALs and Rangers had taken hundreds of enemy off the battlefield, but had also lost ten of their own. It had been a vicious fight against a determined enemy, and he was now back home in his day job, commanding officer of a SEAL Group.

"Scott, who do we have nearby that can be on scene quickly?"

"Sir, we have Jonas Kelsall in Nairobi. He's got a team of about seven SEALs that could link up with the *Bainbridge* within six hours."

I knew Kelsall. He was a SEAL lieutenant commander, a fabulous young man who had done some enlisted time and then gone back to the University of Texas in order to get his bachelor's degree and his Navy commission.

"Bill, this is Shortney."

I heard the familiar voice of Vice Admiral Bill "Shortney" Gortney, the 5th Fleet commander, stationed in Bahrain.

"Shortney, didn't know you were with us."

"I've been listening in," he said, his picture appearing from a conference room in Bahrain. "Just wanted you to know that anything I've got is yours for the asking."

Gortney had become a good friend and a very reliable ally in the war on terrorism. He had no ego when it came to getting the job done.

"Thanks, Shortney. Not sure what we need just yet, but never worry, I won't hesitate to ask."

I returned to talking with Scotty Miller. "Scotty, just so I understand the chain of command here. Am I in charge of this mission?"

"Yes sir," Miller responded, knowing that putting me in charge would give me access to all the military resources I needed.

"Sir, the Chairman would like a Concept of Operations within the hour, but he and the Secretary have authorized me to move whatever forces you think appropriate at this time to set the conditions for the rescue."

"Roger, Scotty. Let me work with my staff and Scott Moore and we'll be back with you in the hour. In the meantime, let's just keep the video teleconference up and running."

"Sounds good, sir. I'll pass on everything to General McChrystal. My guess is that the Chairman will also sit in on the next briefing."

"No problem. See you again in an hour."

There were a dozen or so stations on the current videoconference, from the Joint Staff, to the State Department, to CIA, FBI, NGA, DIA, Fort Bragg, and a number of military combatant commanders—too many folks to have a candid conversation.

I turned to the SAR NCO. "Set up a point-to-point from my office to Captain Moore."

"Yes sir."

I moved to my office next door and took a few of my key staff with me. The office was large, plywood of course, and had room for ten personnel to gather around a video screen for conferences. I often had teleconferences with the White House and Joint Staff from my office to avoid the appearance that my entire staff was listening in.

As Moore appeared on the screen, he began talking immediately. "Sir, we contacted Jonas. He and his guys have all their kit, to include their freefall chutes, and can be ready to launch within the hour."

I always marveled at our organization. Lieutenant Commander Kelsall and his team were in Nairobi as part of our special operations liaison element. They were in Kenya to coordinate our operations against the Somali terrorist organization Al Shabaab. But no matter where SEALs went, they always took their parachutes for contingencies just like this. Rarely were those parachutes needed, but now the policy was about to pay off.

"All right, Scott, let's work with our liaison at 5th Fleet and coordinate a rendezvous between Team Nairobi and the *Bainbridge* as soon as the ship arrives on station."

"Admiral, I would also like to launch the entire hostage rescue package from Norfolk. We can be on station in twenty-two hours."

"How many folks are we talking about?"

"Well, sir," Moore said sheepishly, "about sixty operators and four High Speed Assault Craft."

"Sixty? What in the world are you going to do with sixty operators? It's five guys in a lifeboat."

"Well, sir, I've been thinking."

"Oh, that's probably not good," I deadpanned.

"Sir, my concern is if the pirates take Phillips across the beach we will lose him for months, and possibly forever."

"Continue."

"Well, sir, with the additional SEALs and support from the Cobras on the MEU, we can ensure that there are no pirates left ashore to receive him." Moore pulled up a picture of the Somali coastline and flashed it up on our shared screen. "Almost all the pirates are operating out of Eyl. There are about six or seven different camps spread up and down the coast. Our sources tell us that these guys all report to a head pirate named Alam. We are working with the FBI and the Agency to track down the headman's exact location, but we think he lives inland and is reachable."

I knew Moore was right, but I also thought that the Joint Staff and the White House would never approve that large a force to rescue one man from a lifeboat.

"Okay, Scott. Go ahead and get the large package ready to move.

We have another video teleconference with the Chairman in about an hour. We can broach it with him at that time."

Moore smiled, knowing I liked the concept and would push it hard with the Joint Staff.

"In the meantime, let's get a Concept of Operations knocked out. I want it simple as usual: one slide on the situation showing the location of the lifeboat and the position of the *Halyburton* and *Bainbridge*; one slide on the intelligence regarding the pirates and their chain of command; one slide on the size of the rescue force and your planned movement from CONUS."

My operations officer chimed in from behind me. "Sir, we probably need to let the Chairman know that Team Nairobi is linking up with the *Bainbridge*."

"Roger. Scott, did you catch that?"

"Yes sir. Include the Team Nairobi piece."

"And then let's get the JAGs to do the usual rules of engagement slide." I looked around the room at my staff. "Anything else?"

No one spoke up.

"Okay, one hour. See you then, Scott."

The screen went blank.

Every screen in the SAR was glowing with activity. Kelsall and Team Nairobi were being tracked on the far left display. A map showed the GPS progress of their small plane as it moved from Nairobi to the coast of Somalia. They were two hours from rendezvous with the *Bainbridge*. The next display showed a live feed with the location of all U.S. naval vessels in the area. Marked with tiny icons and a callout box, it presented the ship's name, current latitude and longitude, and estimated speed. The *Bainbridge* and *Halyburton* were steaming at twenty knots toward the lifeboat. On the center screen was a conference room in the Pentagon. I could see Scotty Miller and other members of the Joint Staff preparing for the arrival of the Chairman. To the right of the center screen was the first slide of the Concept of Operations brief, and to the far right was an air traffic control picture of all the drones operating in the Horn of Africa. While we had ongoing missions in Yemen, we didn't have any Predator or Reaper drones available in the immediate vicinity. All the live video would have to come directly from the *Bainbridge's* ScanEagle drone.

On the center screen, I could see Miller and the other officers come to attention. The Chairman had entered the room. Tall, distinguished, with jet black hair, he was dressed in his khaki uniform, the four stars of a full admiral adorning each collar. Mullen always reminded me of the great fleet admirals of World War II. I could envision him on the deck of a battleship heading to Midway.

"Good afternoon, William."

"Good afternoon, sir."

"Who else is on the VTC?"

I went quickly through the roll call, but made a point of singling out General Petraeus, the CENTCOM commander. While I was technically in charge now, as soon as this mission was over, I would go back to working for him, so I was careful to ensure that he was involved every step of the way.

After a few niceties, I jumped right into the brief. "Sir, we have Team Nairobi headed to an at-sea rendezvous with the *Bainbridge*. They should be aboard the ship within two hours. Intel tells us that the pirates are trying to make their way back to their base camp. However, the lifeboat only makes two to three knots, so we won't have a problem intercepting them well before they hit landfall."

I could see Miller showing the Chairman a PowerPoint slide of the current position of the lifeboat and the estimated intercept point by the *Bainbridge*.

"Sir, we also know that the pirates are in communication with a man named Mohammad, who is located in Somaliland. They are asking for a high-speed boat so they can transfer Captain Phillips out of the lifeboat and get to shore before the U.S. Navy arrives."

"What do you need from me, Bill?"

"Well, sir, I have been talking with Scott Moore, and we would like to bring the entire hostage rescue package from the States."

Miller leaned in and whispered something to the Chairman.

"So, that's sixty operators and four boats?"

"Yes sir. And with that large a package we would need to bring the *Boxer* along with the *Bainbridge* and *Halyburton*. The *Boxer* could berth the sixty operators and put the High Speed Assault Crafts on the flight deck."

"What do you plan to do with all these SEALs?" the Chairman asked, his eyes narrowing just a bit.

"Sir, there are over two hundred hostages being held on the Somali coast. Most of them near the anchorage point at Eyl."

Miller was pointing to something on one of the screens in the Pentagon briefing room, and I assumed it was the location of Eyl.

"Additionally, there are half a dozen other pirate enclaves up and down the coast of Somalia."

The Chairman continued to look at the screen in the Pentagon.

"Sir, I think it's time we solved this problem once and for all. If we continue to let these pirates dictate the flow of merchant traffic around the Horn it will distract from our efforts in Iraq and Afghanistan and put hundreds more Americans at risk of capture."

I could see the Chairman mulling over the idea, but he knew it was a stretch for the new President to authorize so aggressive an operation. No matter how well it went, the potential for American servicemen to get killed or wounded was very high. Still . . . the idea had merit and I think the Chairman knew it.

"Okay, Bill. Let's prepare the briefing for the White House and see what they say."

"Roger, sir," I replied, and moments later we signed off from the VTC.

April 9, 2009

"Jumpers away!" came the call from the SAR NCO.

Five thousand feet above the deep blue Indian Ocean, Jonas Kelsall and his men exited the small aircraft. Tumbling slightly forward as they dove off the ramp of the plane, they immediately pulled their ripcords, deploying their main parachutes. Gathering in the air under their square canopies, the SEALs floated down in formation, landing close together in the choppy sea. Bobbing erratically in the water, a small boat from USS *Bainbridge* was standing by to retrieve them. Within the hour, Kelsall and the commanding officer of the *Bainbridge*, Commander Frank Castellano, had developed a plan to gather intelligence in the event a rescue was necessary. Castellano was an exceptional Surface Warfare Officer and would be involved in every aspect of the rescue.

"Sir, the *Bainbridge* has communication with the pirates."

I nodded and watched intently on the screen as the small Zodiac carrying Kelsall and a few other SEALs approached the lifeboat.

"The leader has okayed the transfer of food and water."

We were receiving a video feed from the *Bainbridge*'s ScanEagle drone. Even across the thousands of miles from Somalia to the SAR in Afghanistan, the picture was remarkably clear.

Aboard the *Bainbridge*, a Somali interpreter was talking with the head pirate, Abduwali Muse. Muse's voice was strained and it was clear that the oppressive heat inside the small lifeboat was beginning to take its toll on both Phillips and the pirates. The interpreter had convinced Muse that they should accept the U.S. Navy's offer of food and water to keep their hostage alive. Muse had readily accepted.

"Slowly, slowly," I muttered to myself as the Zodiac edged closer to the lifeboat. The hatch on the lifeboat opened and one of the pirates leaned outward, the barrel of his AK-47 pointed toward the American sailors. Inching forward, the bow of the Zodiac bumped the stern of the lifeboat and I could see the SEALs and the pirates talking. Soon the food and water were transferred and the Zodiac pulled away. Within minutes we were getting reports from Kelsall.

"Sir, the SEALs report that Phillips is fine. But the pirates seem intent on reaching the coast of Somalia."

My intelligence officer chimed in. "Admiral, we're getting intercepts that the pirates are calling for reinforcements from Eyl. They know they can't reach the shore in the lifeboat. Apparently another high-speed skiff is moving in their direction."

Part of me was hoping that the reinforcements would show up. The .50-caliber gunner on the deck of the *Bainbridge* would love the opportunity to show off his skill set. It would not go well for the pirates.

Throughout the day, the *Bainbridge* was in constant contact with the pirate leader, Abduwali Muse. While our interpreter and Muse appeared to be developing a rapport, Muse still threatened to kill Phillips if we attempted a rescue. As the heat of the day wore on, I knew tensions inside the small lifeboat were getting high. With temperatures soaring to over a hundred degrees, the pirates would occasionally jump in the water to cool off. But there was no sign of Captain Phillips.

I straightened up in my chair as Admiral Mullen came on the VTC. "William, the President has authorized the deployment of the SEALs," he said. "But he also wants a deliberate action plan for how you intend to rescue Phillips."

I looked up on my video screen at the tiny twenty-eight-foot lifeboat gently rolling across the ocean waves. It barely had enough room for the five men inside. This wasn't a cruise liner where the SEALs could fast-rope from a helicopter or assault from the sea.

"Sir," I said, with an unintended tone of frustration, "it's a lifeboat."

"I understand, Bill, but the White House wants a deliberate action plan and William—" He paused. "You will give them a deliberate action plan."

As always, Mullen had a sly smile that meant he understood my predicament.

"Yes sir," I said, somewhat reluctantly. "We will get you a deliberate action plan."

"By tomorrow."

"Yes sir, by tomorrow."

Mullen left and we talked through the next steps with Scott Miller and the Joint Staff. Scott Moore and his SEALs would be arriving the following morning, April 10. The sixty SEALs and their four High Speed Assault Craft would parachute from four C-17 cargo planes, land in the water near USS *Boxer*, and be brought aboard the ship.

Vice Admiral Bill Gortney had CHOPed (change of operational control) the small fleet of ships to my control. Surrounding the lifeboat were the large-deck amphibious ship USS *Boxer*, the guided missile destroyer USS *Bainbridge*, and fast frigate USS *Halyburton*. Together they formed Combined Task Force 151 (CTF 151), commanded by Rear Admiral Michelle Howard. Admiral Howard was an exceptionally capable commander, and her leadership throughout the hostage rescue would prove essential to our success.

As the day ended off the coast of Somalia, we just watched and waited, hoping for an opportunity to end the standoff.

I grabbed another Rip It from the small refrigerator in the SAR and took a quick sip. It had been almost forty-eight hours since the beginning of the hostage crisis and I hadn't stepped away from my desk except to use the head. It was almost 0330 in Afghanistan, making it two o'clock in the morning off the coast of Somalia. At that time of the night, the infrared picture of the small lifeboat slowly motoring across the vast ocean was lulling everyone to sleep.

"Admiral, Admiral. Something's happening!"

On the screen, there was a figure in the water, the heat signature strong against the cooler temperature of the ocean. Was it just another pirate cooling himself down from the nighttime heat?

"What's the *Bainbridge* saying?" I asked.

"Sir, they are seeing the same thing we are, but they can't tell who is in the water."

"The boat's turning."

It was clear now that something was happening. The pirates were moving around the edge of the small lifeboat, waving their hands frantically.

"Shots fired! Shots fired!" came the call from the SAR NCO.

On the infrared picture, the water around the lifeboat churned green as the propeller spun hard, the small boat turning abruptly.

"Admiral, the *Bainbridge* reports that Captain Phillips is in the water."

"Roger," I acknowledged, watching as the figure in the ocean struggled to get some distance from the bow of the little boat. Rarely have I felt so helpless. The *Bainbridge* was too far away to be of assistance and no SEAL Quick Reaction Force was going to save Phillips at that moment.

Within minutes the escape had been thwarted. Phillips was dragged back into the lifeboat and any chance of freedom that night was over. I knew that his captors would not go easy on him.

On the *Bainbridge*, the Somali interpreter made immediate contact with Muse. If Captain Phillips was harmed, he told Muse, the pirates would pay a very high price. Muse seemed to understand. This was a business deal for the pirates. They didn't want Phillips to die any more than they wanted to die themselves, but a miscalculation on either side's part could result in tragedy. We continued to play it safe, waiting for an opportunity, an opening, however slim it might be.

"That's your deliberate plan?" Mullen asked.

"Yes sir, that's it," I responded.

During the night I had called Vice Admiral Mike Miller at the U.S. Naval Academy and asked him to provide me their best naval architect, someone who could tell me whether ramming the lifeboat with the bow of our heavily reinforced High Speed Assault Craft (HSAC) would crack the hull and cause the lifeboat to sink. Miller woke up one of his faculty members, whom we spirited away to an undisclosed location so he could do his calculations. By early morning, I had my answer. Ramming the HSAC into the lifeboat would not cause it to sink.

"So, let me make sure I understand this, William. Your deliberate action plan calls for you to ram the lifeboat with the HSAC, sending everyone inside tumbling around, and then the SEALs jump in and shoot the pirates and rescue Phillips. Do I have that right?"

Somehow when Mullen said it, it didn't sound so clever.

"Sir, it's a lifeboat," I said respectfully. "There really isn't going to be an opportunity for a deliberate action."

"So how will this unfold?"

"Sir, sooner or later the lifeboat will run out of gas, probably by tomorrow. Once that happens, we own the tempo of the operation. The pirates will need food and water. That will give us an opportunity to engage with them and possibly convince them to give us Phillips back. If that doesn't work, once the SEALs arrive on scene, we will have snipers available to take out the pirates if the situation presents itself. But however this unfolds, sir, we will be patient and we won't rush to failure."

Mullen nodded. He knew we would do the right thing and not jeopardize Phillips's life.

"Sir, I have been talking with Scott Moore. He says this is the most difficult tactical problem he's seen in his career. It would actually be easier to take down the *Maersk Alabama* than the single lifeboat. The lifeboat has only one main entry point, and trying to gain the element of surprise is very difficult."

Mullen nodded. "Bill, I will be briefing the Secretary and the White House later today. Just keep Colonel Miller posted."

As Mullen rose and left the room, I knew that sooner than later, this crisis would be coming to an end. The pirates were running out of options, and that would give us the opportunity we needed.

Throughout Friday, April 10, we kept up pressure on the pirates. Playing a little good cop, bad cop, we used the helos from the *Bainbridge* and *Halyburton* to buzz the lifeboat, while at the same time offering food and water as we gathered more intelligence on the situation. I wanted to push the pirates to an uncomfortable place, but not push too hard.

At 1800 Friday evening we confirmed again that Phillips was okay, albeit dog tired from the heat and constant harassment. The sun was setting over Somalia and the moon was already up.

"Shots fired! Shots fired!"

I looked at the lifeboat, but nothing seemed to be happening. No one was in the water, and there was not a lot of commotion. Within minutes, the *Bainbridge* reported that Phillips was okay. Apparently one of the pirates had accidentally discharged his weapon. The night ended and the lifeboat continued to motor slowly toward the shore.

Saturday, April 11

"Jumpers away. Jumpers away."

It was a beautiful sight to see. Catapulting off the back of the ramp of the C-17 was a forty-foot High Speed Assault Craft, and behind it dozens of light blue canopies, all following the craft into the water below. The two giant cargo planes that had delivered the SEALs from the States now banked slowly to the left, dipped their wings as a sign of respect, and headed back to Dover. Within an hour, Captain Scott Moore and his sixty-man team were aboard USS *Boxer*, with the four HSACs tied up alongside.

"Admiral, good to see you," came the voice of Admiral Michelle Howard over the VTC.

"Great to see you as well, Michelle," I said. "Thanks for taking care of Scott and the boys."

"My pleasure," she said. "I have my entire flag staff here and we are ready to assist in any way possible."

In the room aboard the *Boxer* were about forty personnel: the key members of Task Force 151 from Admiral Howard's command, Scott Moore, and most of his senior officers and enlisted.

The VTC was being broadcast from the command center deep inside the hull of the ship. The steel frame of the vessel interfered with the communications, causing the picture to freeze periodically throughout the conversation.

Moore began. "Sir, I am moving a fifteen-man SEAL troop to the *Bainbridge*. We'll set up on the flight deck and be prepared to take a shot if we get one."

Moore and I both knew that even the best snipers would find it challenging to hit a moving target bobbing in the ocean, but we had to prepare for every contingency.

"I'm also going to stage the HSACs on the back side of the *Boxer* where they won't be seen by the pirates. That way if we have to execute a deliberate plan, they'll be ready as well."

Howard chimed in. "Admiral, we would like to continue the helo overflights and the occasional fire hose treatment if you're okay with that."

The buzzing helos and spraying the lifeboat had been used to good effect so far. The helos and the hoses were irritating to the pirates, but not too threatening, and the hoses had the positive effect of keeping the lifeboat a bit cooler.

"Sounds good, Michelle. Just let me know if the pirates start getting riled up. I don't want to push them too far."

"Roger, sir. Understand," she replied.

Onscreen I could see that Moore was chatting with his staff, asking them if there was anything else they needed to relay to me. Negative nods all around.

"Well, boss. I think that's all we have for right now. Anything else you want us to do?"

While I didn't think it was really necessary, I reinforced the obvious. "Scott, as always, let's just move slowly and deliberately. We don't want anything to compromise the hostage. Keep up the pressure, own the tempo, and look for opportunities. I know the boys will do the right thing when the time comes."

"Yes sir. I understand."

I knew he did.

We signed off on the VTC and I went back to the SAR. A new crew of enlisted personnel had come on duty to man the computers and video screens, but all of my key personnel were still in their same seats.

"Hey," I said with a tone of authority, "you guys need to get some rest. This could be a long haul and I want to make sure everyone stays sharp."

No one moved. In fact, no one looked up from their computers.

"Is anyone listening?" I asked.

"Yes sir. Heard every word," Copeland said, still typing away on his keyboard.

Still, no one moved.

"Screw you guys," I said. "I hope you all die of Red Bull poisoning."

Copeland snickered and slid me a new can of orange Rip It.

"Just so we don't die alone," he said, smiling.

Sunday, April 12

"Sir, they are out of gas, low on food and water, and starting to get very agitated. I don't know how far we can push them," Moore said.

"Any sense they are willing to bargain yet?" I asked.

"I think the head guy might be willing to talk at this point, but his fellow pirates are getting pretty hostile. They had all hoped for reinforcements from Eyl, but my guess is they know those aren't coming. They're trapped and are looking for a way out, but trapped men have a way of acting irrationally, and we will have to be careful moving forward."

"Scott's right," Howard chimed in. "Last night they threatened to kill Phillips and then they began firing at the *Bainbridge*. They were just in a pissed-off mood. We settled them down, but it was tense for a while."

"So, let's think through this," I said. "What will it take to convince them to give us Phillips back?"

"Money," the intel officer said without hesitation. "That's their mission. If they return to Somalia without a hostage and without money, then they and their families will pay a steep price. Their life is on the line now. They can't back down."

"Okay. Then we convince them that we are willing to negotiate."

"They know the U.S. government won't negotiate," Moore said.

"Yeah, but they probably think Maersk will."

"Admiral," the intel guy spoke up. "Muse seems reasonable enough. I think we can convince him to come aboard the *Bainbridge* and talk about a deal."

"Unfortunately, he may be the only reasonable pirate in the boat, and I hate to leave Phillips with the other three psychopaths," I said.

"Michelle, Scott. What do you think?"

"It's worth a try," Howard offered.

"I agree," Moore said. "And if there is any way to get the lifeboat closer to the *Bainbridge*, we could have an opportunity for a shot."

"Okay, let's lure them in with the chance of a payout and see if Muse is willing to talk."

"Roger, sir," Moore responded. "We'll get on the bridge-to-bridge and see if Muse is interested."

The large flat-screen TV in the SAR seemed to glow brightly as the sunlight reflected off the blue waters of the Indian Ocean. In the middle of the screen, a small black Zodiac carrying a few of the SEAL operators approached the lifeboat. Concealed underneath some blankets were an assortment of M-4s and MP5s, both for protection and just in case the right moment presented itself.

Long into this standoff, I had given the SEALs the authority to take action if they felt a rescue was warranted. You have to trust the guys on the ground, or in this case, on the water. As a commander, you would like to be in ultimate control of all the decisions. But the reality is, you can't be. In a hostage crisis situation, there are too many factors that unfold too quickly to have to ask, *"Mother, may I?"* You set the conditions as best you can. You give the authority to the ground force commander and you hope that the experience and the maturity of the operators will win the day. Most of the time, it does.

Onscreen I could see the SEAL in the Zodiac talking to Muse. As the Zodiac bumped against the bow of the lifeboat, the SEALs began transferring food and water through the open hatch. The conversation lasted for several minutes. Muse, his head visible through the hatch, would talk with the SEAL and then turn to confer with his fellow pirates.

"Sir, the *Bainbridge* reports that Muse is willing to come aboard and talk."

I nodded without answering. Leaning toward the video screen, I squinted and watched as the SEAL held out his hand and grabbed Muse as he leapt from the lifeboat onto the Zodiac. There was a final exchange between Muse and his men and then the Zodiac slowly pulled away, beginning its short transit back to the *Bainbridge*.

Over the next hour, Muse sat on the helo deck of the *Bainbridge*, drank Coca-Colas, and, using a Somali interpreter, talked with the SEALs. Through some very carefully arranged conversations, the negotiator convinced him that it would be best to allow the *Bainbridge* to hook up a towline with the lifeboat. Exhausted from days at sea and realizing that his small boat and men were drifting away from the mainland, Muse inexplicably agreed. It was exactly the break we were looking for.

On board the lifeboat, the situation was getting tenser. The remaining pirates could see Muse lounging on the helo deck, drinking Cokes, eating chow, and seeming to enjoy himself. A short time later the *Bainbridge* hooked up the towline and they were dragging the tiny boat up and down through the ship's wake, making life more miserable for the pirates.

Onscreen, Moore was relaying his plan. "Sir, as expected, the pirates are getting seasick on the long towline, so we have offered to pull them inside the wake to reduce the rolling motion."

"And they agreed?" I said, somewhat astounded.

"Yes sir. They agreed," Moore said, equally amazed.

"Can we get them close enough for a good shot?"

"Well, boss." He paused as if to think through his answer. "I have three of my best snipers positioned on the fantail of the *Bainbridge*. If the shot is there, we'll take it. But…"

"But what?"

"But it's going to be tough. The sun is going down, the boat is moving both side to side and up and down, and the only shots will be through the portholes."

"Yeah, but other than that, it should be easy, right?"

Moore smiled. "Yes sir, other than that—it should be easy."

"All right, Scott. It's all yours."

I signed off. There wasn't anything I could do at this point but trust Scott Moore and the SEALs on the *Bainbridge*.

My executive officer and right-hand man, Lieutenant Colonel Pat Ellis, sidled up beside me. "Sir, it could be a long night. Why don't you head to the gym and get in a short PT. That will help recharge you. I'll come grab you if anything happens."

"Not a bad idea, Pat. But the first whiff of action, come running."

"Will do, sir."

I closed my computer, walked down the flight of stairs, out past the soldier on duty, and back to my B-Hut. The B-Hut was my refuge. Four plywood walls in a room not much bigger than a walk-in closet, but it was home. It was quiet. It was clean. Inside the walls no one was yelling about shots fired or enemy killed or civilians dead or soldiers dying. Inside the walls no one was looking for guidance, expecting a decision, asking for direction. Inside the walls of the B-Hut it was a different world. But I could never stay long. Because outside the B-Hut was where I belonged.

I changed into my PT gear and walked out into the cool evening air. When you weren't getting rocketed by some hacked-off Taliban, the nights in Afghanistan were beautiful. Stars filled the sky, the mountain peaks were visible in the moonlight, and there was a calmness that made you forget there was a war going on all around you.

The giant sprung shelter that housed the gym was filled twenty-four hours a day. It always smelled of rubber mats, sweat, and just a tinge of loneliness. No sooner had I walked through the door of the gym than Ellis came charging in.

"Admiral! Admiral! You need to come. Now!"

I sprinted out the door, across the wooden sidewalk that connected the B-Huts, and back up the stairs of the Plywood Palace. As I rushed back into the SAR, the NCO was calling out the action.

"Sir, shots fired from inside the lifeboat!"

Taking my seat, I stared at the screen. I knew the snipers were looking for an opening. Just one chance. One opportunity. One small window to rescue Phillips.

In the prone position, lying on a rubber mat, they were peering through their scopes, trying to get a good bead on the pirates, each sniper calling out when he had a clean shot. As the lifeboat moved up and down, the shot picture changed moment to moment. For this to work, all three pirates had to be visible simultaneously. All three snipers had to pull the trigger at the same time. One miss and Phillips would likely die. The crosshairs on the scope of sniper number one lined up on the forehead of the largest pirate. Beside him, sniper number two slowed his breathing, squinted into the scope, and prepared to squeeze the trigger. Sniper number three rolled slightly to his right, leaned into the buttstock, and settled in on his target.

"Sniper One. Target One. Green."

"Sniper Two. Target Two. Green."

"Sniper Three. Target Three... Fuck! Red."

The tiny orange boat bobbing up and down in the wake of the *Bainbridge* came in and out of focus, the profile of Target Three barely visible through the scratched glass of the lifeboat's starboard-side porthole.

"Sniper Three. Target Three... Come on, baby... Come on... Shit! Red."

"Sniper One. Target One. Green."

"Sniper Two. Target Two. Green."

"Sniper Three. Target Three... *Breathe deep, good sight picture...* Green!"

"Execute! Execute! Execute!"

"Shots fired! Shots fired! Shots fired!"

Inside my command center, no one spoke. Minutes passed.

"Admiral," came the voice of Scott Moore. "Phillips is alive!"

Folks in the SAR let out a cheer, but quickly quieted down as the information continued to come in.

"What about the pirates?" I asked.

"Sir, they're all dead," Moore answered.

Not bad shooting, I thought.

"We'll do a quick assessment of Captain Phillips and then move him to the *Boxer* for further evaluation."

"Great job, Scott. Please pass on my thanks to the boys."

Moore was trying to maintain a cool composure onscreen, but it was hard for him to hide his grin.

Thirty minutes later, the screens in the SAR were filled with faces from around the interagency. Scott Moore and Michelle Howard provided a quick debrief. Vice Admiral Bill Gortney would be the public face of the rescue, and together we crafted some talking points and a press release from 5th Fleet. General Petraeus and his staff would make all the appropriate notifications and start working the transfer of Muse to U.S. law enforcement.

But there was one final videoconference with the Joint Staff.

Admiral Mullen, dressed in his blue uniform, strolled into the room, took his seat, and pushed the button to talk.

"Well, William, nice job."

"Thank you, sir," I said. "But you know, it was Scott and his guys. They were magnificent as usual."

"I know. Your guys never cease to amaze me. I think the President is going to call Scott and congratulate him."

"Thanks, sir. I know Scott would appreciate it."

"You look tired, Bill."

I smiled and nodded. "It's been a long couple of days."

"Get some rest, William. You never know what tomorrow will bring."

"No sir," I said, smiling at the thought. "You never know."

I thanked the Chairman and signed off the VTC.

Randy Copeland pulled up a chair beside me. "Sir, you haven't been tracking the days, but it's Easter today."

I looked at the calendar.

"So it is . . . so it is."

"It's what I like best about this job," Copeland said. "Every day you get to do some good. Someone is alive today because the guys did their job. Someone will have a lot more Easters because rough men stood ready to do violence on their behalf."

I appreciated the Orwellian reference. Copeland was right. It's who we were: rough men. Rough men who had to do violence to make the world right. On this Easter Sunday, I wished it weren't so, but even two thousand years after the death of Christ, the nature of mankind had not changed. And rough men were still needed to protect the innocent.

Captain Richard Phillips returned to his family in Norfolk and later was the subject of a major motion picture starring Tom Hanks. Abduwali Muse was sentenced to life in prison by the Eastern District of Virginia. A year later, Captain Scott Moore would make one-star admiral and go back into combat. Colonel Scotty Miller would become a four-star general and in 2018 take command of all U.S. forces in Afghanistan. Commander Frank Castellano made captain and continues to serve. Michelle Howard would go on to be the first female four-star admiral in the history of the U.S. Navy. Tragically, Lieutenant Commander Jonas Kelsall was killed in Afghanistan on August 6, 2011, when Taliban fighters shot down the helicopter he was riding in. A room in the Naval ROTC building at the University of Texas bears his name.

CHAPTER FIFTEEN

MANHUNTING

WASHINGTON, D.C.
September 2009

It never ceased to amaze me how a single person operating out of abject squalor in a fourth-world country could wreak so much havoc on his fellow man, but I saw it time and time again.

Saleh Ali Saleh Nabhan was number three on the FBI's most wanted list. In 1998, he was involved in the planning and execution of the U.S. embassy bombings in Dar es Salaam, Tanzania, and Nairobi, Kenya, that left over 250 people dead. Later, in 2002, Nabhan was responsible for orchestrating suicide attacks on the Paradise Hotel in Mombasa that killed three Israeli tourists and ten Kenyan workers, injuring eighty more. During that same operation, two of his men attempted, unsuccessfully, to shoot down an Israeli charter plane.

U.S. and allied intelligence had been hunting Nabhan since 1998, but his tradecraft was exceptional. Nabhan never used any technical device, a phone or computer. He rarely stayed in one place for more than twenty-four hours, and he always used couriers or cutouts to ensure some separation between himself and a potential threat. It was also helpful to Nabhan that after 9/11, our intelligence focus shifted from tracking a terrorist like him to more notable threats like bin Laden, Ayman al-Zawahiri, and Zarqawi.

However, by 2009 the threat of Al Qaeda had metastasized. Terrorist organizations like Al Shabaab in Somalia had aligned themselves with bin Laden and were attempting more global operations to expand their brand. Saleh Nabhan once again became relevant.

★   ★   ★

The Secretary of State, Hillary Clinton, seemed somewhat unsure of my answer. "So, how many operations like this have you conducted?" she asked.

I thought for a moment, paused, and looked at the still frame of the video frozen on the screen in the White House Situation Room.

"Thousands," I responded matter-of-factly.

"Thousands?"

"Yes ma'am, thousands."

I thought again to make sure I wasn't overstating my case. We had been at war for eight years. We were conducting an average of ten missions a day in Iraq and a bit fewer in Afghanistan. At least half of those missions involved helicopter insertions or the use of helicopters for direct assault. Multiply that times 365 days; multiply that times six to eight years. Yep, "thousands" is probably on the short side.

"Ma'am, we do helicopter assaults every single day, multiple times a day. In fact, this kind of direct assault is easier than most."

Minutes earlier the screen in the Situation Room had been filled with two "Little Bird" helicopters swooping in on a fast-moving Iraqi vehicle. The Little Birds, or MH-6s, were the smallest, most agile, and arguably the most lethal helicopters in the special operations inventory. A Plexiglas bubble surrounded the cockpit and inside the cabin there was only enough room for a pilot, copilot, and two passengers. The Little Birds were equipped with skids instead of wheels, and on this mission a pair of SOF operators were sitting on each skid, leaning forward, taking aim at the engine block of the fleeing Toyota Hilux truck.

Moving at over sixty miles an hour, the Hilux rumbled down a dirt road outside Ramadi. A cloud of dust rose fifteen feet in the air as the wheels spun with each evasive turn. Inside, you could see the driver, his face dripping with sweat as he tried to outmaneuver the pursuing helicopters. From the backseat, two men leaned out the window and fired erratically at the helicopters as the Little Birds closed in for the interdiction. Like a well-synchronized aerial ballet, the pilots swung their helicopters into position, each bird on one side of the vehicle, matching the Toyota's speed. From the skids, the snipers took two shots apiece into the engine block of the truck. Within seconds the vehicle rolled to a stop. The helos landed just in front of the truck and the operators unhooked from the skids, jumped from the cabin, and surrounded the two vehicles. The helpless Iraqis tossed their guns from the vehicle and surrendered immediately.

Lasting no more than three minutes, the video had clearly grabbed the attention of President Obama and his national security team. For those in Washington the war was generally viewed from twenty thousand feet. Predator video. Grainy images. Precision bombs exploding on compounds with faceless insurgents killed by technology. For those not used to war, this was a different look—a high-risk chase scene, with real people and real guns. But it also showcased the incredible professionalism and courage of our pilots and special operators.

Everyone in the Situation Room turned to the President. Placing his folded hands on his chin, he looked down at the long table and said thoughtfully, "So Bill, as I understand it, your intent is to move two Navy destroyers off the coast of Somalia." I nodded as he continued. "You're going to use the destroyers as a launch platform for four Little Birds and some SEALs."

"Yes sir."

I could see the President visualizing the mission in his head.

I grabbed the remote and brought up the map of the Somali coast on the screen. "We know from human intelligence that Nabhan travels periodically from Barawe to Marka. While Nabhan doesn't use any technical device, his courier, who we have identified, always carries a phone with him. Our HUMINT source says that Nabhan and the courier will be traveling in a blue four-door sedan on Tuesday of next week."

"Why helicopters?" asked Bob Gates, the Secretary of Defense. "Why not just bring in some fighters and drop a bomb on them?"

It was a question I had anticipated, but I knew the answer would not satisfy those sitting around the table.

"Sir, we don't know exactly when Nabhan will be leaving Barawe. The HUMINT source has given us a compound to watch, but the time window for Nabhan's departure could be anytime throughout Tuesday."

I went back to the map of Somalia. "In order for us to have a fixed-wing strike package overhead, we would have to move the aircraft carrier from the Arabian Sea down off the coast of Somalia. Then we would need two F/A-18 strike aircraft constantly in the air until we identified the blue sedan."

I returned to the map. "It will take two days for the carrier to transit from the Arabian Sea to Somalia—a day to execute the mission and two days for the boat to return. During that time, there will be no Navy aircraft support for either Iraq or Afghanistan. That would put a lot of soldiers in theater at risk."

"Why not just bring a bomber from our base in Al Udeid?" asked one of the back-row participants.

"The problem is twofold. First, timing. We will have about a fifteen-minute window in order to target Nabhan when he is not in a high-collateral-damage area."

I circled the short stretch of road on the map that we had colored green. Our task force targeteers had surveyed every mile of the road to determine the area with the least possibility of civilian casualties. With the exception of that small portion, the rest of Nabhan's route was red—a "no-go" for the operation.

"The second problem is trying to hit a vehicle moving at over forty miles per hour. It can be done, but it's tricky and the potential to miss the target is high."

The expressions on the faces of those sitting around the Situation Room were predictable. *I was not making my case.*

"I'm just concerned about a helicopter raid into Somalia," Secretary Clinton said. "Last time it didn't work out so well."

And there it is. Just as I had worried. Black Hawk Down, October 3, 1993, Mogadishu, Somalia. On that day in October the task force, along with an element of UN soldiers, were attempting to capture lieutenants of Somali warlord Mohammed Farah Aidid when everything went wrong. An hourlong mission turned into the deadliest battle since Vietnam, costing the lives of eighteen American soldiers and the loss of several helicopters. Despite the incredible courage of the special operations forces, the fallout from the battle caused a fundamental shift in U.S. policy abroad, and the memory of that day lingered over every special operations mission involving helicopters.

Now was the time to play my hole card. "I do have a bombing option, but it's experimental, and"—I paused—"at some point I will still have to put helicopters on the ground to retrieve the bodies to ensure it's Nabhan."

Admiral Mike Mullen nodded at me to continue.

"We have been working on a new piece of ordnance that can be dropped from a small airplane and, using laser guidance, can hit a target moving at forty miles per hour. It's only about a thirteen-pound warhead, but it's enough to do the job."

President Obama shifted in his chair and sat upright. "So where would you launch this plane from?"

"Sir, we have a clandestine base in a neighboring country that we would use to stage and launch the aircraft."

"Would that country be witting of our operation?" Clinton asked.

"Yes ma'am. We have already cleared the concept with the U.S. ambassador, who will notify their president before the strike. The ambassador doesn't think there will be any problems getting host nation approval."

Around the table, the mood began to change.

"So, you would drop this small bomb and then the helos would come in and pick up the remains? Is that right?" the President asked.

"Yes sir, that's right. But if I may, sir. I still believe using the helos as the first option is the best approach. If the small bomb misses its target then Nabhan will make a run for it, and that will complicate the mission considerably."

I glanced at Gates and Mullen to see if I had overstepped my bounds. They both remained expressionless. Clinton still seemed concerned, but I sensed she was supportive. Contrary to public perception, I had found Clinton to be almost hawkish. She asked all the hard questions, but never shied away from making the tough recommendations. I liked her style.

"Okay, Bill. Let me think about this," the President said.

"Mr. President, with your permission, sir, I would like to move the destroyers off the coast of Somalia and position the four Little Birds and SEAL assaulters on board. If you decide not to conduct the mission then no harm no foul. But at least they will be in position if you give us the go-ahead."

The President looked at Gates and Mullen, who both nodded in the affirmative. "Okay, Bill. Do what you need to do in order to be prepared."

The President thanked me and then asked me to step out so the principals could talk in private. I lingered outside the Situation Room for twenty minutes until the meeting finally broke up. As the members filed out of the room, General Hoss Cartwright came over to talk.

"I don't think the President is going to approve it, Bill."

I nodded stoically.

"They are worried about helicopters in Somalia." Before I could say anything, Cartwright continued. "I know, I know. But that's just the way it is."

Outside the main entrance of the Situation Room I could see the President still talking with Clinton. He was listening intently. She finished, he thanked her, and then he walked out into the main West Wing corridor.

"Anyway," Cartwright said, "I should have an answer for you within the next day or two."

"Thanks, sir. I appreciate it."

Cartwright departed and Mullen came over to talk with me.

Mullen looked around to ensure no one was listening. "I don't know, Bill. This is a tough one for them. But I think you made a good case. We'll just have to see."

"Yes sir, I understand," I said. "But just so I'm clear. I do have the authority to move the destroyers, the Little Birds, and the assaulters into position off the coast?"

As Mullen started to speak, several senior White House officials were gathering nearby for the next Deputies Committee meeting in the Situation Room. We stepped a bit farther into the corner so no one could hear the conversation.

"Yes," he started. "We discussed the pre-positioning after you left, and everyone agrees that this is a prudent thing to do. The President just needs a day or so to mull over his decision." Mullen smiled. "You're doing a great job, William."

"Thanks, sir," I replied, knowing that when Mullen called me "William," there was no greater expression of his support.

That evening I returned to my headquarters at Fort Bragg. The staff gave me a quick update on all the ongoing combat missions in Iraq and Afghanistan, and by 2200 hours I headed to my quarters on base, exhausted from the overseas travel and time in D.C.

As I opened the front door to my house, I could hear Georgeann on the secure phone upstairs. "He's at work," she said.

"I'm home! I'm home!" I yelled, bounding up the staircase.

Georgeann handed me the phone, covering the receiver. "It's General Cartwright," she said.

I grabbed the phone. "Yes sir."

"Bill, the President gave us the go-ahead."

That didn't take long, I thought.

"Great, sir!"

"But before you take any direct action against Nabhan, you will need final approval from the Secretary."

"No problem, sir. We'll have a twenty-four-hour video tele-conference set up between the Pentagon, the White House, the embassy in Nairobi, and our State Department liaison officer."

"So what's your plan right now?"

"Sir, I am already coordinating with Central Command and Africa Command to reposition the two destroyers off the coast of Somalia. The SEALs and the Little Birds will start moving by C-17 tomorrow, and we should have all the players in place within about seventy-two hours."

"Where will you command the operation from?"

"Sir, I'm heading back to Afghanistan tomorrow. We have a lot going on in theater, but I can easily manage this mission from my headquarters in Bagram."

"All right, Bill, good luck!" Cartwright said and then hung up.

The next morning, I kissed Georgeann goodbye, boarded my jet, and fifteen hours later was back in Bagram, guzzling Rip Its and trying to fight the war.

"He's moving," came the call from the operations officer.

"Roger," I said, watching four people get in the blue sedan and pull away from the compound. The video feed from the Predator zoomed out slightly as the car exited and turned onto a side street.

On another screen was the face of Captain Pete Van Hooser, the commander of the SEAL unit in charge of the mission. Pete had tactical control of the operation. From his command center in Virginia, he could communicate directly with the SEAL assaulters aboard the lead destroyer.

Van Hooser was a remarkable officer. At sixty-two years old, he was the oldest captain in the U.S. Navy. A former Marine, he decided to become a SEAL late in his career. A parachute accident and subsequent complications from the operation left him as a below-the-knee amputee. Still, there was nothing that could stop Pete. He was a good runner, a strong swimmer, and never complained about his disability. He was an inspiration to all who knew him and one of my best commanders.

"Sir, I've got blades turning," Van Hooser said.

"Roger. Blades turning," I responded, watching the blue sedan as it meandered around the small town of Barawe. Van Hooser would keep the helos on deck until we knew for certain that the car was on the coastal road and heading north. The time from launch to interdiction was ten minutes. The flight of the helos would have to be perfectly timed so as not to interfere with the bombing run from the aircraft above, but at the same time be in position to land immediately after the strike. All of this movement would have to be tightly choreographed to occur within the low-collateral-damage area. If Nabhan or one of his lieutenants heard the overhead aircraft or saw the helos before we were ready to strike, he would evade into the nearest town and the mission would be scrubbed. It would be years before we would have another opportunity to get him.

"Is it him?" I asked no one in particular.

My technical intelligence liaison looked at me without expression. "Not sure, sir. All I can tell you is that the device we've been tracking is in that car. I have no way of knowing if Nabhan is with it or not."

This was always our dilemma. We knew Nabhan never carried a phone, and the only way we could identify him was through his courier. If we struck the sedan and it turned out to be the courier and his wife and kids, then I would have to live with that mistake for the rest of my life.

The blue sedan suddenly turned west, heading in the direction of the coastal road. Everyone in the SAR perked up, but for all we knew he could just as easily be going to the market for bread.

"What's the status of Charlie Three Five?"

"Sir, the aircraft is ten minutes out. The Griffin is armed and ready for deployment."

"Joint Staff, this is McRaven," I said, speaking into the small microphone at my desk.

"Yes sir," came the response from an Army two-star manning the video from the Pentagon.

"Request permission to conduct strike operations."

"Sir, Secretary Gates has authorized me to grant approval upon your request. Good luck, sir."

The request for approval was fairly perfunctory. I knew well ahead of time that if the conditions for the operation were met—that is, the blue sedan was heading down the coastal road, strike assets were in place, and low CDE was confirmed—the Secretary would agree to grant permission. But it was a step I had to take to comply with the President's orders. While the blue sedan still wasn't on the coastal road, I didn't want to wait until the last minute.

"Sir, the targeted vehicle has just merged onto the coastal road and is heading north."

I could hear the excitement in the operations officer's voice, but like everyone in the SAR, he tried to remain dispassionate and professional as he called out the checklist for the mission.

"Roger," I replied, watching the blue sedan as it gained speed on the poorly paved road.

If the blue sedan maintained forty miles per hour they would be in the targeted area within fifteen minutes. I looked up at the fifty-inch face of Pete Van Hooser.

"Pete, the Secretary has granted approval. You are cleared hot to execute the mission on your timeline."

"Roger, sir. I understand we have approval to execute the mission," Van Hooser said, repeating the operative words so no one was in doubt of the order.

My staff began providing me minute-by-minute updates.

"Sir, Charlie Three Five moving into position."

"Sir, helos set to launch in five minutes."

"Sir, targeted vehicle maintaining course and speed."

My operations officer leaned over and whispered in my ear, "Sir, it looks like we may have some weather moving in."

"Weather?"

"Low clouds. It's possible they could obscure the target for the bombing run."

On the screen there were patches of light, airy clouds drifting across the coastal road. Under normal circumstances, that wouldn't have presented a problem, but the Griffin's guidance system needed an unobstructed view of the target or we couldn't guarantee a direct hit.

Over the radio, I could hear the weapons officer aboard Charlie Three Five. He was making final preparations for launch and didn't seem concerned about the cloud cover.

"Pete, are you catching all this?" I asked, looking into the large TV screen.

"Yes sir," Van Hooser responded.

I could see Pete's operations officer lean over and whisper in his ear. Van Hooser nodded back to the officer and then pushed the talk button. "Sir, if the Griffin can't be launched, do we have permission to use the miniguns?"

Two of the Little Birds were equipped with highly lethal side-mounted miniguns that put out six thousand rounds a minute. In the SAR, my executive officer, Lieutenant Colonel Pat Ellis, looked at me as if to say, *Sir, be careful before you answer.* In my briefing to the President, I had agreed to use the Griffin as the primary strike platform. The SEALs and the helos were only there to pick up the remains. I had sold the mission as a bombing run, not a direct action mission by the helos and operators. Any deviation from the original plan would be counter to my guidance from the President.

"Pete, let's stick with the plan for right now." I glanced at the screen showing the blue sedan moving down the coastal road. "It still looks like the weather's good for the Griffin."

"Roger, sir."

Before me on five giant screens unfolded all of the action: the blue sedan moving steadily down the road; the helos turning on the decks of the destroyers; the patch of isolated road, now twelve minutes away from the vehicles' arrival; the SEAL command center and the Joint Staff command center. I knew that several other stations were watching me as well—the White House, the State Department, and the U.S. embassy all had video links into my SAR.

Mounted high above the TV screens, the mission countdown clock now read ten minutes. Ten minutes at forty miles per hour and the blue sedan would be in the kill zone.

Van Hooser calmly announced, "Sir, helos launched."

The Little Birds lifted off from the decks of the destroyers, linked up in modified V-formation, and began their low-level approach to the coast.

In the SAR, all eyes were fixed on the blue sedan and all ears on the voice of the weapons officer in Charlie Three Five.

"Alpha Three Three, this is Charlie Three Five, request permission to drop when target is in the cleared area."

Van Hooser, his voice devoid of any angst, responded. "Roger,

Charlie Three Five, you are cleared hot when the sedan reaches the kill zone."

The blue sedan was now two minutes out. Our technical intelligence assets had a good fix on the phone. The aircraft was lining up for the strike.

"Sir, we have clouds rolling in."

Onscreen a patchwork of wispy clouds was moving quickly toward the target area. Van Hooser was seeing it too.

"Charlie Three Five, this is Alpha Three Three, how's it looking?" Van Hooser asked the weapons officer.

"Sir, it's all good on this end. We're about one minute out from release."

The blue sedan, rumbling down the road, was completely oblivious to the fact that in sixty seconds all its occupants would be dead.

Offshore, the helos had established an airborne holding point. Circling just feet above the water, they would maintain their position until Van Hooser ordered them in.

"Thirty seconds. Twenty. Ten. The vehicle is now in the target zone," came the call from operations officer.

The clock continued to count down. The blue sedan continued to move. No one said a word. I knew that on board the aircraft the weapons officer and his crew were lining up the vehicle with the Griffin's targeting system. He had a fifteen-minute window and wanted to ensure success.

The aviators on my staff had an open chat window with the crew and the SEAL command center. My operations officer turned from his computer and spoke in a low voice. "Sir, I'm watching the chat and the crew seems to be having some difficulty lining up the target."

"Roger," I acknowledged and looked at the clock. We still had plenty of time.

Van Hooser looked calm behind his desk, but I knew that, like me, he wanted a bomb in the air—now! The clock continued to count down.

"Ten minutes remaining," came the call from the SAR non-commissioned officer.

On a digital map, the intelligence petty officer was tracking the movement of the blue sedan. It was a third of the way into the kill zone.

Behind Van Hooser there was a small flurry of activity. In my SAR came another announcement. "Sir, Charlie Three Five is having difficulty lining up the target." And another: "Sir, clouds are on the coast. I don't know if Charlie Three Five can see the target."

I resisted calling Van Hooser, but I could see on his face that concern was mounting.

Van Hooser mouthed something to one of his officers and then turned and faced the camera. "Sir, I know you're tracking all this," he said. "I'm going to reposition the helos a mile off the coast. We're talking with the aircrew and they still believe they can get a lock on the sedan before it exits the kill zone."

"Roger, Pete."

I looked at the clock. Seven minutes left.

Inside the SAR came another announcement. "Sir, Charlie Three Five says they will have target lock in two minutes."

"That's cutting it a little close," my executive officer said, pacing behind me.

Seven minutes turned into six and then into five and then into four. Onscreen, Van Hooser was belting out instructions to his staff. We were running out of time. In the SAR, the digital map showed the blue sedan nearing the end of the targeted zone. Soon the car would be entering a small village. Any attack there would surely injure innocent civilians.

My operations officer spoke up. "Sir, Charlie Three Five says they can't get a lock on the vehicle. The clouds are covering the target."

"Shit!" Looking up onscreen, I could see a broken layer of low-lying clouds, the blue sedan coming in and out of view. From their holding point, Van Hooser had directed the helos toward the target.

"Sir, helos are inbound," the ops officer announced. "One minute to the target vehicle."

Van Hooser tapped the talk button and looked into the camera head-on. "Boss, request permission to shift to guns," he said, a sense of urgency in his voice.

On the screen the village was coming into view. The sedan was moments away. If it was Nabhan, this might be our last chance. If it wasn't, I would be responsible for the deaths of four innocent people.

"Shift to guns!" I yelled.

"Roger, shift to guns!" Van Hooser repeated.

Onscreen I could see the four helos in a tight flight formation as they crossed the beach. The driver in the blue sedan spotted the aircraft and immediately began to speed up.

"Sir, the birds are taking rounds!" the SAR NCO announced.

The helos with the miniguns swung into attack formation and returned fire on the now swerving sedan. From the overhead Predator video, the rounds coming from the helos looked like a single unbroken line of red and yellow fire. The bursts of ammunition lasted no more than five seconds. The driver and passengers were killed immediately and the sedan veered off the road into a small ditch, smoking from the impact of the rounds from the miniguns.

No one in the SAR said anything. All we could do at this point was watch. The two gunships stayed hovering in position as the other two Little Birds landed on the road. Even before the skids touched down the four SEALs on each aircraft jumped to the ground and ran toward the smoking car, rifles up, ready to engage any threat that might still be alive.

Two minutes passed and Van Hooser's voice came back over the screen. "Boss, we have four military-aged males, all deceased. We will gather up the bodies and bring them back for identification."

"Roger, Pete. Understand four military-aged males, all deceased. We'll stand by."

As the SEALs pulled the bodies from the wreckage of the sedan, a small group of locals from the village began to gather. I watched as the SEAL officer approached the villagers and asked them to stay back. They all complied and seemed more interested in knowing who was in the vehicle.

Within fifteen minutes the bodies had been placed in body bags and loaded onto the helo. The helos lifted off and began their return flight to the destroyers.

An hour passed before Van Hooser came back on the net. I could tell by the widening smile on his face and slight twinkle in his eyes that he had good news.

"Sir, we sent the photos off to the FBI and have received confirmation that one of the males is"—he paused slightly—"Saleh Nabhan."

I tried not to look overly excited; killing men is not a sport. But when you bring justice to someone like Nabhan who was responsible for the deaths of hundreds, it does feel good.

"What about the other three?"

"All known accomplices of Nabhan."

"Well done, Pete!" I said.

Van Hooser smiled widely and signed off.

The staff in the SAR went to work providing detailed debriefs to the Joint Staff, the White House staff, and others. Later that afternoon I received word that Admiral Mullen wanted to video-conference with me.

"Well, William, congratulations!" I could see that Mullen was genuinely pleased. "The President asked me to pass on his congratulations as well."

"Thank you, sir," I replied.

"There is one thing, though, Bill."

"Yes sir?"

Mullen had a wry grin on his face. "I specifically recall you telling the President that you weren't going to use the Little Birds for direct action."

"Well, sir," I started to answer.

Mullen interrupted. "The President seems to recall that as well."

"Yes sir." I hesitated momentarily. "Unfortunately, the aircraft couldn't get a good fix on the car and I had to make a command decision whether to let Nabhan go or bring in the Little Birds."

Mullen leaned forward into the camera, his face growing larger on my screen. He gave me a fatherly look: a bit of sternness and a bit of pride. "Okay, William, we'll let this one go," he said, his left hand trying to cover the smile on his face.

"Roger, sir." I smiled back.

"Get back to work, Bill. There are still a lot of bad guys out there."

"Yes sir." I gave a short salute and he signed off.

Over the three years to follow, the task force would capture or kill more than two thousand medium- or high-value individuals *every year*—individuals who were threats to our forces in Iraq and Afghanistan and to our homeland. In the course of those operations, more than three hundred special operations soldiers would lose their lives and thousands were injured, some never to live a normal life again.

Not a day goes by that I don't reflect on the sacrifices of those men and women. It's easy to judge the wars today and say they clearly did not deliver the peace or the change we had hoped for. But... how many more Americans, or our allies, would have died in embassies, in airplanes, in towers, in subways, in hotels, or on the streets if we hadn't eliminated terrorists like Saleh Nabhan, or the countless others who were plotting against us? We may never know, but I take some consolation in believing that somewhere out there is a world leader, or a brilliant scientist, or a lifesaving doctor, or a renowned artist, or a loving mother or father—someone who will bring about real change in the world, someone who is alive today because my men did their job.

It is enough to let me sleep well at night.

CHAPTER SIXTEEN

THE NEXT GREATEST GENERATION

THE UNKNOWN INFANTRYMAN

The room had that sterile smell you expect in hospitals: a mixture of alcohol, cold air, and fear. I had stopped at the nurses' station to gown up. The area I was entering was a clean room, which required all visitors to put on a full white overgarment, a mask, rubber gloves, and blue booties.

It was May 2007 in Landstuhl, Germany, home of the military's premier hospital complex in Europe. I was a two-star admiral in charge of all the special operations forces in Europe and Africa. As such, I often traveled from my headquarters in Stuttgart to visit the wounded soldiers returning from combat in Iraq and Afghanistan. Most of these soldiers had severe injuries. So severe that a stop in Landstuhl was required to ensure they were stable enough to make the final journey back to the States.

In addition to seeing the wounded special operations soldiers, I usually stopped by to visit whoever was in ICU.

"What's this guy's story, Doc?" I said, pulling the strap of my mask a little tighter.

"Sir, all I know is that his unit was hit by a large IED. As you will see, he sustained significant blast injuries."

"What's the prognosis?"

"He'll live, but it's going to be a very long recovery."

The doctor paused. "We have a no-contact rule in the clean room. So please don't reach out and touch him, even if he offers to shake hands."

"Roger, understand."

The doctor nodded and I pushed the door open and entered.

Lying on the bed, completely naked, was a young soldier not more than twenty-five years old. His body was swollen from the impact of the blast. Burns covered the upper half of his torso, and below his waist he had lost half of one leg and much of the other. His face was so badly damaged that his eyes were almost sealed shut and his lips burned clean off. Lifesaving tubes extended from just about every orifice in his body and monitors around the room beeped continuously.

"Sir, he can't talk, but he can hear you and he likes to engage people," the doctor said.

I slowly walked up beside the bed, cautious not to touch the young man.

"Hey partner, my name's Admiral McRaven." I could see him acknowledge my presence. "You look like shit!"

He managed a smile and reached out his hand toward the nightstand. The doctor grabbed a clipboard and handed it to the soldier.

"He likes to write his responses out."

Pulling the attached pen from its holder, he scribbled on the notepad, *You should see the other guy.*

I laughed and he chuckled with me.

"Looks like they are taking good care of you. Is there anything you need?"

Once again he grabbed the clipboard: *A beer.*

The doctor looked at me and reluctantly shook his head.

"Well, I tell you what. You get back to the States, get well, and the beers are on me."

He just nodded.

I was struggling with what to say. I had been in these situations hundreds of times before and all you could do was make small talk. Normally, I knew the soldier or his unit and I had something more significant to offer. I walked around to the doctor's side of the bed.

"Is he a Marine or a soldier?" I whispered to the doctor.

"Sir, I don't know. I'm just the attending physician. I can find out for you, though."

"No, not necessary."

Walking back around to my side of the bed, I leaned over the young man and asked, "Are you a Marine or a soldier?"

He seemed agitated by the question. He pointed to a tattoo that was etched on his thigh. He must have assumed that the tattoo was fully visible, but the blast had burned the leg so badly that only a smudged outline appeared.

I looked closely and could see the image of a Big Red One: the 1st Infantry Division.

"You're a soldier," I commented.

He grabbed the clipboard. *Infantry*, he wrote.

Infantry. The toughest occupation in the Army, I thought. The soldiers are always road marching, always carrying a rucksack, always in the line of fire. You have to be strong and fit to last in any infantry unit, particularly during war.

As I glanced at the young man's battered body, I wondered if he fully understood the degree of his injuries.

He noticed me assessing his physical condition, and suddenly a look of defiance came across his swollen face. He rolled in my direction and then wrote slowly in capital letters, *I WILL BE INFANTRY AGAIN!*

I read the note aloud and he nodded, tapping the clipboard for emphasis. "Yes. Yes," I stumbled. "You *will* be infantry again."

He smiled and rolled back over.

Somehow, I believed him. I had seen it time and time again. These young men and women who had joined the Army during the war had a tremendous sense of determination. Nothing was going to stop them in the pursuit of their dreams. And setbacks like this—well, sometimes that was the price of being a soldier.

I left the room and never saw the young man again. I like to believe that he is marching alongside his comrades, two prosthetic legs moving him in rhythm to the cadence. I like to believe that his swollen body is back to normal and that his washed-out tattoo has been replaced with bright new ink. I like to believe he has returned to some sense of normality. I like to believe, because I must. *He left me no choice.*

SENIOR CHIEF PETTY OFFICER (SEAL) MIKE DAY

I've learned that life has a mystical aspect to it. As a man of faith, I have felt the hand of God too many times not to know that it exists. But when you see his handiwork up close, when you examine all the possible outcomes and determine that only one outcome is possible—but then something else happens—that's when you know there is more to life than meets the eye.

The nurse at the Landstuhl intensive care unit was almost speechless.

"I've been in nursing over twenty years," she said. "And I've been here at Landstuhl for the past three years. I've seen some of the worst injuries of the war." She started to tear up, but they were happy tears.

"I have never seen anyone shot up this bad." She paused. "He's got sixteen bullet holes in him"—she took a deep breath—"and he is going to be fine."

I smiled and thanked her and her team for everything they had done to save my fellow SEAL. She looked at me, shook her head, and said, "We had nothing to do with it."

I understood. Life is that way sometimes.

The man in the hospital room was Senior Chief Petty Officer Mike Day. Mike had served with me in SEAL Team Three. He was a character: a bit mouthy, in a funny Team-guy sort of way. Always had a joke, nothing seemed too serious, but he was a great SEAL operator and a good sailor. I had lost track of Mike after I left the West Coast. Now we were reunited in the worst of all possible situations. A hospital.

Talking with Mike's military escort, I got the whole backstory. During a raid on a house in Iraq, Mike had been leading a joint U.S.-Iraqi squad. The squad, led by an Iraqi officer, with Mike following right behind, stacked on a door leading into the kitchen area of the home. On order, the Iraqi officer breached the door and the squad stormed in. The room was not the kitchen as expected, but a smaller anteroom. The Iraqi officer froze; the flow of the squad came to a halt.

Mike knew that time was now of the essence. The bad guys inside would clearly have heard them. Mike yelled at the Iraqis to continue the squad surge into the next room, but fear overcame the Iraqis and they began to retreat out the door.

Mike took charge and led the team through the next door, but it was too late. Four insurgents with automatic weapons lay waiting. They opened up on full automatic, bullets flying everywhere. Mike was immediately hit in his Kevlar chest plate, with several rounds piercing his arms and legs. As the bursts from enemy fire continued, Mike's M-4 rifle was cut from his body by an ensuing round and he crumpled to the floor, having sustained twenty-seven direct hits in a matter of seconds. Behind him three others were killed, including a young SEAL officer who sustained a single shot to the back of the head.

Lying on the floor, bleeding severely, Mike pulled his handgun from his holster and, one by one, killed the insurgents. And then, in classic Mike Day fashion, he got on his radio and called to the team outside to calmly let them know that the house was clear. Medics stabilized Mike at the scene, and within a day he was on his way to Landstuhl. At the time, no one knew whether or not he would survive.

As with so many of my other visits to the hospital, Georgeann had joined me. Peering through the window, we could see Mike lying on his back with the usual array of monitors and IVs protruding from his body. The nurse opened the door and cautioned us not to stay too long. Mike still had another surgery to undergo before they moved him back to the States.

As I entered the room, Mike perked up, raised his hand high in the air, and yelled loudly, "Hey, skipper! Great to see you!"

"Michael!" I boomed back at him at an equally high volume. "Are you lying down on the job again?"

"No sir! Just getting ready for the next fight!"

I shook my head and laughed.

As I got closer to Mike's bedside I was stunned by what I saw. There was hardly any part of his body that didn't have a bullet hole. Only his chest, where the Kevlar vest had protected him, was free of wounds.

I sat for about thirty minutes and listened to Mike's story. As the minutes went by, I could see him struggling to stay awake. Finally, he looked me in the eye and said, "Sir, when do you think I can get back to the guys?"

Looking down at Mike's tattered body and the colostomy bag plugged into his bowels, I knew the answer, but sometimes the truth wasn't always the best response.

"As soon as you can kick my ass on the obstacle course, then you can get back to the guys," I said.

Mike rolled his eyes and smiled. "Well, that shouldn't be too hard."

The morphine started to kick in and he slowly drifted off to sleep.

I look back on the hundreds of men and women I visited in the hospitals. Every single one of them—*every single one of them*—asked me the same basic question: *When can I return to my unit? When can I be back with my fellow soldiers? When can I get back in the fight?* No matter how battered their bodies, all they could think about were their friends, their colleagues, their comrades, still in harm's way. Never once—*never once*—did I hear a soldier complain about their lot in life. Soldiers with missing legs, blinded soldiers, paralyzed soldiers, soldiers who would never lead a normal life again, and yet not one felt sorry for themselves.

Later that week, Mike was transferred back to the States. His injuries were too severe for him to get back in the fight, but that didn't stop him from serving his fellow warriors. Today Mike helps veterans with post-traumatic stress disorder and traumatic brain injury. He gives back to the nation every chance he can. Over the years that followed, I would run the obstacle course every chance I could, knowing that one day Mike would show up to challenge me. I needed to be ready.

Sergeant Brendan Marrocco

As my security detail pulled up to the entrance of Walter Reed hospital in Washington, D.C., Sergeant Major Thompson stepped out from the main building and greeted me with a smile and a sharp salute. "Sir, good to have you back."

"Thanks, Sergeant Major," I said, shaking his hand. "Where is your brother, the other Sergeant Major Thompson?"

He smiled.

It was a running joke. The Thompson "twins" were the two senior enlisted men who provided patient advocacy for the special operations soldiers at Walter Reed. One was black, the other white. But, down deep, they were both Army green and damn proud of it.

"Sir, he's down in the Advanced Training Center talking to our newest patients."

The ATC was a remarkable thirty-one-thousand-square-foot facility that helped soldiers with amputated limbs get back to some sense of normalcy. It was equipped with a state-of-the-art prosthetic lab, the finest rehabilitation technology, and world-class doctors. But what really made it special were the soldiers who, under the most difficult of circumstances, bonded together as a unit, each soldier helping his or her brothers and sisters to heal. I loved to visit the ATC because it was like being on the grinder during morning SEAL calisthenics. Everyone harassed each other. They challenged one another. They wouldn't let you feel sorry for yourself. *Stop your whining. So you lost two legs. So what! Now you can get two new ones that will make you taller. Maybe then the women will notice you.*

After I had spent an hour or so with several of our SOF soldiers, Sergeant Major Thompson pulled me aside.

"Sir, there is one soldier here from the 25th Infantry Division that I would like you to meet. His vehicle was hit by an EFP in Iraq and he is now a quadruple amputee. His unit is still overseas, so he hasn't gotten a lot of visitors yet."

"No problem, Sergeant Major. Just point me in the right direction."

The sergeant major subtly nodded to my left, and it didn't take long to figure out who he was talking about.

Leaning against the wall was a young man balancing on his "shorties," new prosthetics attached to what was left of his legs. The shorties raised him just inches off the ground and were the first step in preparing him for the more challenging full artificial limbs. Not only was he missing two legs, but the blast from the explosively formed projectile had also severed both his arms, burned his neck, and left him with lacerations across his face.

I had seen a lot of amputees, but when the human form is so changed by either nature or the violence of man, it still takes your breath away.

The sergeant major saw the look in my eye.

"I know, sir," he said, acknowledging the sorrow we both felt.

Turning from the sergeant major, I walked over to the young man and took a knee so that I could face him eye to eye.

"Good afternoon," I said, extending my hand to shake what remained of his right arm.

He looked at me, trying to determine what manner of uniform I was wearing. "You're a general?" he asked, looking at the four stars on my chest.

"Well, an admiral, actually," I said, smiling. "What's your name?"

"Brendan Marrocco," he replied politely.

"I understand you're with the Tropic Lightning," I said, referring to the infantry division's nickname.

"Yes sir!" He smiled, trying to stand a bit more erect. "Alpha Company, 2nd Battalion, 27th Regiment."

"Looks like you had a rough go of it in Iraq."

He looked to the ground where his legs would have been and then quickly surveyed the rest of the room packed with amputees. "Yeah, but not as bad as some of the guys."

It was hard to hide my expression. *Not as bad as some of the guys,* I thought. *You're missing all four limbs, have burns and cuts throughout your body, and someone else has it worse?*

Standing next to Marrocco was another young man.

"Sir, this is my brother Mike."

I greeted Mike, but I could tell he was devastated by what had happened to his younger brother. The sadness on his face was heartbreaking. I turned back to Marrocco.

"Are they taking good care of you here?" I asked.

"Yes sir! The docs and the nurses have been terrific and I love being around the guys."

"Anything I can do for you?"

He didn't hesitate for a second. "Yes sir. I would like to get back to Hawaii and meet my company when they return from Iraq."

If you're lucky in life, there is a moment, a moment you never forget, when you meet someone whose entire world has been turned upside down and they find a way to inspire you. They find a way to show you that you can rise above all of life's difficulties. They find a way to make the human condition, regardless of its form, seem perfect. Kneeling face-to-face with young Brendan Marrocco, I had one of those moments. He must have seen something in my eyes—pity, sorrow, regret—because he cocked his head and smiled.

"Sir," he said, touching me with what remained of his right arm. "I'm twenty-four years old. I have my whole life in front of me. I'm going to be just fine!"

I'm going to be just fine.

I never forgot those words, and when life got a little difficult for me, I remembered that moment again and again. I repeated those words over and over. *I am going to be just fine.*

If a nation is to survive and thrive it must pass on the ideals that made it great and imbue in its citizens an indomitable spirit, a will to continue on regardless of how difficult the path, how long the journey, or how uncertain the outcome. People must have a true belief that tomorrow will be a better day—if only they fight for it and never give up. I saw this indomitable spirit in my parents and those who lived through the Great Depression and World War II—and I saw it again in the soldiers, sailors, airmen, and Marines whom I served with in Iraq and Afghanistan. And later when I was the chancellor of the University of Texas system, I saw it in equal amounts in the young students who sat in the schoolhouses across Texas. From the battlefields to the classrooms, I have seen the young men and women of this generation, the oft-maligned millennials. They are supposed to be pampered, entitled, and soft. I found them anything but. They are as courageous, heroic, and patriotic as their parents and grandparents before them. Those who fought and died or were wounded in Iraq and Afghanistan are the same young Americans who are building our bridges, finding the cures, and teaching our youth. They are the men and women who are volunteering to wear the uniform, fight the fires, and protect the people. They are not like my generation. *They are better.* They are more inclusive. They don't see color, or ethnicity, or orientation. They value people for their friendship and their talents. They are more engaged. They will not stand by and watch bad things happen to good people. They are more questioning. They want to know why. Why are we going to war, why are we increasing our debt, why can't we do something new and different? They are risk takers, entrepreneurs, givers of their time and energy. Above all, they are optimists—and as challenging as the times may seem right now, this generation believes that tomorrow will be a better day. I am convinced that history will someday record that these young Americans were the greatest generation of this century, and I know, beyond a shadow of a doubt, that we will all be *just fine.*

Brendan Marrocco got to Hawaii in time to greet the returning 25th Infantry Division. In 2012, he underwent a successful bilateral transplant that gave him two new arms. Today he travels the country telling his story and helping those . . . *less fortunate than himself.*

CHAPTER SEVENTEEN

NEPTUNE'S SPEAR

An undisclosed location in the United States
April 2011

W ith an apostrophe."

"I'm sorry, sir. What?"

"With an apostrophe," I said. "It's Neptune's Spear. With an apostrophe."

The young lieutenant commander looked at me with some surprise. "Sir, the computer doesn't generate names that have an apostrophe."

"Of course it doesn't."

He smiled and nodded. "I like it." Picking up the magic marker, he wrote on the whiteboard in large letters: OPERATION NEPTUNE'S SPEAR. BRIEFBACK TO THE CHAIRMAN.

As silly as it was, I had actually put some thought into the name. I wanted a name that would symbolize the SEAL assault force's maritime roots, that would represent justice in the form of the sea god's three-pronged lance. A name that would resonate with the team of handpicked operators; a name that people might remember if the mission went well and would hopefully forget if it went south. In my office at Fort Bragg there was a small bronze statue, which I had purchased in a curio store in Venice years before. It was the Greek god Poseidon riding on a seahorse. Poseidon had a long-shafted trident spear in his grasp and the seahorse was rearing, his two legs kicking in the front and his tail flowing behind, ready to attack. I didn't normally go in for this kind of symbolism. It seemed ridiculous. But the statue caught my eye and I had to admit—it was

cool. So when the time came to attach a name to our planned operation, I thought back to the bronze figure. I knew I couldn't call it
"Poseidon's Trident" because if the mission failed, every one of my
generation would remember the disaster film *The Poseidon Adventure*, and that would be the mission's legacy. So, Neptune's Spear it
was—with an apostrophe.

Three months earlier, the Deputy Director of the CIA, Michael
Morell had briefed me that the CIA had a lead on the location of
Osama (a.k.a. Usama) bin Laden (UBL). Through a series of courier
follows, surveillance, and technical collection, the Agency identified a large walled-in compound in Abbottabad, Pakistan. The compound was just down the road from the Pakistani military academy
and a mile or so from a major ammunition storage point. Photos
revealed the presence of an individual they called "the pacer," a
tall man in flowing robes who walked around the interior of the
compound, but never went outside the walls. The intelligence was
interesting, but the truth was there had been dozens of bin Laden
sightings since 2001 and none of them ever panned out. Still, I had
to admit this lead seemed much more compelling.

After the Agency briefing I reported back to Secretary Gates
and Admiral Mike Mullen at the Pentagon. Situated on the outer
ring of the Pentagon, the Secretary's office was long and expansive,
with a magnificent view overlooking the Potomac River and across
to the center of Washington, D.C. On the walls were portraits of
Lincoln, Washington, and several unknown soldiers, a constant
reminder that the Secretary's decisions affected the entire nation.

"What do you think, Bill?" the Secretary asked.

"Sir, it's a compound. We do compound raids every night
in Afghanistan. It's not tactically difficult. Getting to the target
undetected will be challenging, but once we're there, it's pretty
straightforward."

"How many men will you need?" Mullen asked.

"Sir, normally a compound raid includes about fifty to seventy guys. You isolate the compound, position small elements at critical blocking points, have an assault force that breaches the walls and gets the high-value target—then you have a medical team, forensics and exploitation team, biometrics, etcetera. But again, this will all depend on how we get to the target."

"What's the minimum number of men you need?" the Secretary inquired.

I thought for a moment. It was a very large compound. Well over thirty thousand square feet. "Probably twenty-five to thirty men. But that's assuming a lot of risk."

"Okay, Bill," Mullen said. "I don't know that we need to do anything right now. The Agency has the lead, but sooner or later they may want your advice and some assistance in the planning."

"No worries, sir. We'll be standing by to help with whatever they need."

"How long are you in town, Bill?" the Secretary asked.

"Sir, I head back to Afghanistan tonight, but I can return whenever the Agency needs me."

"William," Mullen began. "You can't tell anyone else about this mission. If word were to leak out it would be disastrous."

"I understand, sir. But if the time comes that the Agency needs some detailed planning, then I will have to bring others into the inner circle."

The Secretary and Admiral Mullen thanked me, and that afternoon I boarded the command's plane and returned to Afghanistan. One month later, while still in Afghanistan, I received a call from the Vice Chairman of the Joint Staff, General Cartwright, requesting that I return to D.C. for further meetings with the CIA. It was highly unusual for me to keep leaving the battlefield to return to the States, but things were beginning to heat up in Libya and most of my staff assumed I was heading back for classified discussions with the Joint Staff or the White House.

As the commander, every move I made was recorded by the personnel in my operations center and logged into our daily digital notebook. There was no hiding my comings and goings, but the reason for my travel was never noted. My executive officer, Lieutenant Colonel Art Sellers, was the only member of my staff who knew something unusual was in the works. Sellers was an Army Ranger who had been my XO for the past year. He traveled with me everywhere. His job was to ensure that all the decisions required by the command received my attention. He reviewed every piece of paper that came into my office. He coordinated every visit. He screened every call and managed every small crisis that is part of running a large command. He was one of the most valuable men in my command, and I trusted him with my life. But even as trusted as Sellers was, I had my orders.

We landed in D.C. late Monday evening.

"So, sir. What time is your appointment at...the Pentagon?" Art said, drawing out the final word.

"We need to be at 'the Pentagon' at 1300. Call this point of contact and he will ensure we are cleared in." I handed Sellers the number of my CIA contact. "Look, Art, I can't tell you anything right now and I need you not to ask any questions."

"No problem, sir."

"Also, I need you to cover for me with the headquarters staff. Sooner or later they will smell something and start to ask questions. Keep to the story until I tell you otherwise."

Sellers was unfazed. "Roger, sir. Understand."

I knew that he did. Art was the consummate professional, and over the next several months he would be key to the success of the mission—even if he didn't know it at the time.

The next day I headed over to the Agency to meet with my point of contact and review the intelligence on the target. Morell and his team had given me a great overview, but now I needed to look at the Abbottabad compound in detail. The planning team from the Agency was segregated from the headquarters building in an innocuous-looking one-story facility that no one visited. It was perfect.

Sellers drove me through the main gate of the CIA and dropped me off in the parking lot. My command had dozens of folks working at the CIA, and sooner or later I knew one of them would spot me slinking into the facility. By then I hoped to have a better cover story.

My Agency contact met me outside the facility, cleared me into the building, past the lone guard, and walked me back into a large room filled with boxes of paper, cartridges, and ink. The building was a holding area for all the CIA's administrative material. "We're going to get this all cleaned out," he said, waving at the clutter that filled the room.

We made our way to a large table upon which sat a small model of the Abbottabad compound. I was introduced to a number of the CIA analysts who had been developing the intelligence and the Special Activities Division (SAD) officer who was planning the CIA's raid option. For the next hour the analysts used the scale model to outline all that they knew about the compound, "the pacer," the Pakistani military, and the civilians in the area. It was an impressive display of the Agency's intelligence collection and analysis capability. The depth and detail of the intelligence was unlike anything I had ever seen before—on any subject. However, even among the analysts there was no consensus on whether "the pacer" was bin Laden. Some placed the confidence level at 95 percent, others as low as 40 percent.

Next, the SAD officer briefed me on his plan to get bin Laden. SAD was the Agency's paramilitary unit. They were mostly former special operators or Marines who helped train, equip, and run covert forces around the world. They were very good at what they did, but they were a small outfit with no real raid capability. The officer briefing me was a former captain in the Army with some reconnaissance background. He was professional, detailed in his briefing, and interested in my critique of his plan. I offered some small suggestions, but stayed away from any sweeping recommendations.

There was always some professional tension between the Agency and my command. In the world of counterterrorism we had similar equities. Throughout the hunt for high-value targets in Iraq and Afghanistan our HUMINTers, those uniformed case officers who gathered intelligence to support military operations, were often in competition with the Agency case officers. The CIA case officers felt it was their job to gather the intelligence. Legally both agencies were correct. Under Title 10 of the U.S. Code, the Department of Defense has traditional military authorities that allow qualified individuals to collect intelligence that will ultimately be used for military operations. Under Title 50, the Agency has intelligence authorities to do similar missions under covert action. While this distinction is much clearer outside a theater of war, during wartime, such as in Iraq or Afghanistan, the authorities tended to overlap and occasionally caused some bruised feelings. Having said that, overall the military and CIA relationship was very strong. Still, at this early juncture in the mission, I didn't want to be perceived as the "Pro from Dover" coming to preach rightness to the Agency. So I remained quietly appreciative of the briefings and only asked questions to clarify some small points. After the briefings, the team of analysts departed and I sat around the model looking at the compound and thinking through how I would approach the problem.

Two hours north of Pakistan's capital, Abbottabad was a city of approximately three hundred thousand people. It was, by Pakistani standards, fairly affluent. The city was home to the Pakistan Army's military academy, a large ammunition depot, a barracks, which housed a Pakistan Army infantry battalion, and several police stations.

The compound itself was situated down a small dirt road about half a mile from a main highway that cut through Abbottabad. While there were houses around the compound to the north and to the west, there was open space to the south and for several hundred yards to the east. Off to the east was a densely populated middle-class neighborhood. Fortunately, a small canal separated the neighborhood from direct access to the compound. Any young person could easily traverse the canal, but it was a minor obstacle that I knew would dissuade some older Pakistanis from coming to the compound if things got interesting.

The compound itself was irregularly shaped, with a long straight wall on the north side, two walls on the east and west running perpendicular to the north wall, and then, extending from the east and west walls, two long walls that met at a point to the south. On the north wall was a double metal door that opened up to the driveway. Also on the north were two private doors that presumably led into the home. The home itself was three stories high and the windows looked out toward the south. The compound was divided into two areas—a living area with the main house, a smaller guesthouse, and another even smaller building on one side of the driveway, and an open courtyard where some goats and chickens were kept. Each separate area was self-contained within the walls of the compound. You could not easily move from the courtyard to the living area without going through several metal gates, all of which were locked.

While the compound was somewhat unusual, with its high walls, barbed wire, and security lighting, it wasn't out of the ordinary for Pakistan and certainly not for what we had seen in Afghanistan. The only real aberration was an unusually high wall to the south. While the main walls surrounding the compound measured twelve feet high, the south wall had been built up another six feet. At eighteen feet high it was quite difficult for anyone to see inside the compound from any vantage point in Abbottabad.

What the analysts didn't know was the layout inside the living quarters. Overhead imagery could tell you a lot, but it couldn't see through walls. The analysts believed that there were no underground tunnels, but they couldn't be sure. If it was bin Laden, there was a general assumption that he would have an escape route out of the compound. This was common practice, and during my time in Iraq and Afghanistan, we frequently found tunnels where the high-value targets would hide until the security forces left their homes. Additionally, and most disturbing, the analysts didn't know if the house was wired with explosives. Again, this was not uncommon with many compounds we had raided over the years. While the possibility of booby traps, explosively wired houses, pressure plate IEDs, and escape routes loomed large, there were no obstacles that we had not encountered before. I was confident that if we could get to the compound, we could get bin Laden—*if he was there.*

For the next several hours I looked at the bigger picture. How could I get an assault force to the compound? It was about 162 miles by air from the border of Afghanistan to Abbottabad. The Pakistanis had a sophisticated Integrated Air Defense System (IADS), and we knew from experience that their radars could pick up our helos and airplanes when we flew close to the border.

I looked at several other alternatives. Could we do an offset parachute insertion into a remote landing zone and then walk to the compound? Could we pile some commandos into a Trojan horse–like vehicle and drive to Abbottabad? Could we come in under tourist visas, assemble at a safe house, and get the Agency to move us to the compound? Unfortunately I didn't know the answer to any of these questions.

After several hours I left the facility and met up with Sellers. We headed back over to the Pentagon so I could debrief the Secretary and Admiral Mullen.

After a short review of the new intelligence, I said, "Sir, I need to bring at least one more man into the planning effort."

Gates and Mullen exchanged glances. "Who do you have in mind?" the admiral asked.

"Captain Rex Smith, sir. He's a Navy SEAL with extensive combat experience, and he works here in D.C. He can move around the town without drawing a lot of attention."

"All right," Mullen agreed. "But he's the only guy for now. I'll talk to the Agency and the White House. Don't speak with him until I get back to you."

"Yes sir."

"Bill, can you do this mission?" Mullen asked again.

"Sir, I don't know yet. I need to talk to some folks. We will need to do some detailed planning and rehearsals. Only then will I know if it's feasible."

"The President is likely to want a Concept of Operations in a few weeks," the Secretary noted.

"In a few weeks I can have a detailed concept," I said. "But without bringing in the aviation and ground operators to really look at the problem and rehearse the concept, there is no way I can be certain of success."

"Okay," Mullen said. "For now it remains just you, and I will check on your D.C. guy. But no one else is allowed in until the President agrees."

"Understand, sir."

I left the Pentagon and headed back to my hotel. Within an hour I received word that Rex Smith was approved to join my one-man team.

Nicknamed "the Senator," Rex was the spitting image of the 1950s movie star Robert Mitchum. He was always poised, with a coolness and sense of confidence that makes him the man in the room whom everyone wants to listen to. Tall, broad-shouldered, with black hair, he was wickedly smart and exceptionally experienced. The captain had worked for me on several occasions in the past decade, and I trusted his operational judgment implicitly.

*   *   *

I closed the door to his small office.

"Rex, I'm going to tell you something, and I need to ensure that no one, absolutely no one else, learns about this."

As big men tend to do, he was slightly slouched in his chair. He sat up and leaned forward. "Yes sir. No one will know."

"No one," I repeated.

"Yes sir. No one."

"We have a lead on bin Laden." I let it sink in for a second. "The Agency is planning a mission to get him. They have asked us to help with the planning."

Rex nodded. Like me, he had been through bin Laden sightings before, so his reaction was measured.

"I need you to go over to the Agency and listen to what they have to say. They have developed a number of courses of action, only one of which is a raid option. But right now that's not at the top of their list."

He shifted in his chair and asked, "What do you want me to do?"

"Nothing. Just listen. The last thing I want is for the Agency to think that we are trying to take over the mission."

"Should I help with the planning?"

"The SAD guys are planning the ground option. If they ask for your insight then provide it. But stay away from implying we could do it better."

"Okay, sir."

"I head back to Afghanistan tonight. So call me if things begin to develop or you have any questions."

"Yes sir."

I knew that Rex was the perfect man for the job. He was engaging and had a likability that generated openness and partnership. If anyone could gain the Agency's trust, it was "the Senator."

By the next day I was back in Afghanistan. Over the next few weeks Rex called me almost every day with an update. Now that he had seen the intelligence, his enthusiasm was evident. This might just be the real deal and he knew it.

As expected, I received a call three weeks later asking me to return to the States. The President wanted a meeting to review the intelligence and discuss his options. Heading back to the States so soon after returning to Afghanistan would normally have spiked attention, but Libya was falling apart and NATO and the United States were supporting the National Liberation Army fighting against Gadhafi. For the next several months, all my movements and my frequent visits to the White House were assumed to be closely held planning for Libya.

Soon after arriving back at Fort Bragg, I contacted some subject matter experts and, without revealing too much, tried to get answers to my four questions: Could I insert a small team into an offset drop zone and have them walk on foot to the compound? Could we build a Trojan horse truck, fill it with armed operators, and drive across the border from Kabul to Abbottabad? Could we take commercial flights directly into Islamabad, get weapons and gear from the Agency, and drive to Abbottabad? Finally, could we fly the 162 miles from the border undetected by Pak radars and go straight to the target?

My command had one of the finest Air Force aviation squadrons in the military. The pilots from this squadron knew every trick in the book when it came to inserting a small unit of operators onto a parachute drop zone. I called the squadron commander and told him that I needed one of his best pilots for a few days just to do some preliminary planning for a possible Libyan contingency. It was a shallow cover story and it's likely the commander didn't believe it, but he knew not to ask too many questions.

After a day of looking at possible air insertion routes and likely drop zones, it was apparent the offset infiltration idea was not going to work. Next I contacted some of our clandestine operators and asked them to look at the Trojan horse idea. While it had merit, it also had the greatest risk of compromise and took the longest to execute. Finally, I ruled out entering the country on tourist visas because the scrutiny of

Americans entering Pakistan had been significantly elevated after the Raymond Davis incident. Davis was a government contractor who killed two undercover Pakistani policemen after he mistook them for criminals trying to assault him. Consequently, every American was now viewed suspiciously and there seemed to be no way of getting men and weapons into Pakistan without getting caught.

As expected, the Pakistanis had a well-integrated air defense capability. However, the Pakistanis viewed their greatest threat as coming from India. Consequently, there appeared to be holes in the radar coverage on their western frontier that we could use to mask our helicopter insertion.

As I reviewed each option I compared them against an intellectual model I had created twenty years earlier while studying at the Naval Postgraduate School in Monterey, California. The model was based on a theory that attempted to explain why special operations forces succeeded, particularly in light of the fact they are a small force normally going against a well-defended target. Carl von Clausewitz, the great Prussian military strategist, said that the defense is stronger than the offensive, because the defense only has to "preserve and protect" while the offense has to "impose its will upon the enemy." The "defense" in this case was the Pakistani air defenses, the battalion of Pak infantry surrounding the objective, and the Abbottabad compound itself.

Clausewitz asserted that the only way for an attacking force to overcome the natural strength of the defense was through mass and maneuver. But special operations missions seemed to defy conventional wisdom—why was this? I concluded that special operations forces were able to achieve "relative superiority" over an enemy by developing a "simple plan, carefully concealed, repeatedly rehearsed, and executed with surprise, speed, and purpose." And to compare my theory against real missions, I conducted eight case studies and developed a relative superiority model. The model showed how, in the course of a commando mission, the special operations force gained "relative superiority," how long they maintained it, and when they lost it. What is crucial for the success of any special operations mission is to minimize the time from when you are vulnerable to when you achieve relative superiority. Unlike real military superiority, relative superiority only lasts for a short period of time. No matter how I compared each Abbottabad option to the relative superiority model, the outcome was the same. The best approach was the simplest and the most direct: fly to the target as quickly as possible, get bin Laden, and get out. Nothing complicated, nothing exotic, just like thousands of missions we had done before. By the end of the week I knew what needed to be done. What I didn't know was, *could* it be done?

The day prior to briefing the President, the Director of the CIA, Leon Panetta, asked me to meet with him and his key staff members at Langley. Since he had taken over the CIA in 2009, Panetta and I worked together on a number of operations. He was the consummate team player, gregarious, bawdy at times, with a laugh that was contagious. You couldn't resist Leon Panetta's embrace. And no matter what you were doing, it was never about Panetta. It was always about doing what was right for the nation. But Panetta also had a tremendous depth of experience that served the Agency and eventually Defense very well. An eight-term Congressman from Monterey, Panetta had also been the White House Chief of Staff under Clinton and the Director of the Office of Management and Budget. He knew Washington.

In the Director's office, with his senior staff present, we reviewed the current options for Abbottabad. General Cartwright had advocated for an air option to bomb the compound. Having bombed a number of compounds in my day, I knew that to ensure bin Laden was dead, the air option would require a massive ordnance drop. While this might ensure bin Laden's demise, it was likely to have significant collateral damage and leave a large smoking hole in the middle of Abbottabad. Probably not good for

U.S.-Pakistani relations. Even after the bombing raid, we would never know for certain if bin Laden was dead. While this option seemed far-fetched to me, it remained a viable one.

The second option was a CIA-led snatch and grab using a handful of Special Activities Division officers who would quietly enter Pakistan, travel from Islamabad to Abbottabad, and grab bin Laden. However, the flaw in the plan was trying to get bin Laden out of Pakistan, either dead or alive. There was an offshoot to this SAD plan that involved the Pakistanis. No one in the room thought bringing the Pakistanis into our confidence was a good idea, but we wanted to provide the President with all the options. The final option was the special operations raid.

"Well?" Panetta told his staff. "I'm in favor of the SOF raid, but I want to know what the rest of you think."

Going around the room, I was surprised by the responses. Those CIA officers who disliked SOF the most seemed to be our staunchest supporters. Panetta encouraged professional dissent and there was no holding back from some of his senior staff.

"There is no fucking way we can let the Paks in on this. That option should not even be on the table," came one reply.

"What happens after we bomb the shit out of this place and it's not bin Laden? I mean, these guys have nukes and they are already pissed off about Davis."

"Look, the ISI must know bin Laden is there. For God's sake, he's a fucking mile down the road from their West Point."

"While I like our SAD guys, this is just beyond the scope of what they can do."

Everyone had an opinion.

Finally, Panetta turned to me. "Bill, what do you think?"

I looked around the room. Most of the senior staff and I had worked closely together for the past ten years. Iraq, Afghanistan, Yemen, Somalia, Kenya, Djibouti, Lebanon, Israel—somewhere our paths had crossed. They were exceptional patriots and very,

very good at their profession. But there were one or two senior officers who felt threatened by SOF and always tried to undermine our efforts. And in this crowd, those senior officers' opinions mattered.

"Sir, right now I don't have enough information to tell you whether the special operations raid will work. We have a lot of detailed planning still to do and then I need to conduct several rehearsals before I'm ready to give you or the President a good answer."

"What about the SAD option?" one of Panetta's staff asked me.

I hesitated. I really liked the young SAD officer who was planning the CIA mission, but relative to my SOF operators, his team had limited combat experience; and in order for his operation to be successful, he still needed helicopter support.

"Sir, I think the SAD option is workable, but based on their current planning they'll still need a helo to extract their team and bin Laden."

"Then why not just have your guys do the mission?" Morell said, asking the obvious.

I turned to Panetta. "Sir, we can support the SAD guys or we can do a unilateral SOF raid, but we'll need to choose one or the other."

"Look," Panetta said. "I think the only real option we have here is the special operations raid. But let's keep looking at the other courses of action and see what unfolds."

Two of the senior officers present were former CIA chiefs of station in the Middle East, and I could tell by their body language that, while they respected the SAD guys, they thought the SAD plan was unworkable. Panetta tabled the discussion and asked for a further review.

For the next hour, Panetta drilled his staff on finding ways to verify that "the pacer" was bin Laden. Could we get better overhead photos? Could a CIA source plant a camera on the outer wall and look into the compound? Without proof that "the pacer" was bin Laden, the President was unlikely to authorize any direct action against the Abbottabad compound.

As the meeting ended Panetta pulled me aside and reaffirmed his support for the SOF raid. I was pleased that he was so firmly in the raid camp, but I wasn't ready to lead the charge just yet and I didn't want to offer the President of the United States an option that I couldn't guarantee.

Sellers dropped me off outside the White House. I wore my Navy Service Dress Blue, the double-breasted uniform with the gold stripes on the sleeves. I debated wearing a suit to the White House in order to avoid being recognized, but with Libya in full swing, hiding in plain sight seemed to be a better idea.

As I approached the south entrance along the back side of the Old Executive Office Building, I heard my name called. There, waiting to pass through the south entrance, was Karen Tumulty, a childhood friend whom I had not seen in forty years, but who I knew was a reporter for the *Washington Post*.

"Bill!" she said, hugging me. "What are you doing here?"

Just what I needed. A *Washington Post* reporter. What was I doing here? Hadn't I thought through that question? No. Apparently not.

"Oh, well. You know. A lot going on in the world." I smiled.

"Libya, huh?"

"Well..." But before I could stammer any more, I quickly changed the subject and asked about her family and her career. We talked for several minutes, trying to catch up on the past forty years. Karen was an extremely well-respected political reporter, and while national security was not her beat, reporters are curious by nature. The sooner I could break contact the better.

"Karen, it was great seeing you again. I'm in D.C. a lot. Maybe we can get together for coffee."

"That would be wonderful," she said. "No business. I promise I won't ask about your work."

"It's a deal."

I hugged her one final time, picked up my badge from the Secret Service agent, and walked onto the White House grounds. I drew a deep breath. Next time I would be better prepared for the unexpected.

The Situation Room was empty when I arrived. The director of the SITROOM was a Navy captain. He subtly made it known that he was unaware of whatever was transpiring that afternoon. There was no record of the meeting on the President's calendar, and the Situation Room schedule only indicated that the room was blocked.

Moments later my old friend Nick Rasmussen showed up. Nick was one of the few NSC staffers read-in to the planning, and over the next few months he would provide me invaluable insight into the thinking of the President and his national security team.

Before long the room began to fill up. Secretary Gates, Chairman Mullen, and Hoss Cartwright arrived together, followed by Vice President Biden; Secretary Clinton; Leon Panetta; the Director of National Intelligence, Jim Clapper; the National Security Advisor, Tom Donilon; Denis McDonough; John Brennan; and a small briefing team from the Agency. As the junior man present, I sat at the end of the table.

A few minutes after everyone was seated the President arrived without any fanfare. He looked tired. I recalled that he had just returned from a trip to New York City and a big event the night before.

The President slid into the chair at the head of the table, his long frame laid back almost in recline. The CIA team briefed the intelligence. Panetta gave his overall assessment, and then the President asked the principals for their opinions. All agreed that the intelligence was compelling, but it lacked a level of certainty and no one was ready to take any action just yet. Panetta then reviewed the four options.

The President and others quickly dismissed the idea of including the Pakistanis in the mission. If bin Laden was just a mile from the Pakistani military academy, surely they had to know about it. Confiding in the Pakistanis could easily mean bin Laden would run, and then it might take another ten years before we found him again. It was too risky.

That meant that there were only three other options—the bombing option, the SAD snatch and grab, and the special operations raid. Hoss Cartwright walked the President through the bombing option, but it was clear that this course of action made everyone uncomfortable. To completely level the compound and ensure bin Laden didn't survive would require twenty-eight two-thousand-pound bombs. While the size of the ordnance load was of concern, what really bothered the President was the loss of innocent lives. The CIA reports assessed there to be three to four women and up to fifteen children in the three-story house. All of them would die along with bin Laden. And what if it wasn't him? the President asked. What if it was just some Arab sheik with a number of wives?

Panetta briefly discussed the SAD option, but then passed the briefing over to me to outline the special operations raid.

"Good afternoon, Mr. President," I began. "Sir, as briefed, the Abbottabad Compound Number One is 162 miles from the Afghanistan border. I'm confident that once I get an assault force on the ground, we can secure the facility and capture or kill the high-value target. Getting to the compound is the hard part." I paused briefly. "I analyzed a number of options to include parachuting into an offset drop zone and walking to the target, trying to drive across the border in a makeshift vehicle that could hide the operators, and finally, just flying directly to the target as we do every night in Afghanistan."

Panetta chimed in. "Mr. President, Bill is looking into the use of some special helicopters we have that may be able to get past the Pakistani air defenses."

Onscreen in the Situation Room, I pulled up a picture of our specially configured Black Hawk helicopters. "Sir, it's possible that these helos can avoid radar detection and make it to the compound." As I looked around the room all the principals were fixated on the unusual-looking helicopters on the screen. "But there is a lot I don't know."

"Like what?" the President asked.

"Sir, I don't know if the helos can carry enough men."

"How many do you need?"

"At a minimum about twenty men and their equipment."

The President, still looking intently at the photo, nodded for me to continue.

"A lot goes into determining the lift capacity of a helo," I continued. "Fuel, temperature, altitude, and time on target. For example, sir, if the temperature is one degree different than what we forecast it could change the entire load and fuel requirements to do the mission. If the time on the ground is longer than anticipated, then the helo will have to refuel, and that is another element of risk."

I could feel some of the enthusiasm for the raid waning. "In addition, these are untested helicopters. While the MH-60 Black Hawk is a proven airframe, these birds have been so reconfigured that I don't know how well they will perform."

Everyone was quiet. While I wanted to be entirely truthful about the limitations of the helicopters, I also didn't want to completely undermine the raid option.

"But sir, it is also possible that our regular Black Hawk helicopters could use the mountains to skirt the air defenses, and if that's the case then getting to the target is very much doable." I paused to let that sink in. "However, I just don't have the information now to tell you whether any of these helo insertion options are viable."

"What do you need, Bill?"

"Sir, I need to bring in some experts to help me with the air and ground planning phase."

"How many extra folks are we talking about?"

"Sir, I will need five more men read-in to the mission."

The President looked around the room to see if anyone objected. "Okay, Admiral. Do the additional planning and get back to me."

Tom Donilon, the President's National Security Advisor, spoke up. "Mr. President, we have another meeting scheduled for 29 March."

"Okay, let's reconvene on the twenty-ninth. Everyone knows what information I need?" the President asked, looking around the table. "Yes sir," came a collective response. The President thanked everyone and departed the room. Most of the principals stayed behind to ensure they all understood what tasks the President had assigned them.

On the way out of the Situation Room, Panetta pulled me aside and said, "Bill, you know what needs to be done, don't you?"

"Yes sir."

He smiled, slapped me on the back, and said, "Okay, let's get at it." There was always something reassuring about having Leon Panetta in your corner.

That evening I went back to my hotel room and thought through exactly who I needed. The air piece was easy. I would reach out to Colonel John "J.T." Thompson, the commander of our elite special operations aviation unit, and ask for his most experienced warrant officer to lead the tactical portion of the air planning. Additionally, I would need to have the lead pilot from the special Black Hawk unit to provide the technical information necessary to determine if his aircraft could perform as advertised. Finally, I would have to make a decision on the ground assault element. Would I choose Navy SEALs or Army special operations? There were only two men I trusted well enough to lead the ground operation. Both officers were extremely experienced in combat, both superb tacticians, and most importantly, I felt, both were consummate team players. With all the tension that would invariably develop as a result of this high-profile mission, I needed someone who could calmly build the joint operational team and not get overpressurized when the stakes got high.

After checking the Afghanistan deployment schedule, I learned that the Army officer and his squadron had just deployed to Afghanistan. There was no way I could pull the officer and his leadership team out of Afghanistan and bring them back to the States without someone getting wind of a big operation. On the other hand, the Navy SEAL officer and his squadron had just returned from Afghanistan and were on leave for three weeks. Three weeks! It was the perfect cover for action. No one at his command would ask about his whereabouts. No one would miss him at work.

I contacted Rex and told him to call the SEAL officer and his master chief and get them to D.C. the next day. I subsequently called J.T. Thompson and requested the additional air planners. Thompson immediately knew something was up when I asked to have a warrant officer from the special helicopter unit meet me in D.C. Not wanting to be too nosy, but also not wanting to be left out of something important, Thompson inquired if I needed his personal assistance as well. I couldn't help but chuckle. I would have done the same thing. Not now, I told him, but the time might come, so don't go anywhere soon. Thompson was a superb helo pilot and equally impressive officer. I knew that sooner or later I would bring him into the fold.

The next day, Rex rounded up the four new members and escorted them to CIA headquarters. In the back room we had convened the CIA analytical team and the leadership of the SAD element. Rex hadn't provided the new guys with any information on why they were here nor whom they were meeting with.

As the men entered the room I greeted them at the door. The two SEALs I knew well, but the two warrant officers from the aviation unit were new to me. They had no idea why they were at the CIA, but they knew my presence and the fact that we were hiding in some small nondescript building must mean something was afoot. All of the four were exceptionally experienced combat operators.

On the table in the center of the room was a scale model of Abbottabad Compound One (AC-1). After quick introductions with the CIA team, we sat down for a lengthy briefing on "the pacer" and all additional intelligence surrounding AC-1. Once again, the depth of the intelligence and the quality of the briefings were exceptional.

After the intelligence briefings were completed we talked through the four options still before the President.

"Gentlemen, in less than two weeks the President expects a fleshed-out concept for the raid option," I started. "Your job is to tell me whether or not we can do it." They nodded but said nothing. "I've looked at several other options to get to the target, but frankly, I don't think any of them are feasible. I'll give you a day or two to relook at my analysis, but then we have to decide on one course of action and start planning."

"Sir, have you looked at jumping into an offset location?"

"I have."

"How about driving across the border?"

"I have."

"What about just flying into Islamabad and going directly to the target?"

"Yeah, looked at that too. But you guys check my work and let me know if I missed anything."

As expected, the SEAL commander immediately pulled the small team together and said, "Okay, you know what the boss needs. Let's get to work."

Without any prodding, the CIA analysts gathered around the operators and offered their help. For the next two weeks every conceivable bit of intelligence was reviewed and re-reviewed. Experts on Pakistani air defense and radar systems were brought into our planning facility. Imagery analysts answered every question about the compound: the height and thickness of the walls, the outdoor lighting, the living facilities of "the pacer," the possible number of women and children, the surrounding neighborhoods, the location of the Pakistani police and military units. Additional analysts provided detailed assessments of likely Pakistani reaction once we were detected. We knew from previous incursions across the Pakistani border that the Paks would engage our helos and ground forces at the first opportunity. Throughout the course of the next two weeks, the mission planners provided an extensive list of Requests for Intelligence (RFIs) to the CIA analysts. Only one RFI seemed unanswerable: *Was it bin Laden or not?*

It didn't take long for the planners to confirm my suspicion that the only real raid option was a direct helo flight to AC-1. The hard part was trying to determine if we could get to AC-1 with the right number of SEALs, in the right helicopters, without being detected. The only way to test this concept was to exercise the plan against a simulated Pakistani threat. That meant bringing in a lot more folks, and that meant getting the President's approval.

On March 29 we met again with the President and the other

members of his national security team who were read-in to the operation. The CIA briefed the updated intelligence, but they were still no closer to determining the identity of "the pacer." We debated the merits of all the courses of action again.

By this time, however, the Air Force had provided General Cartwright a new kinetic option. Instead of a massive bombing run, it was possible to drop a more surgical weapon that could kill "the pacer" and limit the collateral damage. However, this course of action would require the strike platform to be overhead at precisely the time "the pacer" was in the AC-1 courtyard. Additional overhead photos showed that he always had several children surrounding him during his daily walks.

The new option was compelling. If it worked, then no boots on the ground were required. The Pakistani reaction would likely be stern but short-lived, and the likelihood of killing people in the surrounding houses was eliminated. The nagging fact was that with any kinetic operation we still wouldn't know if bin Laden had been killed. And in this case, children were likely to die.

Finally, the President turned to Panetta and said, "Okay, let's talk about the raid option."

Panetta nodded to me.

On the table in front of the President was a scale model of Abbottabad Compound One. Additionally, I had placed a few PowerPoint slides in front of each member in the room.

I began the brief. "Sir, the plan is pretty simple. When directed, I will move an assault force from the United States to Afghanistan. The force will consist of twenty-four SEAL operators, a CIA officer, two special modified Black Hawk helicopters, and a military working dog. We already have positioned in Afghanistan another two MH-47 medium lift helicopters. They'll provide a Quick Reaction Force and additional fuel if required."

The first slide gave the battlefield geometry, a map showing the distance between the Afghanistan border and Abbottabad. The second slide was a graphic portrayal of the Pakistani air defense radar coverage. Red arcs meant we were likely to be detected. Green was clear. There wasn't much green.

"On order, we will launch the assault force and fly the 162 miles to the Abbottabad compound."

The President's eyes followed the proposed path of the helicopters on the slide. "Can you get by the air defenses?" he asked.

"Sir, I don't know yet. We're still studying the problem. But if we use the mountains as a shield then there is a possibility we can get pretty close to the compound before being detected."

Sitting up in his chair now, the President was focused, and I could see the questions mounting as I continued the brief. "How close?" he asked.

"Sir, once we break out from behind the mountains, it will be two minutes before we can reach the compound. At that point, the sound of the helos will give us away and it's very likely that someone in the compound will hear us."

"Continue."

"Yes sir." I flipped to the next slide, which was an overhead photo of the Abbottabad compound with arrows showing our proposed insertion routes.

"Sir, the first helo carrying twelve men will fast-rope into the center of the compound, clear the small guest quarters, and then breach the bottom floor and clear from the bottom up. The second helo will drop off a small element outside the compound to ensure the escape routes are covered and then lift the remaining men onto the roof of the living quarters so they can clear from the top down."

"What about women and children?" Secretary Clinton asked.

"Ma'am, we expect up to a dozen children in the compound and probably five women. This is a challenge we deal with every day in Afghanistan. The men know how to handle large groups of noncombatants."

"But what if one of them poses a threat?" someone else asked.

"If they have a suicide vest or are armed and threaten the assault force—they will be killed."

The sudden realization that others besides bin Laden could be killed, not by a bomb, but by a U.S. soldier with a gun at point-blank range, seemed to bring the reality of the mission into focus.

I wanted to ensure that there was no misperception about how this raid would go down. "Sir, if there are people in the compound who pose a threat to the operators, they will be killed. It will be dark. It will be confusing. If it turns out that bin Laden is not in the compound, there are still likely to be dead Pakistanis as a result of the raid."

The President nodded. "I understand."

"How long do you think the mission will take?" Brennan asked.

"It's about a ninety-minute flight from the Afghan border to Abbottabad. I intend to spend no more than thirty minutes on target and a ninety-minute flight home."

"How quickly can the Pakistanis react?" Secretary Gates inquired.

"Sir, we're not exactly sure, but we will have intelligence on their movements and we will be able to relay that information to the assault force."

I presented the last two slides, which showed the helo route out of Pakistan and some additional information on our planned rehearsal schedule.

"Can you do the mission, Bill?" the President asked.

"Sir, I don't know yet. This is just a concept. Before I can tell you with any assurance, I need to identify the assault force, do more planning, and conduct several rehearsals. Only then will I know if the concept is valid."

"How much time do you need?"

"Sir, I need three weeks."

Without hesitation the President said, "Okay, Admiral. I think you have some work to do. Pull your team together and get back to me in three weeks."

"Yes sir."

The meeting broke up without a lot of discussion. Afterward, I talked to Panetta, Mullen, and Brennan. The Agency had constructed a mock-up of the Abbottabad compound near my home at Fort Bragg, North Carolina. We would find a cover story to assemble the operators. We would brief them in, do the first set of rehearsals, follow that with a full dress rehearsal, and in three weeks be prepared to brief the President on whether the raid was feasible. It was going to be a busy few weeks.

Within twenty-four hours I had ordered the special operations units to assemble in North Carolina. On the SEAL side, all were senior enlisted from the same SEAL squadron. All were handpicked by the SEAL commander. All had extensive combat experience. The aviation crews were equally experienced and also handpicked. But none of them knew why they were being asked to come to North Carolina on such short notice.

The following day, as we ushered the members of the raid team into the conference room at our North Carolina location, I could see a look of annoyance on their faces. By this time, I had briefed my boss, Admiral Eric Olson, on the bin Laden mission. Olson, along with the Under Secretary of Defense for Intelligence, Mike Vickers, and several CIA senior officers, were also present in the conference room. The operators' body language was unmistakable. Clearly, they thought they had been dragged out of Virginia Beach and Fort Campbell to participate in some kind of no-notice exercise just to impress the brass.

I offered some short welcoming remarks and then turned over the briefing to a CIA officer. He began by handing out nondisclosure forms. I watched with some amusement as the body language began to change. Rarely were nondisclosure forms required for exercises, even sensitive ones.

It took a few minutes before the forms were signed and collected. Then another CIA official stepped up on the small stage and began to brief the target. The operators shifted in their chairs, sitting up to focus on the slides on the screen.

"Gentlemen, for the past several months the CIA has been tracking an individual we call 'the pacer.'" Embedded in the slide was a link. The CIA officer clicked on the link and a video played on the screen. Everyone watched as "the pacer" moved around the compound at AC-1. "We have reason to believe that 'the pacer' is Osama bin Laden."

At the sound of bin Laden's name there was silence in the room. I could see a number of the SEALs glancing around at each other as if to ask, *Are they screwing with us or is this for real?*

The briefing went on for another thirty minutes. After the CIA analyst finished, I pushed away from my table, stood up, and made sure everyone was clear on why we were here.

"Gentlemen, the President has asked us to develop a raid option to capture or kill bin Laden. For the past several weeks a small team has been planning the mission, but now we have to find out whether the plan is executable. We have less than three weeks to test and rehearse the plan. At the end of that time I have to report back to the President on the viability of the mission."

There was no emotion from the operators. No smiles. No acknowledgment of the magnitude of the operation. Now it was all business.

"The Agency has built a mock-up of the compound just a mile from here. You have two days to work through the movements on target. After that we will move to another location out west to do the full dress rehearsals." I offered the other senior officers an opportunity to say a few words, but they recognized that this was about the operators, not a time to wax philosophically about the importance of the mission.

"I will turn you over to your boss and you guys can work out the details." I paused. "Any questions?"

There were none.

"All right. Let's get to work."

The SEAL commander and his master chief immediately pulled

together the other SEALs and helo pilots and began to outline the next twenty-four hours. Within an hour, rehearsals on the mock-up had begun.

Eric Olson, Mike Vickers, and I drove to the mock-up site and watched as the SEALs did a dozen or so ground movements while the helo pilots flew multiple approaches on the compound. The Agency had done a masterful job of constructing the mock-up. There was a chain-link fence built to exactly the height and dimensions of the walls surrounding the real AC-1. In the middle of the fencing was a Lego formation of shipping containers stacked one on top of the other to simulate the living quarters and the small guesthouse. Every key feature of AC-1 was accounted for. However, owing to the short amount of time the Agency had to construct the site, there was no way to exactly replicate the thick concrete walls that surrounded the compound in Abbottabad. Later, this shortfall would come back to haunt us. Additionally, we had no knowledge of what the inside living quarters looked like. The Agency engineers and analysts made some calculations based on square footage and normal construction in the region, but we all knew that until the operators entered the house there was no way of knowing how the rooms were laid out.

Within forty-eight hours we completed the North Carolina rehearsals and subsequently moved the force out west to begin the final set of dress rehearsals. These final rehearsals would tell me whether or not I could stand before the President of the United States and, with confidence, say that we could do this mission. At this point, I was a long way from certain.

The Air Force base was located in a remote area. While the Air Force officers weren't read-in to the mission, they knew that owing to the priority we had been given, something very important was in the works. They were incredibly professional and equally discreet.

Our task force had grown considerably since my last meeting with the President. In addition to the special operations units and my small staff, I brought in a few operational planners and senior officers from Fort Bragg, as well as my Command Sergeant Major, Chris Faris, and Captain Pete Van Hooser from Virginia Beach. All would be needed as we prepared for the mission, deployed forward, and, if directed, conducted the mission.

We set up our rehearsal command post in a small single-story building away from the main base. While the operators continued to exercise their tactical scheme of maneuver, my staff rehearsed the command and control aspect of the mission. The staff prepared detailed execution checklists, reviewed every possible scenario, and looked at every backup plan. I directed the staff to build a decision matrix, so that in the heat of the moment if something went wrong on the mission, I didn't have to think through all the alternatives. We would work through all the possible problems ahead of time and be prepared with options. Most of my decisions were binary:

If we were detected crossing the border would we continue? Yes or no?

If we were detected one hundred miles out? Yes or no?

Fifty miles out? Yes or no?

What if we had mechanical problems with the helicopter one hundred miles out?

Fifty miles out?

Once on target, what if bin Laden was not found within fifteen minutes?

Within thirty minutes?

What if the Pakistanis converged on the target within fifteen minutes?

Within thirty minutes?

The list of possible problems was extensive, but the decisions were easy. Hard to make, but easy to discern. If we were compromised crossing the border we would turn around and try for another day. If we had a helo set down for mechanical problems at a hundred miles out from the target, but the helo was not detected, we would continue on with the force we had. If a helo crashed, but we still had sufficient force to move to the target, we would continue the mission, but alert the Quick Reaction Force and medevac. Everything was binary. On missions like these you don't want emotions to drive your decisions. If we were compromised crossing the border and the Pakistanis threatened to shoot down our helos, you could easily convince yourself that the mission was so important that you must press forward. Decisions like that rarely ended well. We had a backup plan for every contingency and a backup to the backup.

In addition to rehearsing the SEAL ground movements and the command and control, the helos flew against a simulated Pakistani threat, trying to determine if they could mask their approach to the target. The results looked promising, but not conclusive. As I talked with the pilots, who had extensive experience in the region, they were much more confident that by using the mountains, they could hide from the Pakistani radars. While I trusted them, I remained concerned.

By the week's end, we had rehearsed every individual aspect of the mission multiple times, but we still hadn't put it all together. And if my research from the Naval Postgraduate School was correct, a full dress rehearsal was absolutely necessary to find flaws in the plan. Every historical mission I analyzed for my thesis showed that when a particular part of the mission wasn't rehearsed, that portion invariably failed. Unfortunately, time was running out and we would have to conduct our first full dress rehearsal in front of the military and civilian leaders who would ultimately influence the President's decision.

"I'm not sure the Black Hawks can make it to the target and return without refueling."

"What?"

J.T. Thompson looked me in the eye and said again, "Sir, we've done the calculations a dozen times, and with the weight of the operators and the temperatures we expect to have on the night of the mission, I don't think we can make it there and back without stopping to refuel in Pakistan."

I took a deep breath. All along we had planned to fly the two Black Hawks to the target, loiter for up to forty minutes, and then return. Every calculation we made indicated we could do this without refueling. Now, right before our briefing to the Chairman of the Joint Chiefs, the plan was changing dramatically. Refueling the Black Hawks meant bringing in an additional MH-47 Chinook with a Forward Air Refueling Pod (FARP), a large fuel bladder. That meant another helo in Pakistani airspace and it also meant finding an isolated area where the Black Hawks and the Chinooks could land, undetected, and spend twenty minutes on the ground refueling.

"I'm sorry, sir," Thompson said. "It's still possible we could make it there and back, but if there are any variations in temperatures or headwinds, we'll find ourselves landing in Taliban-controlled Pakistan and having to refuel. I'd rather we plan for it now."

I knew Thompson was right. I had been pushing the mission planners hard to find me an option that used only two helos to get the SEALs in and out of the target. The more complex the mission, the more likely it was to fail and, I also knew, the more likely it was to be disapproved by the President.

"Okay J.T., I assume you guys have identified a secure FARP location."

"We have, sir."

"Well, let's make sure the refueling is part of tonight's rehearsal."

"Yes sir. We've already taken that into account."

I slapped Thompson on the back and said, "We'll be fine, J.T. Get back to the guys and let's just ensure we have everything necessary to carry out the FARP." Thompson nodded and left. I had no doubt in my mind that he and his men would make it all work. They were simply the best in the world.

Admiral Mullen leaned forward on the aluminum bench to get a better look at the map on the floor.

"Sir, the second helo carrying Chalk Two will move to a position just outside the compound walls, fast-rope the three SEAL operators, our CIA colleague, and the military working dog. This element will secure the outside of the compound and, if required, keep the locals away from the action."

"How fast do we think the Pakistanis could react once they know we are on the ground?" Mullen asked.

The SEAL chief petty officer briefing the Chairman answered without hesitation. "Sir, there is a police station about one mile from the target and then an entire infantry battalion approximately four miles from the target. We assess that the police will arrive first, but that it would take at least thirty minutes before an armed element from the battalion arrived. Our bigger concern is the locals who live in the houses just across this small ditch." The chief pointed out the ditch on the floor mock-up. "With all the noise from the helos it's highly likely that they will come over to see what's going on."

The chief pointed to the CIA officer who was sitting with the SEAL assault force. "Sir, Mohammad is a Pakistani American fluent in both Urdu and Dari. If a crowd develops Mohammad will tell them it is a Pakistani exercise and to go back to their homes."

The SEAL commander chimed in. "Sir, it's not a very good cover story, but it should buy us a few minutes and that's all we really need."

For the next two hours each special operations unit presented their portion of the mission to Mullen and the other VIPs. Afterward Mullen spoke personally to each man and asked them point-blank, "Are you confident you can do this mission?" Without any reservations, the answer was yes.

Pulling me aside after the brief, Mullen said, "I see we've added another helo to the plan."

"Yes sir." I hesitated a bit. "It might not be necessary if all the conditions are right, but we need to plan and rehearse as though it were necessary."

Mullen nodded. "I agree."

Throughout the entire planning and briefing for the mission, Admiral Mullen had been firmly in my corner. Over my time as the SOF commander, he was very active in supporting dozens of missions we had conducted all around the world. When other seniors in the interagency became weak-kneed about risky missions, Mullen's strong leadership and confidence in the special operations force always carried the day. This mission would be no different. If the Chairman supported the raid, the President was likely to give it much greater consideration.

Over the course of the next five hours the task force conducted a flawless rehearsal. Afterward, the VIPs departed the air base and headed back to D.C. I followed shortly behind and made final preparations for the next day's brief to the President. After tomorrow, there was nothing more I could do to convince the U.S. leadership that we were ready.

Panetta smiled as I finished my briefing to the President. The room was quiet as the President thought through what I had just told him. The mission was executable, I said. And I was confident we could get to the target, capture or kill bin Laden, and get back safely. I explained the need for the FARP and the third helo. The President politely questioned why this was just coming to light now. I explained that it became apparent when we did the additional air planning that if the temperature on target and load variations in the helo were just a few degrees or a few pounds different, then we likely wouldn't make it all the way back to Afghanistan. The additional MH-47 with the FARP would preclude an emergency refueling in the FATA (Federally Administered Tribal Areas). The President acknowledged the change without a lot of concern.

I felt I was answering each of the President's questions to his satisfaction. Without trying to make my case, at the expense of the other options, there seemed to be more appreciation for the raid than I had seen in past meetings. And then the conversation turned abruptly.

"What happens if the Pakistanis surround the compound when the SEALs are inside?" the President asked. Before I could answer he continued. "What happens if we get into a big firefight?" His words were measured but pointed. "What happens if they start shooting at our helos?"

Around the room the principals began to shift uncomfortably in their large leather chairs. *Yeah, McRaven, what are you going to do when* that *happens?*

All eyes turned toward me.

"Sir," I replied, "we have a technical term for that in the military."

Gates and Mullen exchanged puzzled glances.

"We call that"—I paused—"when the shit hits the fan!"

"Exactly!" the President responded loudly.

The Secretary and Chairman broke out laughing, but some of the senior staff seemed unamused by my humor.

I explained that with twenty-four heavily armed SEALs we could hold off the Pakistanis long enough to extract from the target. But in fact, part of our planning was not to engage the Pakistani police or the military so we didn't escalate the situation and create an international firestorm. Clearly, the President didn't want to compromise the success of the mission or the safety of the SEALs by trying to build a plan that was too concerned about the political fallout—which I greatly appreciated.

The President directed me to develop an alternate plan to

"fight our way out" if the SEALs found themselves surrounded by the Pakistani military. "We are not going to have U.S. forces held hostage by the Pakistanis," he said emphatically. This was an easy addition to the base plan. There were ample forces in Afghanistan to provide backup if the SEALs needed the support. Those forces wouldn't need to be notified until the day of the mission, so OPSEC (operations security) could be maintained.

The meeting went for another thirty minutes as we reviewed the timeline for key decisions. Before wrapping up, however, the President turned to Mike Leiter, the Director of the National Counterterrorism Center (NCTC), and asked him to have another group of intelligence analysts review CIA's assessment about "the pacer." Was there too much groupthink? Wasn't this what happened with WMD in Iraq? Maybe other intelligence analysts had another view.

At the end, the President thanked everyone for their hard work, and Donilon scheduled another meeting in a week to review the options one final time.

A week later we reconvened again. The President turned to Leiter.

"Well, Mike, what do your folks think? Is 'the pacer' bin Laden?"

Leiter paused, looked down at the assessment his analytical team had provided him, and very carefully stated, "Sir, the team of analysts think the chance it's bin Laden is anywhere between 60 percent and 40 percent."

When he said 40 percent, everyone in the SITROOM took a deep breath.

"Forty percent!" Panetta exclaimed.

"That's on the low end," Leiter quickly responded. "But that's still thirty-eight percent higher than we've been in the past ten years."

"Mr. President," Panetta launched in, "I am fully behind CIA's assessment, and while I can't tell you with certainty that it's bin Laden, I put it at well above 60 percent. I think it's him!"

The President looked at Panetta and nodded, and while everyone knew the 40 percent figure was the worst-case prediction, clearly the new assessment had brought added anxiety to the mission.

"All right, everyone. Let's go over this one more time," the President said.

After another hour of revisiting the intelligence and the options, the President gave me approval to move the SEALs and helo assault force to Afghanistan, but he made it clear that he had not made any decision yet. I left Washington on Wednesday evening, arriving in Bagram late on Thursday night.

My arrival back in Afghanistan drew no attention from either my forward-based staff or the senior leaders in country. Owing to my constant movements back and forth, my return seemed routine.

I immediately convened the small group of officers who were witting to the plan. Earlier I had directed my deputy commander, Brigadier General Tony Thomas, to travel with the assault force and ensure everything was ready to go by the time I arrived in theater. Thomas, a former Ranger and Army special operations assaulter, had extensive combat experience and was one of the finest officers with whom I had ever served. He confirmed that the force was ready. Additionally, I had given the task of building the Quick Reaction Force (QRF) to Colonel Erik Kurilla, the Ranger Regimental Commander. Kurilla, one of the most aggressive combat leaders in special operations, was already in Afghanistan; and with all the ongoing daily missions, he devised a cover story to assemble the QRF without anyone taking notice.

The following morning, as per my usual Friday battle rhythm, I flew to Kabul to talk with General Petraeus. This was the third time in the past six years that I had worked for Petraeus—first, when he was the commander of the Multi-National Force in Iraq; second, when he was the commander of U.S. Central Command; and now as he headed the International Security Assistance Force

(ISAF) in Afghanistan. Petraeus had always been incredibly supportive of special operations, and I liked him a lot. Unfortunately, there were many in Washington who didn't feel the same, and consequently Petraeus had been left out of the planning for the raid. From the beginning of Neptune's Spear, I had asked to ensure both General Petraeus and General Jim Mattis, the new CENTCOM commander, were kept in the loop. But, because of concerns over expanding the inner circle, they did not participate in the operational discussions. Finally, right before I departed Washington, I was told that General Cartwright would call Petraeus and Mattis and fill them in on the operation. Consequently, when I showed up in Petraeus's headquarters that morning I assumed he was fully briefed on the mission.

"Sir, I understand you've been briefed on the operation," I said as I sat down at the small conference table in Petraeus's office.

Petraeus cocked his head slightly, with a look of mild disdain. "Hoss called me and said something about a cross-border operation."

Something about a cross-border operation? *I am so screwed*, I thought.

I looked at Petraeus. He had no idea about Operation Neptune's Spear. Cartwright hadn't given him any details at all.

"Well," I said, drawing a deep breath. "It's a little more than that."

"What is it?"

I grabbed my set of five slides, got up from the table, and moved to Petraeus's desk. "We're going after bin Laden."

"What?" Petraeus said, almost laughing.

"We're going after bin Laden," I repeated. Laying the slides in front of Petraeus, I walked him through the plan.

"Holy shit!" he said, looking at the distance to the target.

I laid the second slide down.

"Holy shit!" he said again, looking at the compound in Abbottabad.

I finished with a couple more slides.

"Are they really going to let you do this?"

"I'm still waiting on the final approval from the President, but we are ready to go."

Petraeus shook his head and smiled. "Well, all I can say is good luck, Bill. You're certainly going to need it."

Although I thought we had a good plan, I nodded in agreement because you can never have too much luck.

Late for a meeting, Petraeus stood up, shook my hand, and laughed again. It was a reassuring laugh. A friendly laugh. Not what I had expected, and somehow it made me feel better about the mission.

I left ISAF headquarters, hopped on a helo, and returned to Bagram. I called Mattis and found out he knew little about the mission as well. Like Petraeus, he wished me well and offered any help he could provide. That afternoon a congressional delegation was visiting our special operations headquarters in Bagram. Among those in the know, we had debated whether to cancel the visit, but I wanted to keep everything on the schedule until the very last minute. Consequently, I greeted the congressmen and their staffs, gave them a brief of our daily operations in Afghanistan, and provided them a tour of our facility. They departed by early evening without any inkling that a major operation was in the works. Soon after the congressional delegation left, I received a call from Panetta. He informed me that the President had made the decision. Operation Neptune's Spear was a go.

The following day, Saturday, I received a call from our operations center in Jalalabad (JBAD). The weather along our planned infiltration route had some low-lying fog. It was passable and likely wouldn't present a major problem for the helos, but the weather on Sunday looked even better, so I made the decision to delay the mission one day. I passed on my decision to the CIA, who informed the Director and the President that I had rolled the launch twenty-four hours.

Later that evening I received a call from the White House operator that the President wanted to talk with me around 1700 East Coast time. Right before the top of the hour I called the number I was given and was connected with the President's secretary. She politely put me on hold until the President came on the line.

"Bill, how are you doing?"

"Fine, Mr. President."

"How are things going out there?"

"We're all set, Mr. President, but the weather in Pakistan was a bit foggy so I decided to wait until tomorrow. We'll be good to go on Sunday."

"Well, don't push it unless you're ready."

"No sir. I won't rush to failure."

"Well, Bill, I just wanted to call and wish you and your men good luck."

"Thank you, Mr. President."

"I want you to tell them that I am proud of them. Make sure you tell them that, Bill."

"I will, sir."

"What do you think? Is he there, Bill?"

"I don't know, sir. But I do know that if he is there—we will get him. And if he's not, we'll come home."

There was a slight pause on the other end of the line. Maybe I was reading too much into it, but I felt the President understood the risks my men were taking and truly appreciated their courage and their patriotism.

"Well, again, good luck, Bill."

"Thank you, Mr. President." I hesitated just a second, wondering whether I should tell the President of the United States that I understood the difficulty of his decision and that I appreciated his leadership.

"And thank you for making this tough decision," I said.

"Thank you, Bill."

The phone went dead. Now all that was left to do was conduct the mission.

The small twin-engine plane landed with a thud at the airfield in Jalalabad. We taxied to the end of the runway, I got out of the plane, and was met by a young petty officer. He drove us the half mile to the SEAL compound, where I quickly dropped my gear in my room and headed into the small Joint Operations Center, which we had commandeered to use as our command and control hub.

Inside the small plywood building were an array of large flat-panel displays, computers, and telephones. The SEAL Team commanding officer, Pete Van Hooser, and his master chief met me at the door and briefed me on the preparations for the mission.

"We have one final briefing in an hour," Van Hooser said. "After that, the boys will get some rest until it's time to suit up."

As the commanding officer of the SEAL Team conducting the mission, I had placed Van Hooser in charge of overseeing the tactical execution of the mission. He would be in direct contact with the SEAL ground commander and provide me all the updates as the mission unfolded. Along with Van Hooser was J.T. Thompson, who would oversee the helo portion of the mission and report to Van Hooser. Additionally, in the JOC were parts of my headquarters team and representatives from CIA and a small Air Force element to help with the ISR.

At my request, the SEALs built me a closet-sized room inside the JOC where I could have some privacy as I talked to Panetta and his team, but inside the closet I was still in position to look at the tactical action on the large screens and hear the radio communications.

An hour later we convened in a large warehouse where the operators gave me their final mission brief. It was exceptionally detailed and covered everyone's responsibilities. I reemphasized a couple of points to ensure everyone knew my orders.

"I want to make sure we communicate. One of the reasons the 1980 operation to rescue Americans from Tehran failed was that the assault force was overly OPSEC conscious. I want you to communicate to me and with each other so everyone knows what's going on. Do not be afraid to get on the radio and talk. The Pakistanis are not likely to intercept our comms, and if they do, they won't be able to stop us from getting to the target."

Everyone nodded.

"Next, for you pilots, fly safely. Do not try to fly fifty feet off the deck or be so damn close to each other that you create a risky flight profile. Your job is to get the SEALs there safely. If you have problems with the helo, set down in a remote area and work through it. Slowly, methodically, safely."

I looked at Thompson and the warrant officers who were flying. "Do I make myself clear?"

"Yes sir."

"For you SEALs. Do not shoot any Pakistanis unless you absolutely have to in order to save your life. Is that clear?"

They nodded and seemed to understand and appreciate the political complexities of the mission. Being professional also meant knowing when not to shoot.

"Finally, this mission is to capture or kill bin Laden. Capture him if you can, but if he presents a threat at all, any threat whatsoever—kill him."

We had gone over the rules of engagement before, but I wanted to ensure there was no misunderstanding. After twelve years on the run it was thought that bin Laden likely slept with a suicide vest either on his body or next to him. Every SEAL in the briefing had encountered Iraqi or Afghan fighters who inexplicably detonated themselves when the assault force arrived. Consequently, we had clear criteria for what posed a threat. Unless bin Laden was in his underwear with his hands in the air, then it was possible he was wearing an explosive vest and was therefore a threat to the force. In the middle of the night, in a confusing combat situation, with the adrenaline pumping and people moving around the target, the SEALs didn't have time to stop and assess a threat to the force. As I had told the President and his national security team, if there were men, or women, on the target and they appeared to be a threat, then they would die—period.

At the end of the briefing, I stood up from my folding chair and faced the gathering of SEALs and helo crews.

"I think most of you know that I am a basketball fan."

Some in the crowd smiled, having played pickup ball with me on several occasions.

"There is a great scene in the movie *Hoosiers*," I said, waiting a second to let it sink in.

"*Hoosiers* is the story of a small-town basketball team in Indiana that reaches the high school state championship in 1954. They travel to Indianapolis to play a team from the big city. Most of these small-town kids have never been to a city and the stadium in Indianapolis is huge."

I moved away from my chair and drew closer to the men.

"At one point, the coach, played by Gene Hackman, realizes the boys on the team are intimidated by the size of the stadium and the fact that they will be playing on the big stage in front of thousands of people. Hackman grabs one of the players and hands him a tape measure. 'Measure the height of the basket,' he tells the player.

"Reeling out the tape measure, the player announces, 'Ten feet.'

"Hackman grabs another player and tells him to pace off the length of the court. The player does so and tells Hackman that it's ninety-four feet."

Some in the audience were starting to get my point.

"Hackman tells his team that the court is exactly the size of the court at home. That the basket is exactly the height of the one at home."

Now heads were nodding.

"Gentlemen, each of you has done hundreds of missions just like this one. This mission is no different. The court is exactly like the one you've played on for the past ten years. There is no need to do anything differently. Just play your game like you always have and we will be successful."

I thanked them and started to leave. Those sitting stood up, and a few shook my hand as I departed. I would see the SEALs and helo crews off before they launched. I walked out of the warehouse and into the warm night air. It was five hours until showtime.

"It's about time, sir," Faris advised me.

I looked at my watch. The SEALs would be gathering around the fire pit for one final talk from their squadron commander. Then they would load the helos and await my orders to launch.

Faris and I walked out of the JOC and without speaking strolled over to the fire pit. Chris Faris had been my right-hand man for the past three years. There was no finer enlisted man in the military. He was raised in the Rangers and then spent eighteen years as an Army special operations assaulter, rising to the position of Command Sergeant Major. Faris had been in combat since he was twenty—Mogadishu during Black Hawk Down; South America chasing Pablo Escobar; Bosnia and Kosovo; and of course, Iraq and Afghanistan. He was the perfect balance of professional NCO and personal friend. He never stepped over the line with respect to our friendship, and he was fiercely protective of my position as the commander. However, he told me all the ugly truths that a good commander needs to know. He often challenged my decisions, forcing me to defend my position and thereby ensuring a better outcome. But when I made a decision, he accepted it as his own and supported me completely. I rarely made an important decision without Chris Faris. He also knew when not to talk, and as we walked to meet the SEALs, this was one of those times.

The SEALs were clustered around the fire pit. Music was blaring, some hard rock song, and most of the operators were adjusting their kit one final time. There was an air of tension, but that was not uncommon before any tough mission. I sensed no fear, just anticipation and a desire to get the operation underway.

"Kill the music," one SEAL yelled as I approached. They closed in around me and I turned to Faris so he could say a few words. Even though he was an Army NCO, he had the respect of everyone in the SEAL community. Faris reminded them of the British SAS motto, "Who Dares Wins." Tonight we were daring greatly, and he told them he was confident they would come home victorious.

Faris turned to me. I hadn't put a lot of thought into what I might say. But it occurred to me, just moments before, as I was walking from the JOC, that everyone gathered around the fire pit was thinking the same thing.

"Gentlemen, first let me say that I talked to the President yesterday evening and he told me to pass on his thanks and appreciation for what you are about to do."

Most of the men were deep in thought, their heads cast downward, but I could tell that they were beginning to understand the magnitude of what they were about to undertake.

I moved a little closer to the fire and scanned the group of men standing before me. They were rough-looking. Serious. Professional. Focused. They had their game face on, but I knew that beneath the body armor they were like any other men. They had families. Wives and kids. Friends back in Virginia Beach. They were good men. Men you would want as your friends, your neighbors. Men you could count on when things got bad—real bad. Men who loved each other as only those who have experienced combat together can. They didn't know what the night would bring, but they knew they were lucky to be chosen for this mission. And that was my message. It was simple.

"Gentlemen, since 9/11 each one of you has dreamed of being

the man going on the mission to get bin Laden. Well, this is the mission and you are the men. Let's go get bin Laden."

There were no smiles, no cheering, and no contrived jubilation. It was time to get to work.

"Launch the assault force. I say again, launch the assault force."

"Roger, sir," Van Hooser replied. "Launch the assault force."

I could hear Van Hooser relay the order to the SEAL squadron commander aboard the helo.

In my small closet, Art Sellers had set up a video teleconference with CIA headquarters, the U.S. Embassy in Pakistan, Brigadier General Brad Webb, my command's liaison in the White House, and General Tony Thomas and Colonel Erik Kurilla back at Bagram. Additionally, on Sellers's laptop was MIRChat, a means of chatting with everyone on the JOC floor and those around the world who were allowed to monitor the mission. Outside my closet sat my good friend, the CIA Chief of Station in Afghanistan. He and I had been together in Afghanistan many times over the past ten years. There was no better ally in the interagency.

At exactly 2300, I peered out from my closet and looked at the big screen as the two Black Hawks lifted off, followed soon thereafter by two MH-47s. Minutes later they were crossing the border into Pakistan. For the next ninety minutes I tracked the execution checklist as the helos went from point to point, making their way undetected through the mountains and valleys of Pakistan.

Throughout the mission we monitored the Pakistani radars to determine if anyone had picked up on our presence. At one point about halfway through the flight the SEAL squadron commander called the JOC and calmly radioed that a large spotlight was emanating from a nearby city, sweeping the mountainside, apparently looking for something.

Intelligence hadn't detected any Pakistani reaction, and I

relayed back through Van Hooser for the assault force to press on. It appeared to be nothing of concern. Forty minutes later we were closing in on the target.

"Sir, General Petraeus is on the MIRChat," Sellers said.

"What?"

"He's on the chat and wants to know if we are still doing the mission tonight."

Petraeus had left his headquarters in Kabul and walked down the street to the small building that housed my special operations liaison officer. He had questioned the officer about the status of the mission, but the officer, who was not read-in to the operation, didn't have a clue what Petraeus was talking about.

I laughed. "Art, tell General Petraeus that we are ten minutes out from time on target."

Sellers sent back my response, to which Petraeus replied, "Good luck!"

"Sir, General Webb is on chat now."

Brad Webb, my assistant commander, was in the White House in a small anteroom just off from the larger Situation Room. He had full communications with me and also was monitoring the same video feed I was receiving from my overhead assets.

I was looking out my closet watching the big screen as the helos broke out from behind the mountains and began their last two-minute flight to the Abbottabad compound.

"Yeah," I said, somewhat distracted.

"Sir, he says the Vice President just walked into the anteroom."

"Okay," I acknowledged, still eyeing the big screen as the helos approached the target.

"Sir, General Webb says the President just walked into the room."

"Got it, Art."

A moment later, "Sir, he says everyone is now in the room watching the operation."

I had to chuckle. I could imagine Brad Webb sitting alone in the anteroom and then, without warning, the entire national security team converges around him. Webb was a superb officer and he had all the right experience to answer any questions the President or others might ask. I didn't give it a second thought.

"Sir, we are two minutes from the target," I notified Panetta.

"Okay, Bill," came the reply from CIA headquarters.

The first helo approached the compound, moving into position between the three-story living quarters and the eighteen-foot-high concrete wall that bordered the southern fence line. As he maneuvered the Black Hawk into fast-rope position, I could tell the pilot was having difficulty holding position. The helo wobbled and pitched upward trying to maintain altitude.

"They're going down!" someone yelled.

As it spun slowly out of control, I was already thinking of the next step. Less than thirty minutes behind the two Black Hawks were the MH-47 Chinooks. We lagged the Chinooks behind the initial assault force over concerns that owing to its large radar and noise signature, it might be detected and compromise our surprise. But right now, surprise was no longer an issue.

Struggling to maintain lift, the Black Hawk pilot nosed the aircraft down, forcing it over the small interior wall and into the open animal pen just on the other side of the driveway. Bricks and concrete flew in all directions as the tail boom of the spinning aircraft clipped the outer wall, driving the fuselage into the ground and slamming the SEALs and crew to the metal deck of the helo.

It all unfolded in slow motion, but having lost several helicopters during my time in command, I knew the difference between a crash and a hard landing. This was a hard landing.

Three weeks earlier, the Black Hawk pilot and I had talked about the worst-case scenario coming into the compound. We both agreed that the most dangerous point in the mission was when the Black Hawk came to a hover just outside bin Laden's third-story living quarters. The potential for bin Laden or one of his men to fire an RPG into the hovering helo was high. Snipers and door gunners were positioned on the right side of the helo, prepared to engage any threat, but still the possibility of an RPG existed.

The pilot assured me that even if he took an RPG, as long as he survived the initial blast, he could get the helo into the open animal pen and land it safely. As it turned out, the high temperatures that evening and the eighteen-foot-high concrete wall created a vortex effect from the propeller downwash, causing the helo to lose lift. The pilot, true to his word, had gotten the men safely, albeit dramatically, on the ground.

"Sir, we have a bird down," Van Hooser announced unemotionally.

"Roger, Pete, I'm watching. What's the timeline to get the 47 in?"

"Sir, she's thirty minutes out."

"Okay, bring her to a holding position. She will have to be the extract bird."

"Roger, sir."

Thompson contacted the Chinook and maneuvered the helo to within five minutes of the compound. The aircraft would hide behind the ridgeline until it was necessary to call her in.

In the meantime, I contacted Panetta and let him know the status. "Sir, as you can see, we have a helo down," I said. By then the SEALs were already out of the aircraft and beginning to execute an alternate plan.

"The SEALs are continuing on with the mission. I will keep you posted."

Panetta nodded, but there was a real look of concern on his face.

Not immediately knowing what had caused the first helo's problems, the pilot of the second helo landed outside the compound walls. From my closet I watched on the video screen as the SEALs moved toward the main compound.

"Shots fired! Shots fired!"

Flowing in two directions, the first SEAL element approached the small guesthouse and a short burst of gunfire lit up the screen. Moments later came the dispassionate call.

"One EKIA."

At the same time, multiple explosions flashed on the video as the SEALs blew down the hardened steel doors that were protecting the outer and inner cordons of bin Laden's small fortress.

"Shots fired! Shots fired!"

Inside the main building, away from my view, the SEALs engaged another of bin Laden's men. As they made their way to the second floor another call came from the JOC NCO.

"Shots fired! Shots fired!"

I knew from the plan that the assault force was clearing the floors one by one. They encountered a threat on the first floor and on the stairwell leading to the second floor. Both enemy were dead.

Outside the three-story building, I could see the dark figures of the SEALs as they methodically cleared the rest of the compound. Everywhere, beams of infrared light from the weapons' laser pointers swept across the ground, into the windows, across the buildings, and into the shadowy spaces that could be hiding another threat.

"Sir, we have visitors."

"Roger," I replied, watching the small crowd of locals assembling near the entrance to the compound. "What are we hearing from the police?" I asked.

"Sir, it's all quiet right now, but the cell phones in the area are starting to buzz."

Only a mile away, the Abbottabad police were within earshot of the activity in the compound. One of my biggest concerns was that the police, good men just doing their job, would show up and get into a firefight with the SEALs. It would not go well for the Pakistani cops.

Inside the compound a two-man element of the assault force had nearly reached the third floor. From behind a curtain separating the stairway from the third floor, a shadowy face emerged, his dark eyes fixed on the men rushing up the stairway. The lead SEAL, his gun tucked firmly into his shoulder, finger on the trigger, fired toward the figure, but the rounds impacted high. Without hesitation, the SEALs stormed up the last few steps, through the curtain, and into the room. Inside, two young girls stood at the entrance. Nearly certain that the girls were wearing suicide vests, the lead SEAL threw himself on the young women to shield his partner from the blast. Entering the room immediately behind, the second SEAL came face-to-face with a tall, thin man, who was using an older woman to shield his body.

The second SEAL, Senior Chief Petty Officer Rob O'Neill, leveled his weapon and fired three rounds at the man, two to the head and one more for good measure. The tall man crumpled to the floor, dead before he hit the ground.

Inside the JOC, I was getting updates from Van Hooser and Thompson. The SEALs were still clearing the three-story house and the helos were holding their position outside Abbottabad.

I looked up at the clock. Fifteen minutes had passed since the assault began.

"Sir, the squadron commander is on the radio," Van Hooser alerted me.

The voice was unmistakable. Deep, calm, in control. "This is Romeo Six Six." He paused and you could hear a small shudder in his voice. "For God and Country, Geronimo, Geronimo, Geronimo!"

The hunt for the most wanted man in the world was over. *We had gotten bin Laden.*

The JOC erupted in cheers, immediately followed by Van Hooser's booming voice. "Shut the fuck up!" he yelled. "We still have to get these guys home."

The JOC immediately quieted down.

Van Hooser was right. We still had a long way to go. I had

no sense of relief, no internal exhilaration, no feeling of victory. The mission was not over. We were 162 miles from home and the Pakistanis were now beginning to wake up and muster a military response.

I relayed the message to Panetta, "Sir, we have Geronimo." But it suddenly occurred to me that I didn't know if Geronimo meant bin Laden had been found and captured, or killed in the assault.

Yelling out of my closet to the JOC floor, I asked Van Hooser to confirm if it was Geronimo EKIA. Seconds later came the response from Van Hooser. "Yes sir, Geronimo EKIA."

Once again, I passed the information back to Panetta. On the screen in my closet, I could see Panetta and Michael Morell smiling broadly.

I looked up at the clock. The SEALs had been on the ground in Abbottabad for almost twenty minutes now. The plan called for thirty minutes on the ground—no more.

In the courtyard, I could see the SEALs and the helo pilots rigging the downed Black Hawk for destruction. A downed helo was always a possibility on every mission. Consequently, each crew carried sufficient demolition to destroy the classified electronics, and in this case, we brought enough explosives to destroy the entire helicopter. Still, we would have to wait until right before extraction to detonate the charges.

"Sir, the SEALs are requesting some additional time on the ground," Van Hooser said.

"What's the holdup?" I asked.

"Sir, they say they found a whole shit-ton of computers and electronic gear on the second floor."

I looked at the clock. We were now closing in on thirty minutes and my gut told me to stick with the plan, but I also realized that the forensics from a hard drive could be vital to follow on missions.

"Okay, Pete. Tell them to grab as much as they can, but I don't want them to linger too long. Ask J.T. how this will affect our gas situation."

Van Hooser acknowledged and a few seconds later came the response. "Sir, J.T. says we are going to have to refuel anyway, so a few more minutes won't make a difference."

"Roger. Okay."

I checked the clock again and looked at the monitors, which showed Pakistani activity. From my closet I could hear one of the intelligence analysts talking to Van Hooser.

"What's going on, Pete?"

"Sir, the Pakistanis are up on comms. They know something is happening in Abbottabad but they don't seem to know what."

I looked at the clock. "How much more time do they need on the ground?"

"Sir, they are still rigging the helo, but the squadron commander says they can be ready to go in five minutes."

Five minutes was an eternity, but I knew the ground commander understood the situation, and I would leave the decision in his hands.

The Pakistani communications began to light up. The Pakistani leaders were trying to understand what was happening. Was there a helicopter in Abbottabad? Was there a Pakistani exercise ongoing that they were unaware of? Were there Americans involved? How was that possible? Americans in downtown Abbottabad? A helicopter had crashed. In Abbottabad?

The crowd of locals had now grown to several dozen. Our Agency officer was very casually talking with the townsfolk. He informed them that this was a Pakistani military exercise and they needed to stand back. Much to everyone's surprise, the locals bought the story and were very cooperative. No one seemed alarmed by the heavily armed American soldiers who were standing nearby.

"Sir, the SEALs are ready for extraction."

"Roger."

The second Black Hawk, which had successfully offloaded its

SEALs during the initial assault, was now inbound to pick up the first ten SEALs and their precious cargo, the body of Osama bin Laden. Onscreen, four SEALs carried the body bag containing the remains of UBL. The remaining six provided security as they moved to the waiting Black Hawk.

The helo lifted off and began its next leg to the Forward Air Refueling Point located about thirty minutes from Abbottabad. Seconds later, the MH-47 Chinook came swooping into view on the large screen just as the downed Black Hawk inside the compound exploded. The plume from the explosion reached a hundred feet into the air, obscuring my view of the inbound Chinook. I listened to the radio calls, and within thirty seconds all the remaining SEALs were on the last helo outbound for Afghanistan.

I called in to Panetta. "Sir, everyone is out of the compound and headed back to Afghanistan. We still have a long way to go, though. I will keep you posted."

Right about then, I overheard the intelligence officer notify Van Hooser that the Pakistanis were preparing to scramble their F-15s. Van Hooser passed on the intelligence to me. Once again, we had foreseen this possibility, and all the analysts were certain that the state of the Pakistani radars and their ability to find and then direct the F-15s to our position was highly unlikely. Still, I knew they were hunting us now and they could get lucky. President Obama had directed me to fight our way out if necessary; consequently, on the Afghan side of the border I had a "Gorilla Package" of U.S. fighters, radar-jamming aircraft, attack helicopters, the works. Nothing could stop our return now but an unfortunate accident.

Thirty minutes after the second Black Hawk left the compound with bin Laden's body, it set down in a remote area of Pakistan. Soon thereafter, the MH-47 bearing the FARP set down beside it. Nineteen minutes later, the refueling was complete and both helos were on their way back to Afghanistan.

At 0330 local time, the last helo crossed back into Afghan airspace and minutes later landed at Jalalabad airfield. *The boys were safely back home.* But the mission was not completely over.

On the other side of the VTC, I could see that Panetta and others were celebrating the successful mission. The screen on my VTC suddenly changed and the President and his team came into view.

"Congratulations, Bill. Great mission!"

"Thank you, Mr. President, glad everyone is back safely. Sorry about the helo. It looks like I owe you about sixty million dollars."

The President smiled.

"But sir, I still need to be certain that it is bin Laden. I have been on a number of missions before where we called PID," I said, referring to positive identification, "only to be wrong."

"Okay, Bill, I understand. How long before you can confirm it's bin Laden?"

"Sir, the helo just landed with the body. Let me go take a look and I will get back to you within twenty minutes."

As I was heading out of the JOC, the CIA Chief of Station stopped me at the door. "Bill, do you mind if I go with you to PID bin Laden? I have been chasing this guy for over ten years. I'd like to be there just to see it through to the end."

"You bet! You can represent every Agency man and woman who had a stake in this mission."

We loaded up in a small Toyota pickup and drove out to the hangar. There the SEALs were just arriving from the flight line. The joy of the moment was uncontainable. Guys were shaking hands, hugging each other, and yelling excitedly. They had just completed the most successful special operation since World War II.

The pickup truck containing the remains of bin Laden's body pulled into the hangar with a few SEALs riding in the back. I walked over to the truck.

"Sir, do you need to see the body?" one of the SEALs asked.

"I do."

Grabbing the remains, two SEALs pulled the heavy rubberized bag off the bed of the truck and laid it in front of me. I knelt down and unzipped the bag and exposed the body of bin Laden. My Agency colleague knelt beside me. Bin Laden's face was contorted from two shots to the head and the beard was a little shorter and lighter. But it certainly appeared to be him.

"What do you think?" I asked the station chief.

"Sure looks like him," he said.

"It does look like him," I answered with a bit of hesitation.

"It's him. It's absolutely him," one of the SEALs proclaimed loudly. "Look, here is the photo I took of him right after we killed him."

I looked at the photo and we compared it with another likeness the Agency officer had. It was an exact match. Nevertheless, I was about to report to the President of the United States and I needed to be as sure as possible.

"Help me get him out of the bag," I said to no one in particular.

We pulled bin Laden's body out of the bag, but his legs were folded awkwardly in a fetal-like position. Grabbing his legs, I stretched them out until his body was full length. Knowing that reports had bin Laden at six foot four, I eyeballed the remains, and he certainly appeared tall.

Looking at the small gathering of SEALs that surrounded me, I turned to one young operator. "Son, how tall are you?"

"What?"

"I said, how tall are you?"

"Six foot two," he responded.

"Good," I said. "Lie down next to the body."

He looked at me as if to say, *Surely you're kidding.* "You want me to lie down next to the body?"

"Yes... I want you to lie down next to the body."

"Okay, sir."

The SEAL positioned himself within inches of the remains,

and it was clear that the body lying on the hangar floor was a good two inches longer than the SEAL next to him. My Agency friend smiled. "It's definitely him."

I quickly shook a few hands and thanked the guys, but I knew that the President was waiting for my report.

"Sir, I can't be 100 percent sure until we do the DNA tests, but it certainly looks like him, and all the physical features match." I could see the President and his staff nodding their acknowledgment. "While his face was contorted from the impact of the rounds, I did have a SEAL, who was over six foot two, lie down beside the body, and the remains were at least six foot four."

There was a long pause on the other end of the VTC.

"So let me get this straight, Bill," the President deadpanned. "We could afford a sixty-million-dollar helo, but we couldn't afford a ten-dollar tape measure?" In the background I could see the President's staff laughing. I had no comeback and I didn't need one. The smile on the President's face said it all. It had been a good night, and just for a moment we could laugh about it.

"Sir, I've sent the pictures of bin Laden's body back to Langley. They are going to do a facial recognition comparison and that should give us a reliable assessment in short order."

"Okay, Bill, I know you have some things to do before this mission is complete, so I will let you get back to work. Please pass on to all your men and those that supported the mission that this was a historic night and all America will be proud of them."

I couldn't help but get a little choked up. "Thank you, sir," I struggled to say. "I will pass it on."

Within an hour I was on a plane back to Bagram. I landed, got on a waiting surrey, and immediately headed back to my headquarters building. Entering the two-story plywood structure, I noticed something was missing. It was the wanted poster of bin Laden that had hung in the building for ten years. For the thousands of men and women who had worked in this facility, it had been a daily reminder of why we were there. *Now it was gone.* I continued up the steps, strangely fixated on the small poster that had meant so much to so many. Opening the door, to where Thomas and Kurilla were working, I asked abruptly, "Who took the poster?"

Kurilla smiled. He lifted the cheap wooden-framed picture from behind his desk and said, "Sir, we thought you ought to have this?" For the second time that evening, I choked up. Tony Thomas and Erik Kurilla, two men who had given more to this long fight than just about anyone else in special operations, shook my hand and said thanks. For a soldier, when you have earned the respect of real warriors, there is no greater feeling in the world. I thanked them for all they had done that evening and then flopped down in the large Afghan chair and took a breather.

The television was muted in the background, but I could see Geraldo Rivera, a look of uncontrolled excitement on his face, as he announced that the President was going to speak in a few minutes. It was unprecedented that a President would come on television so late in the evening. It must be that Mohammar Gadhafi was dead, Rivera speculated. What else could it be?

As the President walked down the hall toward the podium, I pulled my chair closer to listen.

"Good evening. Tonight I can report to the American people, and the world, that the United States has conducted an operation to kill Osama bin Laden, the leader of Al Qaeda and a terrorist who is responsible for the murder of thousands of innocent men, women, and children."

As the President talked, two Marine MV-22s and a Ranger security detachment, transporting the remains of bin Laden, were flying back into Pakistan and down the air corridor that led to the northern Arabian Gulf. There, waiting at sea, was the aircraft carrier USS *Carl Vinson*. By early the next morning, after an adherence to strict Islamic guidelines, the body of Osama bin Laden slid quietly into the ocean, never to be seen again.

For those who were lost in the Twin Towers, the Pentagon, and in a field in Shanksville, Pennsylvania; for those who had given their lives in Iraq and Afghanistan; for those men and women who, due to wounds, internal or external, would never be the same again; for all those around the world who suffered as a result of this man's evil—justice had been served.

CHAPTER EIGHTEEN

THE FINAL SALUTE

TAMPA, FLORIDA
August 2014

The color guard marched straight up the aisle, turned, and presented the American flag. Beside me on the stage at the Tampa Convention Center was the Chairman of the Joint Chiefs, and my friend, General Marty Dempsey. Standing at attention, we held our salutes until the singing of the national anthem was over and the posting of the colors was completed. At that moment it struck me. This was my last salute in uniform—my last opportunity to officially pay my respects to the flag for which I had served for the past thirty-seven years, my last day on active duty, my very last day as a Navy SEAL.

In the audience were over seven hundred people, all of whom had come to be part of my military retirement ceremony. As I scanned the faces, the stories of my life returned in a flash. My best man, John Scarpulla, was sitting with my fellow high school runners Mike Morris and Mike Dippo. Beside them was Coach Jerry Turnbow. A row back from them were my SEAL training classmates, Dan'l Steward and Marc Thomas. Spread across the aisles were decades of teammates from the SEALs, Rangers, Green Berets, Night Stalkers, Special Tactics, CIA, DIA, FBI, State Department, NSA, NGA, and an assortment of senior officers from the Army, Navy, Air Force, and Marine Corps: men and women who had been with me throughout my career. Admiral Eric Olson, now retired, was sitting on the right side of the aisle, waiting to officiate my transfer of the Bull Frog award, as the longest-serving SEAL on active duty. Our dearest friends, Admiral Joe and Kathy Maguire, were close to the front, sitting near my sisters, Nan and Marianna.

As I stepped before the podium to make my farewell remarks, I glanced down at Georgeann in the front row and could see that she was holding back the tears. Beside her, my daughter, Kelly, and son John, who had borne the brunt of my life in the military, were trying, unsuccessfully, to remain stoic. Halfway around the world, my son Bill, who was on deployment as an Air Force officer, joined us by video. I missed him dearly, but, as always, I was proud of his service. His wife, Brandy, sat with the family.

Grabbing the sides of the podium, I looked down at my speech and took a deep breath.

I began:

My senior year in college, I was the ranking midshipman in the Naval ROTC program. One day, the NROTC executive officer, a crusty old Navy commander named Rummelhart, called me into his office. I stood at attention as he addressed me.

"Bill," he said. "Your mother called and she is worried that you are dating two women. She and I both think that is a bad idea."

I was stunned. "My mother called!" I said, completely embarrassed.

"Yes," Rummelhart replied. "Your mother called."

"My mother called?" I said again, hoping I had misheard the commander.

"Yes," he said, repeating it again. "Your mother called."

I dropped my head. What in the world was she thinking? Mothers!

But . . . it was true. I was, in fact, dating two women. Something I knew was dangerous. The first woman I had

*met on a midshipman cruise the year before. It was a
long-distance relationship, she on the West Coast and I
in Austin, but we had become quite serious. Then in the
spring of 1977, I met Georgeann at school and everything changed...*

As I looked down from the stage, Georgeann appeared morti-
fied that I was telling this story, but to me the story conveyed the
single most important moment in my life—a decision that would
change everything about my future.

I realized then, I told the audience,

*...that the first woman was everything a man of twenty-
one could want. But the second woman was everything
a man could want for the rest of his life.*

*Later that year, when I told my father that I had
asked Georgeann to marry me, he gave me that look
that only a father can and said, "Son, I didn't think you
were that smart."*

*Well, it was the smartest decision I ever made. For
over forty years, Georgeann has been by my side. She
picked me up when I stumbled. She gave me confidence
when I was faltering. She nursed me when I was injured.
She shouldered the burden of my constant deployments, and for all the times that death was at my door-
step, she hid her fear and gave me hope. Nothing in my
life would have been possible without her.*

I paused, knowing I couldn't look at Georgeann or I would lose
it. Deep breath again.

I continued on with my remarks, but my mind began to wander.
Forty years, I thought.

It had been over forty years since I reported for duty at the Naval

ROTC unit at the University of Texas. I remembered that first day as clearly as I would remember this last day. It was to be the beginning of a grand adventure. In the next four decades, I would travel the globe, sail the seven seas, jump from airplanes, lock out of submarines, be shot at, IEDed, mortared, and rocketed. I would crash in a helicopter, a boat, and a parachute and live to talk about it. I would meet with presidents and kings, prime ministers and princesses, despots and terrorists. I would experience the highs of international success and the lows of profound loss. I would confront the worst of humanity and the best of mankind. I would experience the hand of God in little moments and big ones alike. I would constantly be inspired by soldiers—awed by their courage, their humility, and their sense of duty. I would raise a wonderful family with the woman I loved and be blessed to serve the greatest country in the world. It was as though I was the main character in some cosmic adventure. And like all adventures, my odyssey had taught me a lot about myself and the world around me.

In my journey, I found that there was always someone better than me: someone smarter, stronger, faster, harder-working, more talented, more driven, more honest, more pious—*just better than I was*. It was humbling, but at the same time immensely reassuring. There were so many problems in the world that I could not solve, but maybe someone else could.

I learned that life is fragile and that we should take each day as a blessing. A single round from an Al Qaeda sniper, an IED on a road less traveled, a C-130 that never returned, a head-on collision coming home from work, a parachute that never opened, an X-ray that revealed a growing tumor—nothing in life is guaranteed, so make the most of what you have and be thankful.

Many times over I found that my success depended on others. It was the simplest of lessons, one I had been taught in basic SEAL training rowing my little rubber boat. And every success I had from that moment on had been because someone helped me.

I realized that life is actually pretty simple. Help as many people as you can. Make as many friends as you can. Work as hard as you can. And, no matter what happens, never quit!

Along the way, there were moments and people I couldn't forget. I remember leading the funeral procession for Sergeant "Doc" Peney as soldiers from the 1st Battalion, 75th Ranger Regiment marched from the church in downtown Savannah to Peney's favorite pub on River Street. The entire town lined the roads and the streets and the highways, saluting, standing at attention, hats off, heads bowed, and tears flowing. I remembered Ranger Ben Kopp, killed in Afghanistan, whose transplanted heart now beats in the breast of Judy Meikle. I remembered watching the doctors in the combat hospital in Bagram as they tried to save SEALs Jason Freiwald and Johnny Marcum; struck in the chest by multiple large-caliber rounds, both men died on the operating table and I was helpless to do anything about it. I remember the fatal crashes of helicopters Turbine 33 and Extortion 17, call signs that will never be used again and men who will forever be memorialized. I could not forget the sacrifice of a Mike Murphy, Robbie Miller, Ashley White, or the thousands of others, *"all who gave some, but some who gave all."* And I will never forget Section 60 at Arlington National Cemetery, the final resting place of so very many young heroes who fought in the wars after September 11. At times the pain and sorrow of the memories overwhelm me, and they often manifest themselves in awkward displays of emotion in large public settings. I grew to be okay with that.

Most of all, I learned that for all his faults, man is worthy of this world. For every reckless belligerent who seeks war, there are thoughtful wise men and women who strive for peace. For all the unbridled hatred that abounds, there is an even greater amount of unconditional love. For every Al Qaeda torture house in Iraq, every Taliban death squad in Afghanistan, every suicide bomber in Somalia, every righteous zealot who kills indiscriminately, there are countless mothers who care for their children and fathers who raise their young sons and daughters to be honest and hardworking. Man's compassion far exceeds his greed. His caring is greater than his brutality. His courage outshines his cowardice and his sense of hope always prevails.

The audience came back into focus. I was almost finished and ready to be piped over the side. Officially retired.

Just one last story:

There is a great scene in the World War II movie Saving Private Ryan. Ryan, now an old man, returns to the beaches of Normandy, searching for the grave of the officer who saved his life forty years earlier—a man who sacrificed everything so that Ryan could live. Finding the headstone, Ryan, emotionally drained, looks up through weary eyes and asks his wife, "Tell me I've led a good life. Tell me I'm a good man."

I found good men and women wherever I went on my journey through life. I strived to be as good as they were, as good as I could be, so in the end, those that knew me would be proud to call me their friend. All I ever wanted was to be a good man.

I stepped away from the podium, an order was given, and eight soldiers lined up on a short red carpet, ready to render a final salute as I walked off the stage. I thanked General Dempsey, met Georgeann at the foot of the stage, and walked through the honor guard as the words "Admiral. Retired. Departing" were announced. My career was over.

Helen Keller, the wondrous woman who showed us that blindness has a vision all its own, once said, "Life is either a daring adventure, or nothing."

Well, it sure has been *something*!

I can't wait to see what stories tomorrow will bring.

ACKNOWLEDGMENTS

Writing a memoir is not so much about the craft of writing as it is about the people who shared your life with you. For over forty-one years, my wife, Georgeann, has been at my side loving, encouraging, and inspiring me. Whether mentioned or not, she was part of every story in this book. My three children, Bill, John, and Kelly, are the ones who motivated me to write the book in the first place. They are the ones who had to bear the brunt of all my deployments and they did so with remarkable strength and resilience. I hope by reading this book they will understand why I was gone so often and why I loved what I did. To my sisters, Marianna and Nan, I am your biggest fan. Your own remarkable lives always made me proud to be your little brother.

I would also like to thank my editor, Sean Desmond, who not only provided exceptional technical and thematic advice, but was also a constant source of encouragement throughout the process.

Thanks as well to my lawyer and friend Bob Barnett, without whom this book would never have happened. Your advice and counsel was always exactly what I needed, when I needed it.

Finally, thanks to Michael Russo of the Defense Office of Prepublication and Security Review (DOPSR) for all your hard work in getting the manuscript through the government review process. It is a better story because of your efforts.

ABOUT THE AUTHOR

Admiral William H. McRaven (U.S. Navy Retired) is the author of the #1 *New York Times* bestselling book *Make Your Bed*. In his thirty-seven years as a Navy SEAL, he commanded at every level. As a Four-Star Admiral, his final assignment was as Commander of all U.S. Special Operations Forces. After retiring from the Navy, he served as the Chancellor of the University of Texas System from 2015 to 2018. He now lives in Austin, Texas with his wife, Georgeann.